TRIUMPH AND TRAGEDY

For Anne, Clare, Ceri, Anna, Louisa, Sofia and the Prossers of Cefn Brynich Farm in Powys, without whom nothing would have been possible.

TRIUMPH *and* TRAGEDY

Welsh Sporting Legends

PETER JACKSON

MAINSTREAM
PUBLISHING

EDINBURGH AND LONDON

First published in Great Britain in 2011 by
MAINSTREAM PUBLISHING COMPANY
(EDINBURGH) LTD
7 Albany Street
Edinburgh EH1 3UG

ISBN 9781845967765

A catalogue record for this book is available
from the British Library

Printed in Great Britain by
Clays Ltd, St Ives plc

1 3 5 7 9 10 8 6 4 2

CONTENTS

You see things; and you say, 'Why?'
But I dream things that never were; and I
ask: 'Why not?'

— George Bernard Shaw,
Back to Methuselah, 1921

FOREWORD

by Sir Clive Woodward

The road that led to England winning the Rugby World Cup took many twists and even more turns. For me, there would have been no World Cup, no England, no Lions and no rugby had I not been sent to school in Wales.

When I started there at the age of 13, I had not played a game of rugby in my life. I didn't even like it, never mind play it. I was obsessed with football, and had a dream of playing for Everton, or any other big club that showed any interest, and I would never have played rugby had my father not sent me to the HMS *Conway* Naval Boarding School in North Wales. The particular road that led me to Sydney on 22 November 2003 began more than 30 years earlier on Anglesey.

My dad deliberately chose a rugby-playing school, which didn't please me one bit. In fact, I was so displeased I ran away three times, trying to get back home to Yorkshire. I wasn't going to let my ambition of being a professional footballer go without a fight and I couldn't have cared less about my education. Each time I was taken back to HMS *Conway*, I had to face the music. The penny eventually dropped; I got on with it and grew to love my new game.

I was quite small, so they put me at scrum-half and after a while I began to play at fly-half. I found out very quickly that it was a tough school and rugby was a tough game – you got bashed about by a lot of hard characters who were being schooled at HMS *Conway* to go to sea.

I began to get quite good, and when I was in sixth form I went to Cardiff for a final trial before they picked the Wales schools team. I played for the Possibles, and it was no wonder that the opposition were called the Probables because at half-back they had Terry Holmes and Gareth Davies, both of whom went on to have distinguished careers with Wales and the Lions. I must have done reasonably well because a few of the selectors spoke to me afterwards and asked me where I was from. As soon as I said North Yorkshire, they seemed to lose interest, which is why I always find it amusing whenever Wales pick someone from outside Wales.

One of my big regrets is that I never played for Wales as a schoolboy. The schoolmaster who drove me back to Anglesey was spitting blood that I had not been picked and that yet again nobody from North Wales had got into the team. I was pretty chilled about the experience, happy just to have been there. I thought: 'You've got no chance. One, you're English. Two, you're playing for a school in North Wales.'

I made no bones about being English, but I was very peeved not to have been picked. Welsh rugby was then embarking on a golden era and I got swept along by the national fervour. A year or so after leaving school, I played for Harlequins against Cardiff at Twickenham and what an eye-opener that turned out to be.

Bob Hiller, the England full-back, played for Quins, and Gareth Edwards for Cardiff. They had been on the Lions tour of New Zealand a couple of years before and I'd never heard anything like the banter between them. It started in the first minute and they were still at it until the last: a non-stop barrage.

I've always had a passion for sport but going to Wales made me realise there was more to sport than football; for example, I once ran for Wales schools against England in the 400-metre hurdles. My five years in Wales gave me an understanding of rugby and a passion for it without which I would never have got anywhere, as a player or a coach.

As a player for England against Wales, I was definitely behind; as a coach against Wales, definitely ahead, despite what happened in the last minute at Wembley in April 1999 when they smashed our Grand Slam. At the time I was absolutely incandescent that our back-row forward, Tim Rodber, had been penalised for a brilliant tackle and that, of course, led to Scott Gibbs's try and Neil Jenkins' winning conversion. You don't forget things like that, which is why it's still my most painful memory.

You can imagine what the mood within the camp was like that Sunday night. I don't think anyone realises how it feels to lose a big game in those circumstances unless you have actually gone through the wringer yourself. I got up before the crack of dawn and drove to Twickenham, convincing the security people that I was who I said I was before going to my office.

My world was still in a state of collapse when I checked my emails. One was from someone whom I'd never heard of. It read: 'Clive, why are the English the world's best lovers? Because they are on top for 79 minutes and still come second.'

I sent what I thought was an appropriate reply, something to do with sheep. I told the same story when invited to speak at a Welsh rugby dinner in London. A few weeks later, the RFU's then chief executive, Francis Baron, informed me that he'd had a letter of complaint from the Welsh Race Relations Board. To cut a long story short, I rang them up and made it clear that I was not being anti-Welsh, although it did teach me a lesson: don't try to be funny in public.

Far from being anti-Welsh, I have nothing but admiration for a country that has produced, and continues to produce, more than its share of outstanding sportsmen and women. It's a tough country that produces tough, no-nonsense players, and I can pay no higher compliment than that. Rugby in Wales, as I discovered many years ago, has often been a different game from that played in England, and it is this which has enabled it to produce so many great players for both union and league. I always enjoy meeting with the Welsh players, a few of whom I have had the privilege of getting to know better, and excellent men they are, too.

They've also produced colourful characters across the sporting spectrum, from golf to boxing, football to athletics, steeplechasing to Formula One. Peter Jackson has been immersed in Welsh sport all his life, although we on this side of Offa's Dyke managed to distract him a fair bit during his many years as the *Daily Mail*'s rugby correspondent. The stretch of the M4 from his home in Cardiff to Twickenham hasn't been the same since his retirement.

As a highly respected and ultra-professional journalist, Jacko's column was required reading. During my time as England coach, I would start every day in his company, as well as that of a few others, briefing myself with daily cuttings of rugby news. I found his views and his take on events, players, teams, coaches and rugby affairs to be illuminating, and I thank him for many amusing and enlightening conversations over the years.

Nobody, therefore, is better qualified to write about the Welsh greats, and when Peter invited me to write this foreword to the book, I was delighted to accept.

Clive Woodward
September 2011

PROLOGUE

This book has been more than 50 years in the writing. If that sounds an inordinately long time to acquire an appreciation of Welsh sport in its many guises, then all that can be said in my defence is that there has been much to appreciate.

The earliest memories remain the sharpest: of Glamorgan County Cricket Club and a youthful Don Shepherd against Kent at St Helens in 1954, on a rare dry day during one of the wettest summers on record; of the Northamptonshire fast bowler Frank 'Typhoon' Tyson starting his run at what seemed like one end of Ynysangharad Park in Pontypridd and the England wicketkeeper Keith Andrew standing at the other.

Memories, too, of Yorkshire at the Gnoll in Neath; of how every time he beat the bat without getting a touch a disgusted Fred Trueman would give a look as filthy as the coal-black clouds scuttling behind the little pavilion. Other imperishable moments clamour for attention: an expedition to London in the early autumn of 1961 for my first experience of English football. Cliff Jones made it unforgettable, the Welsh wing flying down the touchline like an Olympic sprinter on a balmy September evening at White Hart Lane, when the double-winning Spurs played in the European Cup.

In a hitherto unseen feat of gymnastics, Jones crossed the ball in full flight, and every cross seemed to land perfectly enough on the head of Bobby Smith, for the bustling England centre-forward to head four of the eight with which Spurs overwhelmed the Polish champions, Gornik. Every one, I swear, from Cliff's hanging centres. And those, remember, were the days when the European Cup truly was an elite competition: for national champions only, unlike its twenty-first-century equivalent, the Champions League – a misnomer, if ever there was one.

That sort of luck followed me around, as if I had been blessed by serendipity. My first day as a news reporter on the *South Wales Echo* – Monday, 2 November 1964 – just happened to be the day long jumper Lynn Davies brought his Olympic gold medal home from Tokyo to Nantymoel and they took the conquering hero around in a pony and trap, the next best thing to a chariot of fire.

The first time I saw an international at Cardiff Arms Park, from the terracing in front of the old North Stand, it coincided with Terry Price dropping a goal that climbed to such an altitude that it seemed to come down out of the clouds before clearing the Irish cross-bar by about 30 feet. Wales duly won the Triple Crown at a time when winning it was a far bigger deal than it is now.

My first Wales soccer international later that year proved to be every bit as serendipitous, the might of the USSR picked off in a World Cup qualifying match at Ninian Park by a sumptuous goal from Ivor Allchurch, one of the finest footballers of his generation, or any other. They called him the 'Golden Boy', a classic inside-forward, as they were known in his day, renowned for his artistry and sportsmanship. His image, sculpted in bronze, stands at the entrance to the Liberty Stadium, the twenty-first-century home of Swansea City.

Allchurch belonged to a time long gone when footballers performed before massive crowds for no more than £20 a week, which meant it was just as well that they played largely for the love of the game. Not even the best rugby league players got that much as part-time professionals, which meant they had jobs outside the game. Rugby union players, of course, did it for nothing, or the vast majority did, in compliance with the archaic amateur regulations. In an era when nobody danced to the tune of television, satellite or terrestrial, the winter sports adhered to clear demarcation lines, which gave the summer ones a clear run.

A multitude of Welsh athletes, cricketers, boxers, golfers, jockeys, footballers and rugby players have performed many heroic deeds down the decades, so many that my most difficult task was to limit the final choice. The list is an entirely subjective one, based on my own experiences over almost half a century's observation of the great and the good in my role as a sports journalist privileged enough to have witnessed history in the making.

To do Welsh sport justice, there had to be more to the book than rugby and football; there is so much more to Wales than the two main winter passions. Success in other spheres dictated that the final choice had to be eclectic. After months of agonising, my final choice of seventeen subjects spanned ten different sports and just about every decade since the Second World War.

For the majority, success meant fame and, in some cases, fortune. Others found their pursuit of excellence cut short by serious illness or other traumatic events. Two lost their lives in very different circumstances, each doing what he did best, hence the title: *Triumph and Tragedy*.

All 17 fulfilled the most demanding criterion: that each and every one should have a unique claim to fame.

Jimmy Murphy, a coalminer's son from the Rhondda, the emergency manager who rebuilt Manchester United from the ruins of the Munich air disaster.

Allan Watkins, from Usk, the first Glamorgan cricketer to play in an Ashes Test match.

Don Shepherd, the only bowler to take more than 2,000 first-class wickets and *not* play for England.

John Charles, British football's first, and greatest, export to the Continent; a player never booked, let alone sent off, despite some brutal treatment during his years in Italy.

Billy Boston, one of the all-time greats of rugby league, who tells why he would have given up all his trophies to have played just once for Wales at the Arms Park in his native Cardiff.

Mike Davies, the tennis rebel who left the amateur ranks when professionalism was still a dirty word and revolutionised the sport in America.

Ken Morgans, the youngest of the Busby Babes, who, despite surviving United's crash at Munich, was never the player he had been.

Lynn Davies, the only Welsh athlete to win Olympic gold in track and field.

Clive Sullivan, the first black man to captain Great Britain, at the Rugby League World Cup, which they won.

Mervyn Davies, struck down at the zenith of his career by a brain haemorrhage which denied him the captaincy of the Lions and left him lucky to be alive.

Gareth Edwards, the only rugby player never to miss a match for his country over a period of 11 years, which made him the most automatic of international rugby choices.

Keith Jarrett, the only teenager to flatten England almost single-handedly on his debut a few months after leaving school.

Tom Pryce, still the only Welsh motor-racing driver to win a Formula One race, and a world champion in the making when he was killed in a freakish accident at the age of 27.

Johnny Owen, the last British boxer to lose his life as a result of fighting for the world title.

Ian Woosnam, the one Welsh golfer to win a major.

Carl Llewellyn, on his own as the only post-war Welsh jockey to win the Grand National twice.

Finally, a player who refused to throw in his lot with England and went on to win more Premier League titles than anyone else, irrespective of nationality: *Ryan Giggs* – even if, at the time of writing, he is synonymous with super-injunctions, having been named by an MP in the House of Commons over a sex scandal.

***

This book could not have been written without the cooperation of so many who gave so willingly of their time at homes stretching from Florida to the south of France, Jersey to Humberside, Merthyr Tydfil to Manchester, Wigan to Hull, Ruthin to Cardiff and many places in between.

My thanks to the following interviewees: Allan Watkins, Andy Griffiths, Billy Boston, Carl Llewellyn, Sir Clive Woodward, Dai Gardiner, David Watkins, Dick Tingle, Don Shepherd, Eric Harrison, Gareth Edwards, Ian Woosnam, Jimmy Murphy junior, Jim Mills, Hugh McIlvanney, John Barton, Johnny Freeman, Keith Jarrett, Ken Morgans, Kevin Ratcliffe, Lynn Davies, Mervyn Davies, Mike Davies, Mike Nicholas, Neil McLaughlin, Nella Pryce, Nobby Stiles,

Owen Davidson-Doyle, Paddy Maguire, Peter Walker, Ray 'Chicko' Hopkins, Ray French, Rosalyn Sullivan, Sharon Dixon, Stephanie Morgans, Sean Fitzpatrick and Tony Vlassopulos.

I am also indebted to my old friend and journalistic colleague Steve Bale, for casting a scholarly eye over my prose and rescuing it from grammatical and factual error. A special word of gratitude to the *Daily Mail*, and to sports photograph editor Brendan Monks in particular, for allowing me to use some excellent pictures; likewise to Huw Evans of the Huw Evans Photographic Agency in Cardiff; James Clark, head of media at Hull FC; Dr Andrew Hignell, archivist of Glamorgan County Cricket Club; Edith Hughes, manager of research and archives at BBC Wales, also Louise Hillam and Alison Jenkins; and Georgie Fame, for permission to reproduce 'Ode to Billy B'.

I must also acknowledge the help given by Rob Cole, David Meek, Dan O'Neill, David Sadler, John Stiles, Gareth Jones, David Tremayne, Richard Shepherd, Bobby Wanbon, Steve Groves, Richard Williams, Howard Evans, Clive Lewis, Robin Davey, Terry Grandin, Glyn Potter, Kenny Kahn, Alan Evans, Keith Dewhurst, Paddy Byrne, Jimmy Armfield and Mario Risoli.

Finally, my thanks to Bill Campbell and Graeme Blaikie for their encouragement, to Debs Warner for her editing skills, and to everyone else at Mainstream.

Peter Jackson
Cardiff
September 2011

I

MANAGING MANCHESTER UNITED'S RESURRECTION

Jimmy Murphy

Born: Pentre, 8 August 1910
Died: Manchester, 14 November 1989, aged 79

William Murphy joined the mass emigration from Ireland shortly after the turn of the twentieth century. Instead of taking a left turn out of his native Kilkenny and sailing westwards across the Atlantic, he went the other way, opting for the shorter journey east by ferry to the British side of the Irish Sea.

His search for work took him inland to the booming South Wales coalfield and a job underground in one of the biggest pits of all, the Maindy Colliery in Pentre, at the very heart of the Rhondda Valley. Soon enough, the Irish widower met a Welsh widow, Florence Louisa Eynon (née Scourfield), whose husband's premature death had left her to raise four sons and a daughter on her own.

They married and, on 8 August 1910, Florence gave birth to a fifth son, James Patrick. The year had already been an auspicious one in a more tangible sense for Manchester United Football Club: the young Murphy's birth came just six months after United played their first match at Old Trafford on a site which had been acquired thanks to the largesse of the club chairman, John Henry Davies, in stumping up £60,000 of his personal fortune for its construction. The *Manchester Guardian* acclaimed the playing surface of the 45,000-capacity stadium, describing it as 'as smooth and as green as a billiard table'.

The *Sporting Chronicle* paid gushing tribute to what its correspondent called 'a football ground unrivalled throughout the world'.

It would be a matter of time before the infant James Patrick would play a monumental role in ensuring that Manchester United became 'unrivalled throughout the world' for more than their ground. Nine months after his birth, United had won the Football League championship for only the second time, reclaiming the title one point ahead of Aston Villa and seven clear of Sunderland in third place. They would not win it again until the early 1950s, by which time William and Florence's son was working round the clock to create his very own footballing phenomenon, the Busby Babes.

The Murphys' youngest was still a babe in soccer terms when he began to show signs of musical talent as a pianist and church organist. His mother, anxious for the boy to make enough of his education to avoid a dangerous, back-breaking life mining coal, thought he was destined to become a schoolteacher. As a pupil, he was considered above average, even if he did have a penchant for 'talking too much'.

His other penchant was for football, starting with a team called the Pentre Linnets. From there, he climbed swiftly up the ladder to Pentre Boys, Treorchy Juniors and Glamorgan Boys. A terrier-like wing-half in the days when there were such things, the young Murphy displayed such a precocious talent that by the age of 13 he had been picked for Wales against England in a schoolboy international in Cardiff, where he played with and against boys of 16 and 17. He had found his escape from the pit.

Unlike thousands of his compatriots during the 1920s, Murphy discovered a more rewarding way of life in the West Midlands than working on the assembly lines in the car factories springing up around Birmingham and Coventry – as an apprentice professional in the English First Division with West Bromwich Albion FC. The young Murphy went about his new career with a zeal that meant every ball was there to be won, as though his life depended on it.

They called him 'Tapper', a nickname inspired by his strength in the tackle and the periodic impact that would inevitably have on an assortment of ankles. As one opponent observed: 'You needed two pairs of shin pads against Jimmy . . .' As Murphy told one of his protégés two decades later: 'Remember this, son. They can't play without their ankles.'

He would never have indulged in fanciful talk about 'the beautiful game'. Murphy had been brought up in a tough old school long before they began to dilute the sheer physicality of football as it used to be. 'I'm not happy with our tackling, boys,' he told the Busby Babes at half-time during one of their youth games. 'We keep hurting them, but they keep getting up.'

During more than ten years at the Hawthorns, he played 204 first-team matches for the Baggies, a term of endearment inspired by the generous length of their white shorts. Four years after appearing in their losing FA Cup final against Sheffield Wednesday in 1935 and with twenty-one appearances for Wales to his name, Murphy moved to Swindon with his wife Winnie, their three-year-old daughter Patricia and baby John.

The outbreak of the Second World War, while finishing him as a player, unleashed a long chain of events that would lead to his meeting with another international wing-half from a coalmining background: Matt Busby. The hazardous, roundabout journey that brought them into contact took Murphy to the deserts of North Africa with the Eighth Army, then Tunis, Rome and, ultimately, Bari.

By the time Murphy left to fight Rommel in the campaign that famously marked a turning point in the war, with victories at Tobruk and El Alamein, his wife had given birth to a second son, Philip, with a third on the way. Born in July 1942, James Patrick was named after his father because his mother feared her husband might not survive the war.

By 1945, Murphy was one of thousands of British troops pushing up through Italy after the retreating Germans. With their war virtually over, the soldiers finished up at a camp in Bari on Italy's Adriatic coast, where Murphy's principal job was to keep them occupied by organising football and cricket matches. Busby, a physical training instructor, arrived there with a band of professionals, among them a pair of English internationals who would go on to manage champion teams: Stan Cullis with Wolverhampton Wanderers and Joe Mercer with Manchester City.

One exhibition match pitted Busby and company against Murphy's men. When the little Welshman spoke, Busby had never heard anything quite like it. He made a mental note, there and then, that the fiery Welshman with the Old Testament rhetoric would join him in rebuilding Manchester United at the bombed-out Old Trafford. Sgt Murphy was recruited on the spot, in a part of the Continent to which he would return to conquer, in a footballing sense, more than 20 years later. What Busby heard in that army camp in Bari kept ringing in his ears.

'This little man was talking football with the passion and fervour of a Lloyd George or a Richard Burton,' he said. 'His audience was entranced, as I was. He spoke as if delivering a sermon and we were all transfixed. It was his attitude, his command, his enthusiasm and his whole driving, determined action and word power that caused me to say to myself: "He's the man for me." I asked Jimmy to join me at Old Trafford as my assistant when he had been demobbed and returned to England.'

Long before 'motivation' became a buzzword in sporting parlance, Murphy had made himself a natural exponent of the art; in fact, he was expert by the time he first rolled up his sleeves in his search for the crème de la crème of schoolboy talent during the immediate post-war era. Nobody summed up 'Murphy the motivator' more colourfully than the revered Peter Doherty, then nearing the end of his playing career, festooned by a League Championship medal with Manchester City before the war and an FA Cup winner's medal with Derby County immediately after it. Billy Wright, a colossus with Wolves and England throughout the '50s, always referred to him as 'Peter the Great'.

Doherty, a stylish inside-forward considered by common consent to have been the best footballer produced in Northern Ireland before George Best, said of Murphy: 'When Jimmy talks about football and Manchester United with a youngster, he not only paints a picture but fills in all the details like a Michelangelo or a Raphael.'

The Murphy family reunion at the end of the war did not last long. By the middle of 1946, after introducing himself to James junior, then three years old, the breadwinner was getting stuck into his new job up north as head coach of Manchester United, with special responsibility for all players outside the first team, which remained

Busby's preserve. Murphy coached the reserves every day and then devoted two evenings every week to the younger players, who were either in nine-to-five jobs or still at school.

By the time Winnie and the kids, then up to five with the birth of Nicholas, relocated to Manchester in 1948, with a sixth, Anne, arriving the following year, Busby had taken the decision that would rejuvenate his team as never before and turn them into the youngest champions in Football League history. He put his Welsh right-hand man in charge of youth development, a task that would demand an extensive search-and-find operation throughout the British Isles for the best schoolboy talent.

Murphy set up a scouting network par excellence – but that was only the beginning. Separating the wheat from the chaff, identifying those who he believed would make it from those who would not, was down to Murphy. He then coached them until such time as they were ready for the first team, whereupon they promptly rolled off the assembly line. Busby had an unwavering belief in Murphy's priceless gift for spotting exceptional players and then ensuring they realised their potential.

His eye was so sharp, his instinct so strong that there were times when Murphy could make his mind up in a matter of minutes. Sent during the post-Busby era to run his eye over a centre-half at a lower-division club, Murphy made the journey in the company of Harry McShane, an ex-United player, and his actor son, Ian. They took their seats in good time for the start, whereupon McShane junior went off to buy three coffees. He returned five minutes later to find his father sitting on his own. Murphy had gone, his mind made up about the player before they even kicked off.

'Jimmy's seen enough,' McShane senior told his son. 'He says that the feller he's come to see can't play and won't make it in the First Division. He says there's no point staying, so we're off home.'

Murphy brought a whole galaxy of stars to Old Trafford. There were those who came from Manchester itself, such as Roger Byrne, Eddie Colman, Bill Foulkes and Nobby Stiles. Others came from a little further afield: Bobby Charlton from the North-east; the titanic Duncan Edwards from the West Midlands; Mark Jones and David Pegg from South Yorkshire; Liam 'Billy' Whelan, Jackie Blanchflower

21

and, a little later, George Best from opposite sides of the Irish border.

The Busby Babes swept all before them. Murphy's Marvels would have been a more apposite name for their collective ability, not that their creator would have been the least bit interested, given his aversion to the limelight. The way Jimmy saw it, Busby had given him the 'dream job' and the Welshman was happy to do his bit – and was happier still that his light remained hidden beneath a bushel.

His babes won the FA Youth Cup five times in a row from 1953 to 1957. During this time they had minimal contact with Busby due at least in part to the fact that, pre-floodlighting, all matches kicked off on Saturday afternoons, when Busby would always be on first-team duty. When floodlighting allowed the Babes to strut their stuff midweek, Murphy would finish his team talk with a reminder of who would be watching: 'The Boss is here tonight. So let's show him what you're made of.'

None of those hanging on his every word owed more to Murphy than Bobby Charlton, and certainly nobody has reason to be more grateful. Charlton would never have become one of the all-time greats without his Welsh mentor, and Bobby Charlton would say so himself. Murphy was, to him, simply 'the greatest teacher of football I would know'.

Murphy used his own concoction of the stick and the carrot to turn his protégé into a world-beater from day one. 'Jimmy, as had been so clear from our first meeting, was the man,' Charlton said. 'He was ever-present on the training field in his tracksuit top and shorts, his pot belly protruding with the evidence of how much he liked a pint. He was on to me all the time, standing close to me as a practice match unfolded, chiding me, irritating me. I suppose he was testing my patience when things were not going right, as when he stepped into my path and tripped me when I was in full flight. Jimmy was so intense he used to scare me. He would kick me during practice games to toughen me up. As I moved through the ranks, Jimmy's personal tuition grew more intense and more specialised.

'I learned a lot from Matt Busby and Alf Ramsey. However, everything I achieved in football I owe to one man and only one man, Jimmy Murphy. Matt and Alf were good to me but Jimmy really got to my guts. Jimmy was simply sensational.'

The shy Geordie boy and the sergeant major from the Rhondda spent endless hours in shooting practice, Murphy teaching his pupil the art of shooting for goal without looking at the target, thereby reducing the goalkeeper's chances of stopping the shot. England would never have won the World Cup in 1966 without the younger Charlton brother's mastery of a technique taught by the coalminer's son from Pentre.

'Even today, I pour beer into the mug and raise it to the memory of the man who taught me everything he knew.'

By investing heavily in producing their own players at a time when other clubs were increasingly reliant on buying ready-made material for escalating sums via the transfer market, the club saved themselves a fortune by relying on Murphy's intuition. A consequence of their philosophy was the family atmosphere created at Old Trafford, where every young player was assured an apprenticeship in better conditions than he had sampled in his time between the wars. The club took painstaking care over the players' welfare, especially that of the young ones, by accommodating them in digs run by landladies who had been chosen by the club for their strong sense of family values.

By the start of February 1958, when the Babes were going for their third League title in a row, while fighting on a Continental front for the European Cup, there were some 40 professionals on their books. Of those, only five cost a transfer fee: Harry Gregg from Doncaster Rovers, Johnny Berry from Birmingham City, Tommy Taylor from Barnsley, Ray Wood from Darlington and Colin Webster from Cardiff City.

Murphy, who had been upgraded to assistant manager three years earlier, had built a dynasty capable of extending United's domination of the English game for years to come and challenging Real Madrid's hegemony in Europe. With that in mind, Busby and United took off for a European Cup quarter-final against Red Star Belgrade. Fate, for once, decreed that they would make that fatal trip without Murphy.

As the part-time manager of Wales, he headed to Cardiff to prepare for a play-off against Israel at Ninian Park on the same Wednesday afternoon as United's match in Yugoslavia. The clash of fixtures, which coincided with Wales clinching qualification for the

World Cup finals in Sweden that summer, saved Murphy's life. The man who sat in the Welshman's seat next to Busby on the plane, Bert Whalley, was among the 23 who perished when their chartered aircraft crashed on take-off at Munich. The death toll included eight players, three officials, eight journalists, two crew and two other passengers.

Jimmy Murphy junior, a 15-year-old pupil at St Bede's College, heard about the crash on the radio and read about it in the late editions of Manchester's two evening newspapers after returning from school to the family home in the south Manchester suburb of Whalley Range.

'My mother threw her hands up in horror,' he said. '"Oh dear God," she said. "Your father . . . your father's on the plane."'

'I must confess that, in the initial shock, the same thought went through my mind. Dad had wanted to go with United because he always felt that was where he ought to be. Fortunately, Matt was adamant that, much as he wanted my dad with him, he had a job to do with the Welsh team and that was that. Once I'd gathered my thoughts, I calmed my mother down and assured her that Dad had gone to Cardiff and he'd be home any minute.'

Murphy arrived back in Manchester that Thursday afternoon by rail from Cardiff and took a taxi from Piccadilly station to Old Trafford unaware of what had just happened on a snowy airfield in southern Germany. Alma George, Busby's personal secretary, gave him the news as soon as he got to his office.

Seven players – Roger Byrne, Mark Jones, Tommy Taylor, Billy Whelan, David Pegg, Eddie Colman and Geoff Bent – were killed in the crash. An eighth, Duncan Edwards, survived but died a fortnight later. Of the eight, all bar Taylor, who had been signed from Barnsley, were Murphy babes.

Nothing in his life could possibly have prepared him for a crisis of such magnitude. Murphy acted swiftly and decisively. He caught the first available flight to Munich and rushed straight to the Rechts der Isar Hospital, where 'the Boss', Matt Busby, lay with such severe injuries that he was twice given the last rites.

Somehow, Murphy had to cope with an overpowering sense of grief and not lose sight of the fact that he had to find a team to tackle an ever-rising backlog of fixtures, starting with Sheffield Wednesday in the fifth round of the FA Cup 13 days later.

Harry Gregg, the goalkeeper who performed heroics in leading the rescue of passengers trapped in the doomed aircraft, saw Murphy at the hospital.

'Jimmy was on the stairs, his shoulders shaking as he sobbed and sobbed,' he said. 'He mourned the loss of so many people, especially the fine young men he had turned from schoolboys into footballers admired throughout the whole of Europe. He recognised the enormity of the task ahead.'

As soon as he had let the grief pour out and regained control of his emotions, Murphy was taken into the ward where Busby lay. 'I remember it vividly,' he said some years later. 'The pilot was in the bed on the left. Across from him was Matt in an oxygen tent and when I went across they lifted the flap. He turned his head and said: "Oh, it's you, Jimmy. Keep the flag flying."'

Back in Manchester, as a fleet of hearses waited to collect the coffins at Manchester airport, Murphy pushed his sorrow aside to carry out what he feared had been Busby's dying wish: to ensure that United would still be there when 'the Boss' came back – if he came back.

According to Jimmy junior, the immediate effect was to double his father's daily cigarette consumption, from one packet to two. Almost a whole team had been wiped and now, within a matter of days, Murphy had to find a new one. Of the 11 in action in Belgrade, only Gregg and full-back Bill Foulkes would be fit to play.

'These were the darkest days of my life, but I recall the superhuman strength and resilience of Jimmy Murphy as he undertook his gargantuan task,' Foulkes said. 'How he survived emotionally, I will never know. Those boys were like sons to him and so many had been snatched away. I have no idea how he coped with all the problems. He had the weight and expectations of the world on his shoulders.

'Jimmy was a firebrand of a motivator who lifted those around him by his sheer passion and energy. He was an inspiration to everyone – players, wives and staff.'

One of his first decisions was to take the survivors and those lucky enough to have missed the Belgrade trip away from the pervading sorrow that enveloped Old Trafford and decamp to Blackpool. In between comforting relatives and discussing arrangements for the many funerals, he signed the England international Ernie Taylor from Blackpool and shored up his defence by recruiting Stan Crowther from his old club, West Bromwich Albion.

He filled the other seven vacancies by promoting the next class of his babes on a night when United rode a tsunami of emotion to win, against all the odds, 3–0. One of the babes, Shay Brennan, scored twice in a victory that Gregg acclaimed as 'a great act of man-management. Jimmy had a very distinctive knack of knowing just what to say. It is why the wee Welshman was so invaluable to Manchester United.'

Murphy went on defying the odds for the remainder of that shattered season. He made such a good job of putting United together again that they reached a second successive FA Cup final and if that failed to produce the fairy-tale win everyone wanted – save for those with an allegiance to their opponents, Bolton Wanderers – Murphy's revivalist power had transformed Manchester United and turned them into a club that would forever stand apart from the rest because of Munich.

Foulkes summed it up succinctly: 'Before the crash, Manchester United belonged to Manchester. Afterwards, the club belonged to the world.'

That summer, Murphy devoted himself to managing Wales, using his miraculous powers to coax and cajole the national team to a place they had never dreamt of going before: the quarter-finals of the World Cup in Sweden. They managed it in spite of the haphazard organisation that has tended to be a hallmark of the Football Association of Wales down the decades.

They had booked their squad into a sports camp in London for a few days prior to departure for Stockholm, or at least they thought they had. When Murphy and his troops arrived, they discovered that they had nowhere to practise, the pitch having been declared out of bounds after re-seeding. Undaunted, Murphy whisked his 22-man squad to Hyde Park. In the finest tradition of schoolboys the world over, they peeled off their tracksuit tops and used them as goalposts.

No sooner had they started than a park ranger called a halt to training and pointed to a large sign: 'No ball games allowed'. Imagine Sir Alf Ramsey or Sir Alex Ferguson pleading with a council flunkey to let his players use a public park in preparation for the World Cup finals. Using the same powers of persuasion that had convinced a pyjama-clad 15-year-old Duncan Edwards to get out of bed and sign for United because the Welshman in the front room refused to leave without getting his autograph on the dotted line, Murphy talked the ranger into letting them stay – on the guarantee that they would be gone in an hour.

His team talks were the stuff of legend, as the players discovered on his appointment to the part-time role of national manager in October 1956. Before sending Wales out to face England – and Duncan Edwards – at Ninian Park twelve months later, Murphy went through his players one by one, telling each in turn how to match and better his English opponent. When he had finished, Murphy said: 'Right, anyone got any questions?'

Reg Davies, the Newcastle United inside-forward, spoke up.

'Yes, boss. I've got one.'

'Fire away, Reg.'

'I'm up against Duncan Edwards, but you haven't said what I should do.'

Murphy looked at Davies, a slight figure who would be made all the slighter by the sheer power of the mightiest Busby Babe, and thought for a few seconds in anticipation of the unequal physical contest.

'Reg, do yourself a favour. For ****'s sake, keep out of his way . . .'

Murphy could mix brutal candour with his ability to make players feel ten feet tall. Colin Webster, a Manchester United striker who joined the club from Cardiff City, said: 'By the end of his team talk, you wanted to run through a brick wall for him. He was a hard taskmaster and a wonderful motivator. If Murphy hadn't been at Old Trafford, the Busby Babes would never have existed. What he achieved after Munich was fantastic. I don't think Busby could have done it. Murphy was a one-off.'

Wilf McGuinness, another Busby Babe, who played for England and later managed United, can vouch for that. Murphy's very own brand of *hwyl* ensured the United teenager would make the most of a challenging first-team debut, against Wolves, with the task of marking their England international inside-forward, Peter Broadbent.

'Jimmy told me in his passionate way that Peter would be trying to take the win bonus out of my pocket,' McGuinness said. 'I'd be giving some of that money to my mother, and Jimmy rammed home the point that, if I wasn't able to do that, it would be because Broadbent had stolen it from her. Being the true gentleman that he was, Peter Broadbent came over to me just before kick-off to wish me all the best for my career. I was so wound up by Jimmy's speech that I screamed at him: "Take your thieving hands out of my pockets."'

Nobody held Murphy in higher esteem than John Charles, then in his second of five years at Juventus. His time in Italy would confirm his status as the finest all-round British player of his generation. Playing for Wales in a play-off against Hungary, Charles took such a battering that the national squad had to line up against Brazil without him. The quarter-final was won by the first World Cup goal from a 17 year old who would prove himself greater even than Charles – Pele.

'All the players thought the world of Jimmy,' Charles said. 'He was the best manager I ever came across.'

Over ten months at Old Trafford, Murphy carried out a masterly rebuilding of the shattered club. By the end of 1958, the foundations had been laid of what would become a global business. 'Things were going so well, I could have sat in my office for the next ten years,' Busby said later. 'Everything was in place.'

Once he had recovered sufficiently to resume full control for the second half of the 1958–59 season, his No. 2 happily ducked back out of the limelight to devote his energy to creating another FA Youth Cup-winning team of Babes, which he duly assembled, as promised, in 1964. By then, the 'pot-bellied wee Welshman' had turned down a variety of jobs to manage clubs from Arsenal to Juventus and a fair few in between. For those who questioned why he declined every approach, Murphy answered with a stock question: 'How can you put a price on loyalty?'

His sons inherited the same love for the United cause. Phil was briefly a Babe in the weeks after Munich before concentrating on a career in accountancy, while Nicky, Murphy's youngest son, played as a professional in United's reserve team for three years during the late 1960s before transferring to Reading.

Their father, meanwhile, was busy revelling in the responsibility of presiding over the next generation of United stars, one of whom turned out to be the brightest in the galaxy, as Murphy knew he would be when he first saw what he could do with a football. One look at the then waif-like 15 year old, dispatched to Old Trafford by the club's Belfast scout, Bob Bishop, prompted Murphy to advise Busby: 'Matt, don't coach this boy, George Best. He's a genius.'

The world at large realised that a few years later, when, in 1968, with Best ultimately unplayable, United at last got their hands on the trophy they had been pursuing on their tragic way home from Munich ten years earlier. What the world at large did not realise was that Best considered Murphy to be his mentor and it was Murphy, not Busby, whom he turned to for advice.

'There has been a lot of talk about Matt being like a second father to me,' Best said. 'He was good to me, but I never went to Matt with my problems. If I went to anyone for advice, it was to Jimmy Murphy. He would call me into his office or, sometimes, phone me and ask: "George, what's up?" And we would talk through my problems.'

Murphy, still scouring the British Isles for talent, pleaded with Busby to sign a young centre-half from Blackburn Rovers, Mike England, and long after his recommendation had been rejected, the tall Welshman enjoyed many successful years with Tottenham Hotspur.

While his family remember a man 'of his time' who placed a high premium on loyalty and hard work at the expense of personal glory, he was also, in some senses, a man far ahead of his time. Importing the best foreign players into English football is a comparatively recent phenomenon; nobody had thought of doing it way back in 1956, when communications were so primitive that connecting a phone call from Britain to anywhere behind the Iron Curtain could take hours. The only non-British passport holders at Old Trafford in those days were from the Republic of Ireland.

When the 1956 uprising in Hungary raised questions over the future of its mighty home-based players, Murphy urged United to sign the mightiest of them all: Ferenc Puskas. Whether or not Busby and the board found it a bit too daring for their liking, the recommendation fell on deaf ears and the 'Galloping Major' galloped off to Real Madrid, then in their pomp as undisputed champions of Europe.

Murphy's influence at United had been waning by the time Busby stood down in 1971 and he retired two years later. However, in 1974, when the unthinkable happened – Denis Law, then playing for, of all clubs, Manchester City, back-heeled a goal which sent United down into the Second Division – Tommy Docherty, who had succeeded Frank O'Farrell as manager, duly reinstated Murphy, albeit in a part-time scouting capacity.

'I brought Jimmy back for his experience and his judgement,' Docherty said. 'He found outstanding players such as Steve Coppell and Gordon Hill. He'd say one of two things to me. It'd either be "Sign him," or "Don't sign him." I was happy to take his advice because I never doubted him . . . Jimmy didn't get half the credit he deserved. In my opinion, he was as great as Busby. Matt was wonderful, but he would not have been half the man without Jimmy.'

Sir Alex Ferguson, or plain Alex as he was then, had clearly done his homework on the men who had made United great before his appointment in November 1986. As an acknowledgement of Murphy's success before and after Munich, the new manager wasted no time beating a path to the Welshman's front door in the small town of Poynton, some ten miles south of Old Trafford.

'That was one of my last memories of my father,' Jimmy junior, said. 'Within a couple of weeks of getting the job, Alex called to see my dad. He asked him: "What's wrong with this great club?" My dad told him: "You want to go back to basics and get the youth policy sorted out. The whole system needs a good shake-up." You could say my father knew a bit about both . . .'

Within a few years of putting Murphy's advice into practice, Ferguson had laid the foundations on which to build the most successful club in the history of British football. How strange, therefore, that one of the architects of United's rise in the '50s, the man responsible more than any other for their salvation post-Munich, should remain its unsung hero.

Murphy's innate aversion to being caught under a spotlight of any kind meant he would not have had it any other way. When, in 1966, United were to mark his first 20 years at the club by presenting him with a canteen of cutlery and a silver salver, Busby's No. 2 flatly rejected the club's plan to present it to him out on the middle of the pitch immediately before kick-off. Instead, it was done behind closed doors in the boardroom.

According to Jimmy junior, Busby 'always said there would be a treasured place' for his father at Old Trafford. How sad, therefore, that his long association with United should end with the club refusing to pay a home telephone bill that he had run up talking to scouts all over the British Isles and parents of prospective United players. What a shame that nobody at the club saw fit to pay what was no doubt a piffling sum set against the untold millions Murphy had made by turning an array of schoolboys into priceless superstars.

'My father had a great affection for Matt. He was, after all, the man who had given him what he called his "dream job". He was in love with United and Matt Busby. They were a great partnership because my father could do things Matt couldn't do and vice versa.

'Matt was the architect. Bert Whalley laid the foundations. And my dad was the master builder. Between them, they created a magnificent mansion. And if it's even bigger today, then that is down in no small way to what my dad achieved immediately after Munich. Matt himself said that, without him, United might have collapsed and sunk out of sight for many years.

'When Matt was well enough to take the reins again after the crash, my dad was very happy to be going back to being the No. 2. As long as he had a pint and a ciggy, he was happy. He was a great dad to all of us. He'd always be first up in the morning, lighting the coal fire and getting us breakfast. He'd leave about 9.30 and we wouldn't see him for 12 hours. He was such a workaholic that I only ever had two holidays as a kid. We had a week in Rhyl when I was thirteen, and about six years after that we had two weeks in Newquay.

'He never said anything derogatory about Manchester United, but he did feel in later years that his worth to the club over the 25 years during which he served them had not been recognised. Deep down, he probably did feel let down, that he should have been treated better in recognition of the great conveyor belt of talent which he produced and which didn't cost the club a penny in the transfer market.

'I think the family feel, like a lot of old Manchester United people, including players, that nobody knows who Jimmy Murphy was these days. If you talk to Manchester City fans about the great days of the past, they'll talk about Joe Mercer and Malcolm Allison. United fans talk about the Busby years without any mention of Murphy.'

George Best, for one, felt Murphy deserved better. 'Jimmy was pensioned off in 1971,' he said. 'He was given a scouting job but felt let down by Matt Busby, to whom he had been so loyal, and he expected more in return. Jimmy Murphy, a trusted lieutenant and loyal sidekick for many years, was dumped and hurt by [Busby's] ruthless streak.'

In Busby's defence, it has to be pointed out that he was never less than generous in praise of his other footballing half. 'No one outside the club will ever know how important Jimmy was to the huge success and fame of Manchester United,' Busby said. 'Without doubt, Jimmy was the inspiration of the Manchester United that rose like a phoenix after Munich.'

Even so, the suspicion lingers that Murphy was taken for granted, that his role remains a strangely underplayed one. Years after putting a statue of Sir Matt up outside Old Trafford, they got round to commissioning a bust of Murphy, which was unveiled in the Munich Room at the stadium.

'One of Dad's main qualities was his humility,' Murphy junior said in his speech at the unveiling. 'He was a humble and straightforward man who never forgot his roots in the Welsh mining community. He had no interest in big houses, fancy cars, exotic holidays, restaurants and clubs. As long as Mom was happy, the family healthy and he had enough money for a pint and a cigarette, then he was contented.

'He hated fuss and, if alive today, he would be waiting in one of the local pubs for someone to pick him up on the way home from this function. To Dad, Manchester United was not about Matt Busby. It was not about Busby and Murphy. It was about the whole club. Everyone was important. He tried to find time for everyone. He never forgot the important work done by Walter Crickmer and Les Olive, by his great pal Bert Whalley and the other coaching staff, by the lovely Joe Armstrong and the other scouts, by everyone connected to Manchester United.

'We would like to feel that this bust represents not just Jimmy Murphy but is a symbol for all the backroom staff – the family that was Manchester United.'

On 23 March 2009, a ceremony in South Wales eliminated any risk of Murphy becoming a footballing prophet without honour in his own land. Family, friends and old internationals from near and far, including Nobby Stiles, gathered for the unveiling of a plaque at 43 Treharne Street, Pentre – where William Murphy's youngest son grew up.

For Murphy, the essence of any winning football team lay in its ability to win the ball in the tackle. No international player exemplified Murphy's ethos more strikingly than Stiles, the win-it-and-give-it specialist of England's victorious 1966 World Cup team. 'England would never have won the World Cup without Jimmy Murphy,' Stiles said on a chilly winter morning in Manchester. 'Bobby Charlton was the best player in that entire World Cup tournament and he would never have been that good without Jimmy's coaching.

'He had this brilliant knack of making you believe you were the greatest player he'd seen. He loved me because I won the ball in the tackle. I couldn't hit a 40-yard pass like Bobby or Duncan Edwards, but I'd win it and then I'd give it to people like Bobby. I cannot overstate how much I owe Jimmy Murphy.

'He was a truly amazing man. I never met anyone who had greater passion for the game ... I can remember how he used to get Duncan Edwards ramming the ball against a brick wall and controlling the rebound for hours on end just to improve his touch and feel. I really loved playing for Jimmy. He loved me because my game was to win the ball and give it. For Jimmy, it was all so simple – pass and move, pass and move.

'If it hadn't been for him, I honestly do believe that there wouldn't have been a Manchester United, at least not Manchester United as we know it today. If it hadn't been for Jimmy working non-stop after the crash, I don't think there would have been a Manchester United. I was so proud to be there that day for the unveiling of the plaque at the house where he grew up because I owed him so much.'

Bobby Charlton could not be there on that cold spring Monday morning in the Rhondda, but he prepared a speech read out on his behalf, which paid suitable tribute to a son of the Rhondda who gave '90 per cent' of his life to Manchester United.

'Jimmy Murphy was the best coach I could have wished for,' Charlton had written. 'He would call me in to Old Trafford on a Sunday morning for sessions one-to-one and I found them very hard and uncompromising. And he'd say: "Never moan that you are tired. Hard work on the pitch never really hurt anyone. You could be in a factory or down a pit." All this tuition turned me from an amateur into a professional and a team player.

'Jimmy loved a drink! He hated to go to bed and if you were unlucky enough to catch his eye, you had to stay and listen to him. Jimmy was all football and even though you were tired and wanted to go to bed, Jimmy's words were pure magic.

'His talks would make us better players. He always told me that I was a good listener. The listening probably made me a better player. Jimmy Murphy was full of passion and determination, with a relentless streak to him. Jimmy was the best teacher the young players could wish for. A lovely man . . .'

Only a native son of the Rhondda, where so many paid so dearly for working so long underground, could achieve what he did and still keep an almost subterranean profile.

2

SEEING BRADMAN OFF

Allan Watkins

Born: Usk, 21 April 1922
Died: Kiddiminster, 3 August 2011, aged 89

At the Oval cricket ground in London, shortly before six o'clock on the evening of Thursday, 14 August 1948, Don Bradman came out to bat in a Test match for the last time in his baggy green cap. The crowd rose as one in a standing ovation. When the captain of Australia got to the crease, his opposite number, Norman Yardley, acknowledged the magnitude of the occasion by issuing a spontaneous command to the England team encircling the little chap in the size-five boots: 'Three cheers for the Don!'

The English admiration still ringing in his ears, with a little Welsh thrown-in for good measure, the greatest batsman of them all took guard, acutely aware that his invincible team would almost certainly win the match on their first innings alone.

England had made such a hash of their innings – skittled for 52 after a start delayed by a sodden outfield – that Australia's openers had more than doubled that miserable total by the time Bradman emerged from the pavilion in the early evening sunshine at the fall of the first wicket. When the second would fall was anyone's guess.

In twelve completed innings for Australia at the Oval since first appearing there in 1930, Bradman had compiled three double centuries and four single centuries – 252 not out, 244, 232, 146, 143, 128, 103, 77, 77, 61 not out, 27, 16 and 7. Anything short of 125.20, therefore, would be decidedly below average. As the close-wicket fieldsmen crouched more in hope than expectation, the one closest to the new batsman wondered whether he, too, would be accompanying Bradman through the exit door of Test cricket.

Allan Watkins had made the long, winding pre-motorway journey from Cardiff to London two days earlier in readiness for the distinction of becoming the first Welshman to play in an Ashes Test. 'I was amazed when they picked me,' he said, in his last interview two years before his death in August 2011. 'I'd been overlooked all the way through the series. You get a feeling when you think you have a chance and when you haven't. I didn't think I had a hope.'

His form during the three weeks prior to the Test hardly demanded his inclusion. His last seven innings had yielded the princely total of 69 runs, including a top score of 23 against Somerset at Weston-super-Mare and 19 against the Australians at Swansea, where bank holiday crowds of more than 50,000 had turned up, despite rain finishing the match mid-afternoon on the second day. He had fared better with the ball in the matches immediately before his England selection, taking 13 wickets at an average of 13, but took just the one during the tour match.

The majority of the many summoned that summer in the hope of, at the very least, delaying Australia's remorseless march through the series failed to make much of a difference, and Watkins found out all too soon the difference between a debut of the fairy-tale variety and the one he was in the throes of suffering at the Oval.

Batting at number seven, he fell leg before to Bill Johnston for a duck. To add insult to injury, he hung around long enough to be struck on the shoulder by a bouncer from Ray Lindwall in the course of the Australian fast bowler's assault on the English batting. Whatever hope Watkins had of redeeming himself by sharing the new ball with Alec Bedser had gone with the blow which meant he could bowl no more than four overs.

While everyone knew that Bradman was playing his last Test, the new all-rounder feared it was only a matter of time before they realised he was playing his first *and* his last. Being a pragmatic sort of bloke, he saw himself returning to Glamorgan as soon as England had been put out of their misery, never to be required for national service again.

When Bradman played back to his first ball from the Warwickshire spinner Eric Hollies, Watkins picked the ball up at short-leg and in doing so ensured himself a place in cricketing folklore – the last man in a Test match to field a shot from Don Bradman.

The next one from Hollies darted between bat and pad and hit the off-stump. All the great man needed in order to bow out with a Test batting average of 100 amounted to a solitary boundary. Instead of getting the four runs for a triple-figure career average, he had to make do with 99.94, the price he paid for being undone by the Hollies googly, a leg-spinner's standard trick; it spins the opposite way to the normal leg break, turning into the right-hander instead of away from him.

One explanation trotted out down the years for a duck almost as famous as Walt Disney's Donald was that Bradman was a victim of the emotion that swirled around him every step of the way from the boundary gate to the crease. No less an authority than John Arlott gave it some credence: 'I wonder if you see the ball very clearly in your last Test on a ground where you've played some of the biggest cricket of your life and the opposition stand around to give you three cheers,' he said. 'I wonder if you really see the ball at all.'

Len Hutton, later Sir Leonard, said that Bradman told him: 'It's not easy to bat with tears in your eyes.' But another England batsman from that match, Jack Crapp of Gloucestershire, gave the sob story short shrift: 'That bugger Bradman never had a tear in his eye in his whole life.'

Watkins was firmly in the Crapp camp in dismissing the notion of a batsman as hard-nosed and ruthless as Bradman becoming a nervous wreck. 'He didn't say anything to anyone the whole time he was at the wicket, but that was nothing unusual,' Watkins said in an interview. 'I was very close to the bat, about five yards away at short-leg as usual, and I didn't say anything to him.

'After the skipper called for us to give him three cheers, he knuckled down as usual and we all thought we'd be lucky to stop him making another hundred. Bradman was not a man to get emotional. He was probably nervous, but he was far too disciplined to let anything distract him. And then, when Eric bowled him second ball, he walked off, and again I don't remember him saying anything.'

Others who were there that day held Bradman in such awe and wonder that it seemed as if something sacrilegious had happened. The spontaneous reaction of one England player articulated their sense of loss: 'My goodness, Eric,' he said in a half-congratulatory, half-admonishing way. 'What have you done?'

Bradman said in his autobiography, *Farewell to Cricket*: 'That reception stirred me deeply and made me anxious – a dangerous state of mind for any batsman to be in. I played the first ball, though not sure I really saw it. The second was a perfect-length googly which deceived me. I just touched it with the inside edge of the bat and the off bail was dislodged. So in the midst of my great jubilation at our team's success, I had a rather sad heart about my own farewell as I wended my way pavilion-wards.'

Up in the press box, Jack Fingleton and Bill O'Reilly, two of Bradman's Australian teammates from pre-war tours and the main thorns in his side over the years, celebrated as if they had won the lottery. The guffawing pair, from a similar Irish Catholic background, admired 'Bradman the voracious run-getter' but not 'Bradman the man'. When Bradman was out, said a fellow commentator who was with them at the time: 'I thought they were going to have a stroke, they were laughing so much.'

According to one of Bradman's biographers, the brutal side of Australian cricket had never been so openly on view. 'Bradman's riposte came much, much later,' Charles Williams wrote in *Bradman: An Australian Hero*.

Bradman himself recalled: 'O'Reilly nakedly exposes the disloyalty I had to endure based purely on jealousy and religion. Fingleton was the ringleader. He conducted a vendetta against me all his life and it was most distasteful because he was a prolific writer of books and articles. Conversely, with these fellows out of the way, the loyalty of my 1948 side was a big joy and made a big contribution to the outstanding success of that tour.'

In his wake, Bradman left behind a scorecard of historic proportions:

England 1st innings:
L. Hutton c Tallon b Lindwall 30
J.G. Dewes b Miller 1

W.J. Edrich c Hassett b Johnston 3

D.C.S. Compton c Morris b Lindwall 4

J.F. Crapp c Tallon b Miller 0

N.W.D. Yardley b Lindwall 7

A.J. Watkins lbw b Johnston 0

T.G. Evans b Lindwall 1

A.V. Bedser b Lindwall 0

J.A. Young b Lindwall 0

W.E. Hollies not out 0

Extras (b 6) 6

Total (42.1 overs) 52

Bowling:

R.R. Lindwall 16.1-5-20-6

K.R. Miller 8-5-5-2

W.A. Johnston 16-4-20-2

S.J.E. Loxton 2-1-1-0

Australia 1st innings:

S.G. Barnes c Evans b Hollies 61

A.R. Morris run out 196

D.G. Bradman b Hollies 0

A.L. Hassett lbw b Young 37

K.R. Miller st Evans b Hollies 5

R.N. Harvey c Young b Hollies 17

S.J.E. Loxton c Evans b Edrich 15

R.R. Lindwall c Edrich b Young 9

D. Tallon c Crapp b Hollies 31

D.T. Ring c Crapp b Bedser 9

W.A. Johnston not out 0

Extras (b 4, lb 2, nb 3) 9

Total (158.2 overs) 389

Bowling:

A.V. Bedser 31.2-9-61-1

A.J. Watkins 4-1-19-0

J.A. Young 51-16-118-2

W.E. Hollies 56-14-131-5

D.C.S. Compton 2-0-6-0
W.J. Edrich 9-1-38-1
N.W.D. Yardley 5-1-7-0

England 2nd innings:
L. Hutton c Tallon b Miller 64
J.G. Dewes b Lindwall 10
W.J. Edrich b Lindwall 28
D.C.S. Compton c Lindwall b Johnston 39
J.F. Crapp b Miller 9
N.W.D. Yardley c Miller b Johnston 9
A.J. Watkins c Hassett b Ring 2
T.G. Evans b Lindwall 8
A.V. Bedser b Johnston 0
J.A. Young not out 3
W.E. Hollies c Morris b Johnston 0
Extras (b 9, lb 4, nb 3) 16
Total (105.3 overs) 188

Bowling:
R.R. Lindwall 25-3-50-3
K.R. Miller 15-6-22-2
W.A. Johnston 27.3-12-40-4
S.J.E. Loxton 10-2-16-0
D.T. Ring 28-13-44-1

Umpires: H.G. Baldwin and D. Davies

Australia won by an innings and 149 runs.

The landslide win, with a day to spare, reinforced Watkins' fear that his England career had finished four days after it had started and that he would never be picked again.

'It was bloody awful, to be perfectly honest, and when it was over I thought: "Well, that's it." I thought that was the end of me, as far as Test cricket was concerned.

'It was a very different world back then. Nobody made a fuss, the way they do now. Norman Yardley gave me my cap. It was a very proud moment and one or two said: "Well done." He was a nice lad, Norman. And I'd always been friendly with Denis Compton. We were both soccer players, so we had a lot in common, but I felt very disappointed when I first joined the England team.

'They could have made me feel more welcome. Instead I was left with the feeling that I wasn't wanted. Apart from Denis, I didn't know many of them. The selectors were trying people out to see if they were up to it.

'I used to suffer a lot from nerves and that was a big problem for most of my career. Very often in my sleep, I'd suddenly wake up and shout: "Catch the bloody thing." In my mind, I was playing cricket all the time and sometimes it was impossible to get to sleep. I found it very difficult to switch off. My wife Molly was my greatest supporter and she'd often say: "For goodness sake, try and relax."

'Then there was the time I threw out my left hand to make another catch in my sleep and I caught my dear wife on the nose. No wonder she was always on at me to relax. More often than not I couldn't get to sleep. If I did, it was only for a very short time and then I'd feel tired the next morning before a day's cricket.'

Just as Fingleton and Bradman were never bosom pals, the same could be said of Watkins and Hutton. It was no coincidence that the Welshman's international career ended with Hutton's appointment as England's first professional captain in 1952, a year before they regained the Ashes from Australia and then defended them down under during the winter of 1954–55.

By then, Watkins had become far more than a one-cap wonder. After three more failures with the bat at the start of the five-match series in South Africa a few months after the Oval debacle, the policeman's son from Usk began to justify his inclusion in the team. An unbeaten 64 in the third Test at Newlands in Cape Town paved the way for a maiden century, 111, in the drawn fourth Test at Ellis Park, Johannesburg, in February 1949.

Watkins lost his place to Trevor Bailey, a young all-rounder from Essex, and it took him almost two years to get it back. A match against India in Delhi proved to be his finest hour. Batting a second time, more than 200 behind, England pushed their Glamorgan all-rounder up one to number four and he responded with a match-saving 137 not out, duly acclaimed in *Wisden*, the cricketers' bible: 'An heroic rearguard action led by Watkins, who batted for nine hours, enabled England to draw a match which India should have won.'

He followed that with 80 in the second Test, 68 in the third and 66 in the fourth. If only his results with the ball had been half as good, England would have been hard pushed to find an excuse for dropping him. Hutton's installation as the new skipper, against the same opposition later that year, marked the beginning of the end for Watkins. Scores of 48, 0, 4 and three wickets as a support bowler to Bedser and the newly capped Fred Trueman led to Watkins being replaced by the dual international footballer-cricketer Willie Watson during the series. This time, there would be no coming back.

There are those who blame Hutton for that, including Watkins himself: 'Every member of Glamorgan wanted to know why I was dropped. The powers-that-be can be a funny lot. They never give you reasons and I had no idea. Not good enough, I suppose, [though] I must admit that [Hutton] and I didn't get on that well. We were never on the best of terms. He came across to me as a dour Yorkshireman. I certainly had the feeling that he didn't want me in the England team. I had a feeling that I was the wrong man, as far as he was concerned, certainly from the way I was treated.

'I'm afraid Len's cricket wasn't my cricket. He spoke very quietly, almost as if he was talking to himself. Whenever we played against each other on the county circuit, there wasn't much said.

'I was certainly getting enough runs. I was never really quick enough to open the bowling, not at Test level. I was medium pace, but I was never given the ball often enough to do myself justice and prove myself as a Test match all-rounder. I was only used in short spells.

'The other thing was that I was playing for the wrong county, wasn't I? Half the England team during my time came from the posh counties, as we called them – Surrey, Middlesex, Yorkshire, Lancashire. Glamorgan weren't fashionable and I do believe the better players suffered because of that.

'We were still unfashionable, despite winning the County Championship. The general attitude elsewhere was that we were very lucky to win it.

'We were out of it, out on our own, and in that respect nobody was treated as badly as Don Shepherd. They'd go on about his batting, but his bowling was so good, and England's batting in those days was strong enough for them to have picked him.

'What kept my career going was my fielding at short-leg. It was a new position in those days. Glamorgan were playing in Cardiff one day and I was in the slips. Johnnie Clay was bowling off-spin and one delivery popped up on the leg-side with nobody there. I looked at the skipper [Wilf Wooller] and he looked at me and said: "Go on. Get over there." And I stayed there for the rest of my days.'

Not for nothing did Fingleton pay fulsome tribute to Watkins' acrobatics and hawk-like catching within striking distance of the bat. The incomparable John Arlott gave a vivid, eye-witness account of the feline qualities behind one of Watkins' more stupendous efforts to get rid of the South African opener Dudley Nourse in Durban at the start of the 1948–49 series.

'The wicket, for the first day of the match, was plumb and Nourse was seeing the ball well. Then came a ball from [Doug] Wright, which came in to him a little. Lunch was near and Nourse decided not to risk an attacking stroke but to allow the ball to fall away from his bat on the leg-side.

'He directed it well wide of Watkins and its arc was shallow and short. But, suddenly, we saw Watkins at short-leg dive, feet higher than head, and seeming to lie in the air four feet off the ground, he coolly reached out and took the catch. Nourse was out – and, by the expression on his face, astounded to boot. The deciding factor in his selection must have been his brilliant fielding.'

He held the catch, what's more, without losing his floppy white sun hat, which Watkins presented later in the tour to a 12-year-old boy who would use it as an inspiration to become a specialist close-wicket fieldsman of the highest quality in his own right. Peter Walker, who would emulate Watkins as an England all-rounder, albeit briefly, grew up in South Africa and he was there at Kingsmead in Durban to see the famous catch for himself.

'Allan had given me the memento when, later during the MCC tour, he had come to dinner at the family home, following up a suggestion from Les Spence, the honorary secretary, that when in

43

Johannesburg he should contact an old Canton High School pal of his, Oliver Walker – my father. Allan Watkins was my mentor and inspiration.'

His acrobatics had been a crucial factor in Glamorgan's anointment as county champions for the first time a little later during the summer of 1948. They had the satisfaction of leaving the fashionable quartet of Surrey, Middlesex, Yorkshire and Lancashire to occupy the four positions immediately beneath them. Glamorgan wrapped it all up against Hampshire in Bournemouth a few days after Bradman's duck, but without their new England all-rounder, temporarily rendered *hors de combat* by the continuing effects of Lindwall's bumper. By the time the new champions were treated to a match against a South of England XI in honour of their status, Watkins had recovered sufficiently to win the strictly unofficial Wales–England Test match with an unbeaten century.

Five years later, during the early stages of a season in which he topped the Glamorgan batting averages, showing his determination to prove he was good enough for England again, Watkins had another run-in with his bête noire.

Hutton, partnered by Frank Lowson, had put on more than 170 for the opening wicket at Bramall Lane on 30 May 1953 and got to within two of a century when Watkins caught him off another England hopeful, off-spinner Jim McConnon. Fingleton did not call Watkins 'the best close-wicket catcher in the world' for nothing.

'The incident began when Hutton played the ball round the corner,' Watkins said. 'I was fielding at short-leg and it went sharply to my right. I stuck my hand out and caught it. He stood there as though nothing had happened. I couldn't understand that, because I'd caught the ball almost waist-high.

'It wasn't as if there was any doubt about the ball being grounded. I'm standing there, trying to think what the umpire must be thinking. And with that the umpire, I think it was Laurie Gray, said: "You're out, Len. He's caught it." Hutton had to go, but he didn't like it.

'People ask me who was the greatest batsman I played against and, bearing in mind that the only time I played against Bradman was in his last Test, I'd say Hutton. He always looked safe. Even when he got out he looked safe, like that day at Sheffield.'

Gray did umpire on that occasion at Bramall Lane but, according to one of Watkins' teammates, the decision to give Hutton out fell to the other umpire, Alec Skelding. 'Len wouldn't go,' Don Shepherd said, years later. 'Poor old Alec was the umpire who had to give Hutton out. When we left the field, we walked through a hail of cushions.'

Later that year, Hutton had the last laugh – at the expense of his rival's Test future. Wilf Wooller, then an England Test selector, as well as the autocratic captain of Glamorgan, returned from a meeting at Lord's, where they had finalised the 17-strong party for the defence of the Ashes in Australia. Don Shepherd tells what happened next.

'Wilf came back and told Allan: "Congratulations. We'll have a drink tonight."'

'Allan said: "Congratulations on what?"'

'You can pack your bags. You're going to Australia with England.'

Wooller had got his man the trip as the second all-rounder alongside Trevor Bailey, or so it seemed. Watkins waited for official confirmation from the MCC, and waited, and waited. Instead the invitation was sent to the uncapped Yorkshire batsman Vic Wilson, who retired some years later, still uncapped.

'According to Wilf, Hutton had insisted on making one change to the original selection, which meant Vic was in and Allan was out,' Shepherd said. 'Vic was a fine cricketer, but he was not in Allan Watkins' class, and Allan had done so well on the previous tour in South Africa. It does make you wonder. I should imagine Wilf would have been very annoyed. It put him in a very embarrassing position.'

Wooller and Watkins made an odd couple. Their backgrounds could hardly have been more contrasting, the latter a Cambridge-educated private schoolboy, the former a working-class lad who belonged to that dying breed, the cricketer-footballer, before it followed the dodo into extinction. Wooller, who died in 1997 in his 85th year, ran Glamorgan with a rod of iron for decades – as captain, secretary, then president, whose myriad tasks included negotiating a television deal with BBC Wales on condition he would do the commentating.

A controversial figure, not least because of his strident stand for the maintenance of sporting links with South Africa at the height of the despised apartheid regime, Wooller was at his best fighting against the odds, even when they proved to be every bit as hopeless as they looked. His 'over my dead body' attitude was never more evident than in his backing of the recently retired England captain Ted Dexter as the improbable Conservative candidate who stood against James Callaghan in his stronghold of Cardiff South-East during the general election of 1964.

Watkins, born ten years AW (After Wilf) on 21 April 1922, moved to the beat of a different drum. 'Wilf was, how can I say, a most peculiar person. He was an MCC man and a real Establishment man. His attitude on many things was diametrically opposite to mine. He had a domineering manner.

'We used to have some arguments, did Wilf and I, on a variety of subjects – about bowling and field-placing generally. Being a senior player, I'd very often have a word with Wilf. What I found difficult to understand, what with him being so high up in the selection of the England team, was why we didn't have the selectors looking at us more often. There were a few arguments, all right.'

One of them was in full flow when a callow youth from Neath Grammar School – and future England captain – Tony Lewis first ventured into the hothouse atmosphere of the Glamorgan dressing-room during the mid-'50s. Senior players, such as Haydn Davies and Watkins, were in the midst of a ding-dong with Wooller over something which had, or had not, happened out in the middle.

When Wooller caught sight of the 17-year-old schoolboy, he broke off from the row.

'Hello, Tony,' he said, cheerily. 'Welcome to the madhouse.'

On at least one occasion, the dressing-room took on the appearance of an alehouse brawl, without the ale. Peter Moss, my predecessor as the *Daily Mail*'s resident Welsh sports journalist, was an outstanding newspaperman from tip to toe, which was saying a lot because there was at least 6 ft 4 in. of him. He went on to become the paper's distinguished boxing correspondent, an apprenticeship that may have begun in the Glamorgan dressing-room at the Arms Park long before the move to Sophia Gardens.

Peter Walker had a ringside seat.

'Peter [Moss] tapped on the dressing-room door and asked Wilf if he could get a quote from one of the Glamorgan batsmen who was experiencing a bad run of form. Wilf leapt across the dressing-room and, to our astonishment, grabbed Peter by the throat and wrestled him to the floor.

'The senior players managed to pull Wilf off and a dishevelled Moss rapidly exited. Peter could so easily have laid a charge of GBH against Wilf, but he didn't. However, particularly to the junior members of the team, it was a graphic illustration of what would happen if we crossed the captain.'

Moss swears to this day that he was ahead on points, but that's another story.

As for Albert John Watkins, he changed his name because of Wooller: 'We were signing autographs somewhere on the county circuit. I wasn't too sure whether to sign it Albert or John, and Wilf was in a rush. So when I tried to explain it to him, he said: "For God's sake, sign it Allan." I did and it's been Allan ever since.'

Like Wooller, Watkins made his debut in first-class cricket for Glamorgan before the war, at the age of 17. Hitler having put a stop to all that, the budding cricketer-footballer served King and country in the Royal Navy, based at Devonport, reappearing at scrum-half for Pontypool in a wartime match against a team of New Zealand All Blacks.

The would-be sailor spent the entire war on dry land, denied the opportunity of being sent to help the Australian Navy because of his sporting prowess. 'I joined the navy because I wanted to go to sea,' he said. 'I'd never been on a ship in my life, so I was excited at what lay in store for me.

'I was in what they called a fire-fighting barracks at Devonport and that's where I stayed. Then a few of us were drafted to go to Australia. We got packed and the officer in charge, who was mad on sport, said to me: "Where do you think you're going, Stoker Watkins?"

'I said: "To Australia, sir, with the other lads."

'He said: "Take all your kit back to the barracks. You are going nowhere. And if you're disappointed, Watkins, it's your own fault. You shouldn't have been so bloody good at football and cricket."'

Back on civvy street, Watkins signed for Plymouth Argyle in the old Third Division (South). When the Argyle manager agreed to release him from training during the final fortnight of the season, Watkins was back where he had been so rudely interrupted seven years earlier. And he made the most of it, marking his return to Wales with a maiden first-class century at Cardiff Arms Park. The seasons were defined clearly enough for other dual professionals, such as Arthur Milton and Willie Watson, to play both sports at the highest level.

Watkins' hopes of making himself more than a journeyman wing-half ended when England chose him for their South African tour in the winter of 1948–49, by which time he had joined Cardiff City.

'Playing both sports was perfect for me because there was very little overlapping of the seasons,' he said. 'I played cricket from the end of April to the end of August and football in between. I was back in training with Cardiff City at Ninian Park in the September of that year when I found out by accident that England had picked me for South Africa.

'Sir Herbert Merrett was both president of Glamorgan and chairman of Cardiff City. I was doing quite well in their Welsh League team and there was talk about me getting into the first team. Then one day Sir Herbert came into the dressing-room at Ninian Park after training.

'He started off by congratulating me. I couldn't understand it. I thought: "What the hell are you talking about?" That's how I learnt I'd been picked for the England tour. The news was still sinking in when he said: "You realise that your soccer career is finished, or at least it is as far as Cardiff City is concerned. You won't be playing for us any more."

'A few weeks later, I was on the boat to South Africa with England.'

Despite playing the last of his fifteen Test matches at the age of thirty, Watkins kept going on the county circuit for another nine years before a worsening asthma condition contributed to his retirement at the height of the 1961 season. His form had deteriorated to the point where only a few weeks earlier he had bagged a pair for the first time in his professional life, against Lancashire at Neath. His last match, against Kent at Gravesend in the first week of June that year, proved to be a sadly anticlimactic one – no wickets, no runs, no catches.

Watkins deserved something far better as befitting the finest all-round Welsh cricketer of any post-war generation. The statistics speak for themselves: 484 matches, 20,361 runs, 833 wickets, 464 catches – and that by a man denied the opportunity, like so many of his time, to start until he was 24. Imagine how much more formidable his figures would have been had the Second World War not wiped out the first six summers of his life as a county professional.

He stayed in the game as a coach, but not of Glamorgan. Instead the old England all-rounder imparted his wisdom to generations of pupils at two English public schools, Framlingham and Oundle, the Northamptonshire town where he would have been far too modest to explain to the locals why his wife Molly had their house named after a stadium in Johannesburg more famous for its rugby than its cricket. It was at Ellis Park in February 1949 that he batted himself into history as the first Welshman to make a century for England.

The passing of Arthur McIntyre in December 2009 and Alec Bedser in April 2010, both aged 91, meant Watkins was the second-oldest surviving England Test cricketer behind the former Nottinghamshire opening bat Reg Simpson. The gallant Welsh all-rounder who saw Bradman off more than sixty years earlier died in Kiddiminster on 3 August 2011, more than three months into his ninetieth year.

3

A SHAMEFUL TEST CASE

Don Shepherd

Born: Port Eynon, 12 August 1927

Don Shepherd bowled his first ball in county cricket on Saturday, 29 April 1950 at the Oval against Surrey. He bowled his last on Tuesday, 25 August 1972, against the same opposition at the same Test venue, signing off with a pair of international scalps, John Edrich of England and Younis Khan of Pakistan.

Before he could start work on proving himself the greatest bowler England never picked, the shopkeeper's son from Port Eynon, towards the western edge of the Gower Peninsula, harboured fleeting hopes of a career in professional football.

Leeds United gave him a week's trial on the strength of a recommendation from the scout who had sent John Charles to the club a season or two earlier. A Yorkshire League match against Sheffield Wednesday gave the budding centre-forward from Swansea YMCA an improbable chance to persuade Major Frank Buckley that he had unearthed another rough Welsh diamond. Leeds' formidable manager sent Shepherd to the barber for a haircut, then confirmed what the young fellow had known all along: that he was too 'ordinary' a footballer to justify a professional contract. Homeward bound, he became an extraordinary cricketer instead.

'Shep' grew up with cricket from the age of five, when the family left Port Eynon for nearby Parkmill, where his father ran the village store. 'My grandfather was the local postman for 50 years and he used to score for the local cricket club, so I'd be with him on a Saturday. I have a vague memory of bowling a few balls in the outfield during the tea break. I can honestly say I never had a day's coaching in my life. That sounds like conceit, but it's not, because I couldn't think of a logical reason why I should have been a bowler.'

Nor did that change despite his winning a scholarship just before the outbreak of the Second World War to Gowerton Grammar School, where two pupils, teenagers Willie Davies and Haydn Tanner, joined forces as Swansea's half-backs when the Whites famously defeated the All Blacks. During his years there, Shepherd played surprisingly little in the way of competitive cricket.

'We used to have a slog-about on the concrete yard,' he said. 'We'd bring out a few old bats and balls, run down to the field and play during the lunch break. If I played half a dozen organised matches during the war years, that would have been it. I can recall playing against Neath Grammar, against Dynevor School in Swansea, in Llanelli and Ammanford – six at the very most.'

By the end of the war, the teenage Shepherd had spent several winters trying to perfect the art of fast bowling during long hours of often solitary practice on the beach at Three Cliffs Bay not far from home. To have claimed that it was all part of a grand plan to take more wickets than any other Welsh bowler in cricketing history would have been stretching the imagination too far. There was no grand plan.

In late 1945, at the age of 18, he enlisted in the Fleet Air Arm for the compulsory two years' national service. 'I did an aptitude test, as we all did, and I was told I had no mechanical ability,' he said. 'So I was promptly made an air mechanic. I did the basic training to learn air-craftsmanship, and again the opportunity presented itself to play a bit of cricket, especially when I was stationed in Worcestershire. Somebody must have seen something in me.'

Whoever he was saw enough to put the young Welshman in the station team for a match against the Gentlemen of Worcestershire at Pershore. Somebody else, Major M.F.S. Jewell, a former Worcestershire captain, also saw something and arranged a 'little trial' at New Road, which consisted of Shepherd bowling at a set of stumps and Syd Buller, Worcestershire's new coach, who would appear in the Test arena as an umpire, keeping wicket.

'They said: "Bowl." I bowled and that was about it.'

He made enough of an impression for Worcestershire to offer him a contract, guaranteeing a place on the Lord's groundstaff for the 1948 season. When word of the English county's interest filtered back across Offa's Dyke, Glamorgan, anxious to avoid the embarrassment of losing one of their own, made the 20 year old aware that there would be only one place for a Welshman to play county cricket.

Worcestershire's plan was to groom Shepherd to succeed Reg Perks, their veteran fast-medium bowler who was in his mid-30s when cricket resumed after the war. Against all the odds, Perks kept going until the mid-'50s, retiring in his 44th year with 2,233 first-class wickets, a total made all the more remarkable given that he lost six of his best seasons to the war.

'Worcester wanted me to understudy Reggie and take over when he'd finished,' Shepherd said. 'Thank God I didn't, because Reggie seemed to go on for ever. Had I gone to Worcester, I probably would never have smelt 1,000 wickets, never mind 2,000. Don Bradman always seemed to get 200 or 300 every time he played there. It was that sort of a pitch.'

When he reported for duty at the home of cricket, Shepherd had never attended a county match of any description. 'I didn't know anything about Lord's,' he said. 'In fact, I'd never been to London before. At first I stayed in Kent, which meant a long bus journey at the start and end of every day, until a relative of the groundsman got me digs within walking distance in St John's Wood.'

The apprenticeship at Lord's kept him busy all day, every day. 'You did your own work in the nets in the morning. Then whenever any member of the MCC wanted a net, he used to whistle up the bowling staff and you took it in turn to bowl for half an hour. Then after half an hour's rest, you were back in action.

'It was quite a long day because we didn't finish until seven in the evening, but I loved it. I got to meet famous players like Denis Compton and Bill Edrich, whom I got to know well in the coming years. "Compo" always used to make a point of coming to the young pros' room in the pavilion before a Middlesex match and having a chat. He was a very kind soul and sometimes he'd bring an old bat, which he'd give to one of the lads. What he really liked was a game of shove-halfpenny. Nobody could beat him at that.

'The big thrill would be when a member came out and put half-a-crown [two shillings and sixpence in old money] on top of one stump under the bail. If you hit the right stump, the money was yours. Some of the groundstaff lads did well by knowing the good tippers. Denis Noble, the old opera singer, was one.

'I got £100 for the summer and Glamorgan augmented that by another £100. It was a really hard grind, which is missing from the game now, but an invaluable experience. I was there to play cricket, although in the back of my mind there was always the safety-valve of the little family shop in Parkmill, which meant I wouldn't fall on hard times.

'I was a very, very quiet boy in those days and Sunday was a very, very quiet day. All I did was walk the streets. I'd never had a drink in my life, not even when I was in the services. I remained teetotal until Wilf Wooller told me: "You'll never bowl furiously fast on orangeade."'

A Second XI match for Glamorgan towards the end of the 1948 season pushed him within Wooller's substantial sphere of influence for the first time. He could hardly have joined at a more auspicious period, the county having won the championship for the first time a few days earlier.

'I'd reached my 21st birthday at Lord's but, compared with a 21 year old today, the amount of cricket I'd played was almost nil. I knew nothing and it's certainly true that I knew nothing about batting. I was just a natural bowler who could run up and bowl, and bowl and bowl. They were quite happy with what I was doing at Lord's, but nobody knew whether I'd get any better.'

It would be a little longer before they found out. The home part of Shepherd's apprenticeship continued throughout 1949 in the Second XI and in club cricket for Swansea, where he joined forces with another local boy whose name would become synonymous with the all-rounder's craft of batting, bowling and close-wicket catching, Jim Pressdee.

While Pressdee made his Glamorgan debut at the age of 16 towards the end of that summer, Shepherd had to wait for the start of the decade, by which time he was well into his 23rd year. The scarcity of new talent during the immediate post-war years, particularly in the fast-bowling category, makes his delayed entry all the more surprising.

Once he began his marathon stint, Shepherd rapidly made up for any lost time. He went on and on and on, until a fortnight beyond his 45th birthday, when he decided that he'd done enough.

By then, he had got through the best part of 10,000 miles in the course of delivering 132,562 balls over 23 summers and compiling a monumental tribute to his accuracy, skill and perseverance. In doing so, he left a record that made a mockery, of monumental proportions, of the selectors' perennial refusal to pick him even for one Test match.

Shepherd's stack of 2,218 wickets puts him seventh in the post-war list of leading wicket-takers in first-class cricket. The proliferation of truncated forms of the game, and consequent reduction in the traditional county fixtures, ensures that Glamorgan's marathon man will never be overtaken.

Derek Shackleton	Hampshire	2,857	7 Tests
Tony Lock	Surrey	2,844	49 Tests
Fred Titmus	Middlesex	2,830	53 Tests
Derek Underwood	Kent	2,465	86 Tests
Fred Trueman	Yorkshire	2,304	67 Tests
Brian Statham	Lancashire	2,260	70 Tests
Don Shepherd	Glamorgan	2,218	0 Tests
Trevor Bailey	Essex	2,082	61 Tests
Ray Illingworth	Yorkshire	2,072	61 Tests
Norman Gifford	Worcestershire	2,068	15 Tests

Every one of the six above him and the three immediately beneath him played for England, all but Shackleton and Gifford on a regular basis. While making every allowance for the ferocity of the competition, it is a staggering coincidence that various selection committees excluded Shepherd year in, year out, while picking 14 other spinners – Jim Laker, Lock (Surrey); Malcolm Hilton, Roy

Tattersall, Tommy Greenhough (Lancashire); Johnny Wardle, Bob Appleyard, Illingworth, Don Wilson (Yorkshire); John Mortimore, David Allen (Gloucestershire); Martin Horton (Hampshire); Titmus, Pat Pocock (Middlesex); Gifford (Worcestershire); Robin Hobbs (Essex); Peter Walker (Glamorgan); and Underwood (Kent).

In 1956, when the Australians were Laker'd by the Surrey off-spinner's 19 wickets at Old Trafford, Shepherd reaped the richest harvest of all: a staggering haul of 177 wickets for the season, which included twelve in a match on two occasions and a whole clutch of analyses that had to be read more than once to be appreciated, like this one from the second innings against Hampshire at Bournemouth – 16 overs, 11 maidens, 6 runs, 4 wickets.

How close Shep came to a Test place will remain a mystery because the man best qualified to reveal all, Wilf Wooller, has long since gone to the celestial pavilion reserved for departed England selectors.

'How close? I honestly don't know,' Shepherd said. 'I can honestly say I never lost one night's sleep wondering whether I would be chosen. We were not really a side very much in people's minds, although, having said that, Wilf was a selector for all those years. So, in one sense, I couldn't have been closer to one of the selectors.

'There were a lot of good bowlers about at the time. Without being unkind to those concerned, I think I could have done as good a job as quite a lot of those who did play for England. When it came to overseas tours, there was a theory that off-spinners had to throw the ball in the air and buy their wickets and, by and large, they didn't have much success.

'One of the little motivational things which kept me going towards the end of my career was when we played Kent and came up against the young Derek Underwood. Derek was like me in reverse, in that he bowled left arm medium-fast spin. He was one of the great bowlers of all time and I used to gee myself up to see how my figures compared with his. Derek was only 20-odd at the time and I was nearer 40, so it was a big struggle.'

Had Shep not made a radical change and reinvented himself as a fast off-spinner, his career in Wales would probably not have survived the mid-'50s. Three lean years following a haul of 120 wickets in 1952 left him, in the words of one teammate, with twelve months on his contract and a final chance to avoid finishing up with the dreaded P45. As Shepherd's luck would have it, England did not tour that winter, and when the Australians arrived in 1953 England had found a new pair of fast bowlers.

'I bowled pretty well, seam up, to get all those wickets, but others were coming through who would be around for years,' Shepherd said. 'Brian Statham and Fred Trueman were beginning to establish themselves. Peter Loader was on the way. And then there was the fastest one of all, Frank Tyson, who had begun to make his mark with Northants.'

The summer of 1956 turned out to be one of the wettest in memory and yet it marked Shepherd's rebirth as a bowler of such deadly accuracy that over the course of eight seasons he took more than a thousand wickets, conceding fewer than 20,000 runs from almost 10,000 overs.

For all his decades in the game, there would never be another year like 1956. 'My first year of off-spin was as good as I could have wished for,' he said. 'I was new. I suppose I caught people unawares. After one season, they get to know you.'

His total would almost certainly have been all the more imposing had Glamorgan's last two matches, against Lancashire at Neath and Essex in Cardiff, not been almost completely washed out. Incessant rain during the Lancashire match at the end of August restricted play to three and a half hours and more foul weather the following week reduced the Essex fixture to one day. Earlier in that sodden apology of a summer, the Derbyshire match at Chesterfield in the middle of pouring June had to be abandoned without a ball being bowled.

A paragraph from Lancashire CCC's annual report reflected the national mood: 'The sharp fall in public support is disappointing for a season when the team greatly improved its position but the weather was appalling and largely to blame. It cannot be denied that the players have the future of the game in their own hands. The cricket they play must be the cricket the public want to see and, at the same time, be successful, too.'

Towards the end of the previous season, Shepherd had found himself wrestling with a problem that was rapidly degenerating into a crisis. 'My figures were tailing off,' he said, ignoring the fact that, against Northamptonshire at Cardiff in 1954, he had taken a career-best 9-47. 'Halfway through one match at Cardiff Arms Park in 1955, they said: "Why don't you try to bowl off-spin?"

'Haydn Davies had said to me just before that: "Did you ever see Johnnie Clay bowl?" I said: "No, why?" Haydn said: "Because you run around with the same floppy wrist as Johnnie." Wilf told him to keep out of it but I thought the idea was worth trying.

'For the penultimate game of that season, I changed my grip and shortened my run. I began bowling medium-fast off-spinners and I found that it came reasonably easily. That's not meant to sound conceited, but it did. I got ten or twelve wickets in that match and then worked on it in the nets at the indoor school in Neath that winter.'

The match in question, Somerset at Weston-super-Mare, brought him 12 wickets, 6-42 in the first innings, 6-49 in the second. It produced the startling match figures of 61.3 overs, 26 maidens, 91 runs, 12 wickets. The real Shepherd had only just emerged. 'I didn't do a vast amount of practice during the winter, just enough to tick over,' he said. 'I had no idea when I started the 1956 season that all kinds of records would be broken.'

Twice more he took 12 wickets in a match, against Surrey and Hampshire. He took seven in one innings on three occasions, against Lancashire at Old Trafford (7-67), Nottinghamshire at Trent Bridge (7-61) and Somerset at Weston, again (7-90). For good measure, he took 5-38 against Warwickshire from 26 overs at another Test ground, Edgbaston.

One hundred wickets by the end of June proved so tall an order that a sponsor offered a brand-new saloon car to any bowler who could manage it. Shepherd's total had reached 91 when he reported to Trent Bridge with Glamorgan for a three-day match against Notts starting on Wednesday, 27 June. At best, there were four days of cricket left for their newly converted first-change bowler to hit the jackpot and improve his mobility away from the game.

On the second day, Shepherd made the most of a rain-affected pitch to take 7-61 off 38 overs. The weather then ruined what was left of the game, sending Shepherd across country to Kettering, needing two wickets against Northamptonshire on the last day of the month to reach three figures. As fate continued to conspire against him, Glamorgan won the toss and batted out the day.

Shepherd's two wickets, his 99th and 100th of the season, duly arrived on the second day, 1 July. He had missed the deadline and the fancy new car by less than 24 hours. 'One hundred wickets by the end of June had only ever been done once before and, with a bit more luck from the weather, I would probably have done it in time,' he said. 'Don't forget, a brand-new car was worth a good many years' wages for a county professional in those days.'

The following summer, when the West Indies came for a five-Test series as reward for leading England a merry dance seven years earlier when Sonny Ramadhin and Alf Valentine spun their web, the MCC chose Shepherd for their pre-series match against the tourists at Lord's. The optimists interpreted it as a sign that he had played himself into contention; the cynics shrugged it off as nothing more than a gesture – or, as one Glamorgan player called it, 'a sop'.

'The team would consist of some hopefuls and some established players,' Shepherd said. 'When the invitation came through, Haydn Davies, our wicketkeeper, said: "Don't go." Wilf was adamant: "You've got to go." Haydn had experienced one of those MCC games a few years earlier, against South Africa. Whatever he looked like, Haydn was a very fine wicketkeeper. He'd gone in as nightwatchman, got 50 overnight and never heard another word, which is why he said to me: "It's just a sop."

'Anyway, I went.'

The MCC chose a strong team, with a distinct Test look about it. In batting order, it read: Brian Close, Tom Clark, the Revd David Sheppard, Tom Graveney, Colin Cowdrey, Doug Insole, John Murray, Frank Tyson, Malcolm Hilton, Don Shepherd, Alan Moss. Everyone had either been capped by England or was about to be, except Clark, the Surrey opener who never scored heavily enough to push himself into contention, and Shepherd, who most certainly did.

'It rained a lot, I didn't get any wickets and Clyde Walcott got a big hundred,' Shepherd said. 'Only a few years ago I bumped into him in the West Indies and he told me that was the finest innings he had played. He tonked all of us all over the place, but the fielding of that MCC team was abysmal compared to Glamorgan.

'Clyde offered one chance to deepish mid-off and the man on the boundary never came in to go for it. I've never said who the player was but it was the sort of chance which would have been swallowed by a Glamorgan fielder. When you get one wicket, you always think you're going to get two or three at least, but it didn't happen.

'I remember attending the welcome dinner on the eve of the match and sitting next to Wes Hall. He was a very distraught young man who couldn't bowl a legal ball because he was constantly over-stepping. I said to him: "Just persevere and you will become a great fast bowler." He duly did and became so good that I almost wished, for England's sake, that I hadn't said anything!'

Denied by England on an almost perennial basis, Shepherd duly made the most of opportunities to make his mark against international opponents, notably Australia. As a prelude of what was to come, he did so initially by rescuing Glamorgan's match against the tourists at St Helens, Swansea, in May 1961 from disappearing down the commercial plughole. Had it not been for their tail-ender using the long handle as only he could, albeit once in a blue moon, the match might well have been all over in two days, with the consequent loss of gate revenue.

Shepherd top-scored with 51, which was outrageous even by his swing-and-hope standards. The innings was confined to eleven strokes – six sixes, three fours, one two and a single. Those who were there swear that the Aussies were driven to such utter despair that they dispatched one of their fielders to stand halfway up the steep steps from the boundary edge to the pavilion.

'We were eight down for fewer than a hundred early in the morning on the second day when I went in,' Shepherd said. 'There must have been ten or twelve thousand in the ground, with the prospect of more to come, if only we could make a game of it. I batted as I usually batted, trying to slog whatever came my way. I just laid about me and had a few swishes. I played a reasonably good shot at 47 to get my 50 when they switched Richie Benaud to round the wicket. Instead of playing the usual cow shot, I tried to hit it square and found the middle. Unfortunately, it was the middle of the edge and Bobby Simpson, the skipper, took the catch at slip.

'All I heard Simpson say as I went off was: "I've been trying to tell those dull buggers to go round the wicket for the last half-hour." I'm glad they didn't listen because it was good fun while it lasted. When I got to the dressing-room, all Wilf said to me was: "Well done, you've saved the gate ..."'

They saved the match, too, with a little help from the traditional Welsh summer bank holiday weather. When Simpson came back to meet largely the same opponents at the same venue three years later, on a sunnier August bank holiday weekend, Glamorgan turned a gripping three-day event into a Welsh victory as grand as any achieved in the country's larger theatres of sport. The sound of 'Calon Lân' and a few other old Welsh hymns washing over Swansea Bay from a choir of some 20,000 in number made it truly a national occasion.

The Aussies had never experienced anything quite like it. A duel fought with rare intensity from the first ball on Saturday morning to the last the following Tuesday afternoon ended with the tourists finishing 36 short – Glamorgan 197 and 172; Australia 101 and 232. Every Glamorgan player did his bit, not least Alan Rees, the former Wales outside half and rugby league professional whose famous catch at mid-wicket ended Bill Lawry's five-hour vigil and opened the floodgates.

In the end, two bowlers stood head and shoulders above the rest: a pair of local lads who had joined the club at the same time fifteen years earlier – Pressdee and Shepherd. Between them they took 19 of the 20 Australian wickets, finishing with match figures that have long been enshrined in the pantheon of Welsh sport.

Pressdee took 10-123 from 43.3 overs, 11 maidens. Shepherd finished with 9-93 from 69 overs, 41 maidens. Their joint figures, as preserved for eternity, read: 112.3 overs, 52 maidens, 216 runs, 19 wickets. Pressdee captured six in the first innings and four more in the second; Shepherd four in the first, five in the second, when the only Australian to avoid the pair, Norman O'Neill, succumbed instead to another slow bowler, Euros Lewis from Llanelli – one of nine home-grown players in a team that included a West Indian raised in Cardiff, Tony Cordle, and an Englishman, Ossie Wheatley.

Simpson reminded an ecstatic crowd that the Aussies had long memories and that they would be back in four years' time. Pressdee and Shepherd would have made the Aussies feel a little better with their exploits against Yorkshire at St Helens the following season, 1965, when it took them only two days, 9–10 June, to take the white rose apart, petal by petal.

The formidable visitors fielded no fewer than ten England players – Geoff Boycott, Ken Taylor, Doug Padgett, Phil Sharpe, Brian Close, John Hampshire, Ray Illingworth, Jimmy Binks, Fred Trueman and Don Wilson. Pressdee shot them out for 96 almost single-handedly, returning figures of 9-43 from 23.3 overs. In the second innings, when the Tykes staggered to 134, Shepherd mopped them up with 9-48 from 27.5 overs, making it a unique double – the first time in County Championship history that two bowlers in the same team had taken nine wickets in the same match.

In 1968, when the Australians pitched up for their usual August bank holiday date at Swansea, the men in the daffodil caps had a familiar look, with six of them eager to start where they had left off last time, one of whom, Shepherd, captained the side in the absence of Tony Lewis.

This time, Glamorgan more than doubled their winning margin, to 79 runs. The acting skipper led the side responsibly, if anything under-bowling himself to give his young understudy, Brian Lewis from Maesteg, long enough stints in both innings for the 23 year old to bag seven wickets. Once again, Glamorgan's collective ability to make the sharp catches stick, as exemplified by Walker, Roger Davis, Majid Khan and wicketkeeper Eifion Jones, proved decisive.

The massed choirs, again in full flow all around St Helens, stopped long enough for Australia's acting captain, Barry Jarman, to earn an ovation for his fair-dinkum honesty.

'We've been beaten again by Glamorgan,' he told the cheering crowd. 'So what's new?'

Alan Jones laid the foundations with a first innings 99 and still England refused to pick him. When they eventually did, against the Rest of the World at Lord's, it was on the understanding that the five-match series, arranged to replace the South Africa tour that had been abandoned for political reasons, had been granted Test status.

Having kept the Welsh left-hander waiting a good ten years, the selectors then dropped him after two failures, 0 and 5. The fact that he had made five more runs than Graham Gooch would make on his Test debut against Australia three years later is neither here nor there. Jones was never to get a second chance.

Worse still, some years later, the authorities did a volte-face on the status of the Rest of the World matches and declared them non-Test.

Officially, therefore, Alan Jones is the phantom batsman: the man who played for England in what was then a Test match, only to find his name subsequently erased from the official list of Test cricketers. A shabby form of treatment, but then they had been treating Shepherd every bit as shabbily for years on end.

Wooller had finished his stint on national selection by then, shortly after retiring at the age of 47. His bravery under fire and refusal to be the least bit cowed by the fastest of bowlers were never more evident than when facing a bruising barrage from Frank Tyson, whose nickname 'Typhoon' said everything about his pace.

'You don't frighten me, Tyson,' Wooller called out, disguising the pain from another nasty blow. 'And while we're at it, how the hell did I ever come to pick you for England?'

As county secretary, Wooller directed operations off the field with the same belligerence he had shown on it. Once, when Somerset, under Brian Close, batted on too slowly and too long for his liking at Swansea, Wooller seized the tannoy and told the crowd: 'We apologise for the negative cricket being played by the visitors. Any spectator wanting his money back should come to the office.'

It did not turn out to be Wooller's finest hour. '"Closey" was a fine captain who had his head screwed on,' Shepherd said. 'They took their time to get the runs he required, but they got them. And then they beat us.'

What they did to the secretary's frustration is best left to the imagination. 'There was never any halfway house with Wilf,' Shepherd said. 'I can remember once in my early days dropping a catch down in Kent. We all sat down for lunch and nothing was said until he looked at me and said: "What are you doing here? Get out and get some catching practice. And don't come back if you're going to drop another."

'Wilf wasn't a psychologist, although he may have thought he was.

But he knew how to sort people out and if you could play under his conditions, you could play under any. If you couldn't take the criticism, you were no good to Wilf and by extension you were no good to Glamorgan.

'There is no question that he would go out of his way every now and again, when the situation demanded, to upset opposition players and opposition captains. He would do it as a tactical ploy. There were times when we got hammered but, as a team, we never went down without a trace. We always fought to the very end because Wilf wouldn't have it any other way.'

The never-say-Dai attitude underpinned their second county title in 1969, an achievement made all the more satisfying as belated reward for their most faithful bowler and number eleven bat, except when promoted to the dizzy heights of number ten. Even then, at the age of 42, Shepherd got through more overs than anyone else during a season when Glamorgan's batsmen scored their runs quicker than anyone else and their catchers matched the acrobatic standards set by the previous generation in 1948.

Then, over the course of 32 matches, a quartet of close-wicket fieldsmen held 135 catches between them: Allan Watkins (40), Wooller (38), Len Muncer (31), Phil Clift (26). Those statistics compensated for the relatively few championship centuries – a mere seven, with two each by Willie Jones, Emrys Davies and Gilbert Parkhouse, and one by Watkins.

As Wooller said in *Wisden*:

> We are aware we cannot compete, for instance, with Middlesex in batting or Derbyshire in bowling. But in fielding, we give first to no side. We have attempted to make each fielder, be he a deep long-on or a short-leg, an integral part of a machine. Each man comes off the field with the knowledge that he fulfilled his part by saving runs in some way or another.
>
> The interest was competitive and no small measure of praise came from the team itself if one or another player did something spectacular.
>
> If a man failed in batting or bowling, he still knew he had

an important part to play. Therefore, his enjoyment of the battle itself was increased. Tactically, also it has been a playing policy to encourage each member of the side to study tactics. Cricket is a game requiring thought and brains. Any thinking player may see something a captain has missed. It detracts nothing from a captain's discipline to accept sound advice.

In 1969, from eight fixtures fewer than in 1948, another quartet of Glamorgan players again proved the old adage about catches winning matches. Bryan Davis (34), Roger Davis (33), Peter Walker (29) and Tony Cordle (23) held 119 during a summer when Eifion Jones out-caught and out-stumped every other wicketkeeper with 74 dismissals.

Appropriately, the unbeaten champions seized the title on the last day of the last home match of the season, against Worcestershire at Sophia Gardens on 5 September, with who else but Shepherd delivering the final blow. A game during which he took his 2,000th first-class wicket ended with Worcester's last man, Brian Brain, falling to Port Eynon's finest.

Shepherd had long yielded to Wooller's diktat two decades earlier about the new boy needing something stronger than orangeade. 'I had my first drink some years later on a Saturday night in Brentwood. There was nothing to do the next day and someone suggested that a drop of port wouldn't do me any harm. Then someone else poured me a glass of cider. It could have been arsenic, for all I knew. It led to quite an uncomfortable night.

'People have said that Trueman was a big drinker. If you ask me, he poured a fair bit of the stuff into the nearest flower pot. He looked after himself, did Fred. There wasn't much time for celebrating when we won the title because we still had one match to play, Surrey at the Oval. I did learn something that day – not to drink cold champagne on a hot tummy.'

More champagne followed as soon as Glamorgan had comfortably averted any danger of Surrey preventing them from becoming the first unbeaten champions for 40 years. A distinguished old friend of Shepherd's from Swansea, Harry Secombe, sent a crate of the stuff to the visitors' dressing-room. And thereby hangs a tale revolving around the 12th man, Kevin Lyons.

'Kevin takes the blame because he was one of those in charge of the bags,' Shepherd said. 'We gave him the crate of champagne to put on the taxi taking the kit to Paddington for the train home. Unfortunately, Kevin got everything off except the champagne. We got in touch with the police. They assured us everyone was on the case but nothing ever turned up.'

In his time, Shepherd bowled against most of the greats during the first 20 years of the post-Bradman era, including the West Indian three Ws (Frank Worrell, Everton Weekes, Clyde Walcott), whose combined box-office appeal can be gauged by the fact that on one day, Bank Holiday Monday, 7 August, a crowd of 32,000 paid to see them play, a figure without precedent in Welsh cricket.

Even now, after all these years, Shepherd is unable to come up with a definitive answer to the question of who was the best batsman he played against. 'I've never been able to come down to one name, mainly because of the change in my technique,' he said. 'Who was the best when I bowled seam as opposed to the best when I bowled off-spin? From memory, I got them all out except Len Hutton. He gave me some stick once in a county match at Hull, not too much but enough to get his message over: "Come on, son. Give someone else a bowl."

'I'd like to have played more against Hutton after I'd switched to spin. The three Ws were mighty by anyone's standards, and mightier still on a flat pitch at St Helens. It had to be flat because three days' revenue from that one fixture was essential for the financial well-being of the club. Everton had a bet with Len Muncer, one of Glamorgan's finest players, that he'd score a hundred before lunch, which he duly did on the second morning.

'For me, the best professional, day-in, day-out, was Tom Graveney. His technique made him very difficult to bowl to because he got so far forward and he never played across the line. Of the great amateurs, Peter May and Ted Dexter stood out. I was able to get both out, but you knew that if you got it wrong, the ball went straight back over your head, whereas with Colin Cowdrey it wouldn't.

'He was a wonderful player, but there was never the fear that he would take you apart. Strangely enough, Denis Compton's best against Glamorgan was no more than 60-odd.

'Then there were the great South Africans, Graeme Pollock and Barry Richards. I played against Graeme only once or twice, and while I did get Barry out a few times, it was largely through a lack of interest on his part because every so often the game wasn't a challenge to him. He was that good.'

Shep, 84 not out in August 2011, took six Nottinghamshire wickets in eleven overs without conceding a single run at Newport in June 1961. He was that good . . .

4

THE MESSIAH

John Charles

Born: Swansea, 27 December 1931
Died: Wakefield, 21 February 2004, aged 72

Ned Charles and his wife were sitting at home in Alice Street early one evening during the spring of 1948 when a stranger knocked on the front door of their house in the Cwmdu district of Swansea.

The caller introduced himself as Jack Pickard, a scout for Leeds United Football Club. Considering the enormity of the discovery that he had made, it might have been more apposite had he announced himself as a flat-cap Yorkshire version of Christopher Columbus or Marco Polo.

Pickard asked if he could come in and discuss a matter concerning their eldest son, then a 16 year old on the groundstaff of Swansea Town, having left Manselton Junior School the previous year on the off-chance of making a name for himself as a professional footballer. Being hospitable people, the Charleses invited the stranger in and listened to what he had to say. Fortuitously or not, the approach came at a time when a lack of recognition from the boy's home-town club made him susceptible to the ideas planted by the Leeds scout, even if Pickard represented a club that appeared to be a world away.

Pleasantries having been exchanged and the visitor's bona fides accepted, Pickard got down to business. He spoke directly to Ned's wife, Lill, perhaps on the sensible basis that his call would have been a waste of everyone's time without a mother's blessing for her son's proposed redeployment.

'Mrs Charles,' Pickard began, 'we think John has a big future in football and we would like to send him to Leeds United.'

'He can't go,' she said. 'Out of the question.'

'Why not?'

'He hasn't got a passport.'

Pickard probably could not believe his luck at spiriting the uncut diamond away from his very own backyard. Once it had been explained that the independent socialist republic of Yorkshire was most definitely still part of Great Britain, the family agreed that it might be a good idea for their boy to start afresh. During two years at Vetch Field, Charles, like other groundstaff boys, doubled up as a general dogsbody whose menial tasks ranged from sweeping litter off the terraces to weeding the pitch.

And so began a career that won John Charles universal acclamation as the most complete all-round British footballer of his generation, a colossus whose towering achievements in Italy continue to have such an enduring impact that he is still revered almost half a century since he last played there.

Pickard's visit took Charles from a little house in a modest Swansea suburb to a seventeenth-century villa in the hills above Turin. It set in motion a chain of events that made the humble steelworker's son the original soccer superstar, a pioneer whose success with Juventus won him more public adoration than Sophia Loren and Gina Lollobrigida put together.

Two other Swansea boys, Bobby Henning and Harry Griffiths – Griffiths would return to devote his life to the Swans, as player and manager – kept him company on the long drag to the West Riding. Pickard had watched all three in underage football and had been struck by the thought that Charles had something special. Major Frank Buckley, a colourful figure in football management, who had done much to revive Wolverhampton Wanderers during the 1930s, rapidly came to the same conclusion.

When Charles signed at Elland Road as a professional at the age of 17 for a weekly wage of £6, 'the Major' gave him a new suit and an overcoat, as protection against the ravages of the northern winter.

The gangling youth got something else, too: a £10 signing-on fee. Ten years later, Leeds broke the British transfer record, selling him for 6,500 times as much, which made Pickard's swoop on Alice Street a contender for the steal of the century.

'I must have done well because the Major told me he was satisfied and that he would like me to join the Leeds United groundstaff,' Charles said. 'He promised to find me good digs and give me all the coaching I required. He kept both promises.

'He didn't do much coaching on the training field. Instead he would call me into his office after a match and say: "Jack" – he never called me John – "you shouldn't have done so and so." But he'd also tell me that I'd done other bits right and suggested one or two things I might like to try.'

At Swansea, Charles's specialist position was left-half – or left midfield, in modern parlance. Leeds began to play him in their junior teams at right-back before experimenting with him at centre-half in a Yorkshire League match against Barnsley. As if to make up for the lost time back home, Charles made such swift progress that he was only a few months past his 17th birthday when Major Buckley picked him for his first-team debut, a Second Division match against Blackburn Rovers on 23 April 1949.

Two years later, Charles the centre-half had given way, temporarily at the start, to Charles the centre-forward. A 4–1 beating by Manchester City did nothing to ease the teenager's reluctance to redeploy himself into an alien position. Then two goals against Hull City in the next game left him at a loss to understand how he had scored them. The Major, then in his 70th year, had no doubts, telling Charles: 'Well done, lad. You'll stay at centre-forward.'

He didn't. Circumstances demanded that he revert to shoring up a leaking defence, and there he remained until a chronic lack of goals during the autumn of 1952 forced a tactical rethink. Home crowds had shrunk to 13,000 when the Major reintroduced Charles the striker in a West Riding Senior Cup-tie against Halifax Town. Leeds won 2–1 and their man for all seasons scored both goals.

By then, the scrawny schoolboy had grown into a powerful figure, standing 6 ft 3 in. tall, his aerial strength reinforced by a physique of more than 14 stone. 'Big John' was on his way, and how. In his first six

League matches leading the attack, Charles scored eleven goals, including hat-tricks against Hull City on 1 November and against Brentford four weeks later. His third goal against the West London club, on an icy pitch at Elland Road, encapsulated the very essence of Charles, with his rare mix of raw power, exquisite touch and a ballet dancer's finesse.

'I got the ball in my own half and set off for goal,' he recalled of the hat-trick goal. 'Three times I was tackled and three times I managed to slip away. Then I had only the goalkeeper to beat. I managed to swerve past him. Unfortunately, I was going at top speed and the foothold was very slippery, so there was still a chance that I would fluff an open goal, especially as I saw one of the Brentford defenders come across the goal-line to block my view of the net. Luckily, all went well and we won 3–2.'

The following week, a strange thing happened back at Elland Road. Waiting to greet him was Sam Bolton, chairman of a Leeds board very relieved that Charles had saved them from having to fork out a fortune in the transfer market for a goalscorer. Bolton introduced him to a fellow director who owned a garage.

'John,' the director started, 'we are so delighted with what you've done that I want you to take your car along and get some free petrol. Three gallons of the stuff, one for each of the three goals you got last Saturday. Just go to the garage and we'll fill her up.'

'That's very kind of you,' Charles said. 'There's only one problem. I don't own a car . . .'

Even before he had turned 21, Leeds knew they had struck gold in the shape of the Welsh giant who would walk to training from his digs in a terraced house on Beeston Hill, overlooking the stadium. 'Here we have the most brilliant Association footballer in the game today and one of the most outstanding I have seen in my 50 years in football,' Major Buckley declared. 'Charles is the best in the world.'

Not content with 26 goals in 28 League matches at centre-forward that season, Charles followed up with 42 more in 39 appearances during 1953–54. He got four in the first match, at home to Notts County, three more in the second, against Rotherham United, and added three more hat-tricks. His strike rate was all the more extraordinary given that his total included a mere four penalties and that he was part of an otherwise very ordinary Leeds team, hence their very ordinary finishing position of tenth in the Second Division.

No wonder they called Leeds 'Charles United'.

Years later, the 17-year-old international centre-half who succeeded Charles – Jack Charlton, no less – vouched for the veracity of the one-man-team theory.

'John Charles was a team unto himself,' Charlton said. 'People often say to me: "Who was the best player you ever saw in your life?" I say: "Probably Eusebio, di Stefano, Cruyff, Pele or our Bob." But the most effective player I ever saw, the one that made the most difference to the performance of the whole team, was, without question, John Charles.

'He could defend. He could play in midfield. He could attack. He was quick. He was a very, very strong runner and he was also the greatest header of the ball I ever saw. His power in the air was phenomenal. Normally, when a player heads the ball his eyes close automatically, but John's didn't. They stayed open.

'If you tried to challenge John in the air, he'd always jump a fraction of a second earlier and he seemed to be able to hang in the air. The balls you used to head in those days were nothing like the ones today. The balls today don't absorb water. In those days, a keeper often had difficulty punting the ball out of his own half because it was so big and heavy.'

He was still too good for the best defenders in English football, even after yanking Leeds into the First Division in 1956. Harry Johnston, the Blackpool and England centre-half, was only half-joking when he talked about a pair of stepladders as essential equipment for any defender hoping to beat him in the air.

Raich Carter, one of England's finest footballers before and after the Second World War, succeeded Buckley as Leeds manager in April 1953, and he responded in no uncertain terms to questions from reporters about Charles's availability: 'John Charles is not, I repeat not, for sale. You just cannot afford to sell players like him because money cannot buy a replacement.'

But, as soccer has shown since time immemorial, everyone has his price. Before the end of that season, Juventus had smashed the British transfer record by paying £65,000 for '*Il Gigante Buono*', as the Italian fans soon christened him. The deal, finalised in a room on the second floor of the Queens Hotel in central Leeds after lawyers and accountants had spent hours poring over the small print of the contract, made Charles British football's first truly global superstar – not that he ever behaved like one.

When the big beasts of the European jungle began to make noises about signing Charles, the man himself responded to news of their enquiries with endearing ignorance of his potential new employers. When Raich Carter informed him that Madrid had been on the phone, Charles said: 'Madrid who?'

When told it was Real Madrid, who had turned the European Cup into their private property, he said: 'I've heard of them.'

Charles told Carter he didn't want to go, but, as the bidding soared ever higher, Leeds knew they could not afford to resist indefinitely, not when they needed money to build a new stand and replace the one that had been destroyed by fire.

Recalled to the manager's office shortly afterwards to be informed that Lazio were in for him, Charles said: 'Where's Lazio?'

Later that week, Leeds told him about an offer from Juventus. Again, Charles asked who they were. 'I'd never heard of them, but it was different then,' he said. 'You didn't have the television and press coverage you get now.'

He may have known nothing about them, but they knew everything about him. Juventus left nothing to chance. When Charles went to Belfast in April 1957, joining his 21-year-old brother Mel on Wales duty, in a goalless draw against Northern Ireland in the old Home Championship, one of the richest men in Italy made the journey via London to see him for himself. Umberto Agnelli, whose family owned the massive Fiat automobile conglomerate, as well as Juventus, liked what he saw and negotiations for the Welshman's capture went into overdrive.

Agnelli flew home, his mind made up to buy the elder Charles whatever the price and to avoid, if at all possible, watching Wales play again. He thought little of the other ten players, although Arsenal raided the bank for the £40,000 to buy younger brother Mel from Swansea two years later as a goalscorer in his own right. Agnelli was sold on the Leeds centre-forward: 'I said to myself: "What a player." In flashes he showed what he could do in a good side. Some of those who were with him were not good.'

One week later, on 17 April, Agnelli was back in London embarking on a car journey north with an entourage that included Luigi 'Gigi' Peronace, a dynamic little Italian wheeler-dealer who would change Charles's life forever. Spanish rules at the time, which restricted any one club to a maximum of two foreign players, meant Real Madrid were never in the running. Had they been, the price for Charles would surely have smashed the world record of £75,000, paid by AC Milan, when they splashed out on the Uruguayan Juan Schiaffino.

Internazionale, for reasons that never became clear, refused to turn it into an auction, suspecting, perhaps, that Agnelli had too much clout. As the Fiat magnate and the Leeds board thrashed out a deal, Charles kept out of sight in the Queens Hotel, with his entourage of two. There was his agent, Teddy Sommerfield, a Lancastrian who acted on behalf of several television personalities, and Kenneth Wolstenholme, the BBC commentator.

Even with negotiations clearly at an advanced stage, the Leeds directors kept assuring their prize asset that they had no wish to let him go, that they really wanted him to stay. When word reached Charles that a transfer fee had been agreed, it took him and his advisers a further two hours to shake hands on personal terms. By then, chairman Bolton and his fellow directors could not be seen for dust. According to Wolstenholme, they had rushed off with the cheque without staying to toast what was then the most profitable transfer in British football history.

The ebullient Peronace had not taken long to persuade Charles that the riches on offer in Turin would change his life forever, that by the time he had finished with Italian football he would never need to work again. The nuts and bolts of the personal terms behind the record transfer fee of £65,000 tended to reinforce his point.

Leeds at this stage paid Charles £16 a week. Juventus gave him a signing-on fee of £10,000, divided into monthly instalments over the two years of his initial contract, and a flat wage of £28 a week, with three-figure win bonuses, unheard of in the British game.

'I knew nothing about Turin, but the money was a pull. The main thing was the signing-on fee. Then there were the bonuses. If we beat teams like Torino, Inter and Milan, we'd get £100, £200, maybe even £300.'

Charles did not waste any time showing them what they were getting for their money. His first three matches in Serie A were against Verona, Udinese and Genoa, and he scored the winning goal in all three. A hat-trick of hat-tricks followed, against Atalanta, Lazio and the other Genoese club, Sampdoria. Juventus won the league, the treasured Scudetto, and *Il Gigante Buono* ended up winning the coveted Italian Footballer of the Year award at the first attempt.

When he walked out of Elland Road for the last time, like a latter-day Pied Piper, taking scores of young fans with him, English pundits feared the worst. They thought he would be stifled by the suffocating defensive nature of the Italian game on the field and his inability to make himself understood off it. After that season, those same pundits spent the whole summer long being treated for severe indigestion, caused by eating their own words.

'I admit I didn't know where Turin was to begin with, but I was determined to make it work,' Charles said. 'I did get homesick, but I'd made up my mind to stick it out and enjoy it. I settled in quite quickly and I think that was because I'd left Swansea for Leeds when I was 16. Going from Leeds to Italy was nothing in comparison. I learnt to speak Italian because you've got to get on off the pitch as well as on it.'

Inevitably, he got some things wrong, like buying himself a car without realising one of the perks of playing for a team owned by Fiat included a top-of-the-range model free of charge. By his second season, Signor Agnelli showed his appreciation by putting two such cars at his family's disposal.

At one stage, Charles almost had enough Fiats to fill a showroom. Whenever his friends gathered to reminisce, they would tell the tale about an Italian Cup tie against Napoli and how Agnelli had offered every Juventus player a brand-new car if they spared him the embarrassment of losing to a club whose president did not happen to be one of his favourite people. Juve won 3–1, and the players collected their brand-new automobiles, as well as their more modest cash bonus.

The Torinese loved Charles, and not simply because he scored goals galore. They loved him because he showed them that sportsmanship still had a place, even in the cut-throat world of Italian football. What Charles did in his first derby match against Torino endeared him as much to the rest of Italy as all the goals he rattled in for Juve. To show their appreciation, a small army of Torino fans drove their cars in convoy to the hilltop villa where the 'Gentle Giant' lived with his wife, Peggy, and the first of their four sons, Terry.

'I beat the centre-half but, accidentally, struck him with my elbow and knocked him clean out. I only had the goalie to beat, but it didn't seem fair. So I kicked the ball out for a throw, so the fella could have treatment. From that moment on, the Torino supporters always treated me with great respect. I remember one Sunday they beat us 3–2 and I missed a penalty. Maybe that was why I was so popular. Anyway I was woken up about three the next morning by this incredible din of car horns. When I went out on to the balcony, there was a traffic jam of Torino fans hanging out of the windows waving their red flags.'

Once he had pushed back the frontiers for future generations of the best British players, many followed in his footsteps, but none ever came close to inspiring the love with which fans embraced Charles the length and breadth of Italy. He formed a bewitching double act with Omar Sivori, a tricky little Argentinian whose transfer from the Buenos Aires club River Plate for £91,000 made him, at the time, the world's most expensive footballer.

During the course of five seasons in tandem at Juventus, their partnership was the crucial factor behind *La Vecchia Signora* – the Old Lady – winning Serie A three times. In the most defensive league in the world, Charles scored 93 times from 155 matches.

Nobody summed him up better than Don Davies, a distinguished sports journalist on the *Manchester Guardian*, who was to lose his life in the Manchester United air disaster in February 1958. He wrote: 'Charles was as powerful as Hercules, as authoritative as Caesar.'

This was a player who was never booked, let alone sent off. He answered the snide fouls and more overt physical intimidation the only way he knew how: by taking it without complaint and hitting the opposition where it hurt them most – in the back of the net.

'They defended differently in Italy,' Charles said. 'They would mark close, very close. They knew all the tricks. If you went for a corner, one defender would step on your feet and another would pull your shirt.

'Training was also different. Ball skills were valued more highly in Italy. The theory in Britain was that if you starved a player of the ball during the week, he'd be chomping at the bit on Saturday afternoon. I often found the British system makes a player, even if you are hungry for the ball, incapable of using it.'

In the early days, the Italians assumed Charles was English. After all, he had played in the English League. Even Umberto Colombo, his first captain at Juventus, was at a loss to understand why he had not played for the England national team. So, as if to show the whole of Italy his true allegiance, Charles spent that first summer as a Juve player putting Wales into the quarter-finals of the World Cup for the first and only time. They had to play Hungary twice to get there, drawing with the 1954 finalists 1–1 in Sandviken on 8 June before beating them 2–1 in the play-off decider at Stockholm nine days later. Charles had been subjected to systematic hacking from the merciless Magyars, which he took without losing his temper despite what his teammates considered a disgraceful lack of protection from the 44-year-old Russian referee Nikolay Gavrilovich Latyshev.

Against all the odds, Wales made it to the last eight and a tie against Brazil, but they would have to manage without the man whom manager Jimmy Murphy called 'the Messiah'. Charles, rendered *hors de combat* by the Hungarian hit men, could only sit and watch Wales defy the eventual winners until the 17-year-old Pele scored his first World Cup goal late in the second half.

Back in Italy, Charles's fame knew no bounds. 'It was mad out there. I was looked on as a personality. You'd go into the city and people would come up and ask you for your autograph. They'd follow you as well, just to look at you.'

He was even talked into recording a version of the Tennessee Ernie Ford classic 'Sixteen Tons', which met with rather less success than the songs subsequently released by a goalkeeper from Modena who proved better at singing Puccini than stopping shots – Luciano Pavarotti.

'When we were at Juve, the two most important people to most Italians were the Pope and *Il Gigante Buono*,' Sivori said. 'For the 40 per cent who were Communist, the two most important were Stalin and *Il Gigante Buono*.'

A second Scudetto followed at the end of his third season, as the more cherished part of a league and cup double.

By now, Charles and his expanding family had a second villa, this one on the Mediterranean, at Diano Marina. He had also invested some of his money in a restaurant in Turin, the King's, which he co-owned with his sidekick at Juventus, the mercurial Sivori. It would cost the Welshman a fortune and force him to admit some years later: 'I was a good footballer. People tell me I was great. But I was also the worst businessman.'

Despite a third League title, life for the Charles family was not the bed of roses it may have looked on the surface. The tendency at Juventus to install their players in training camps for days, away from home and their families, did nothing to ease the strain on Charles's marriage. The commercial failure of the restaurant venture did even less for his bank balance.

By then, a coterie of top British players, inspired from afar by his success, followed Charles in pursuit of *La Dolce Vita*. None of the exclusive brotherhood – Jimmy Greaves, Denis Law, another who considered Charles the best header of a ball he had ever seen, Joe Baker, Gerry Hitchens – came close to matching the Welshman, although Hitchens, an England striker who broke into League football with Cardiff City, did stay for six years, serving no fewer than four clubs.

'Big John' played his first match for Juve at the age of 25 and his last, against Venezia, shortly after turning 30. After five seasons in Turin, he and his family packed their bags and returned whence they came. It was a decision that baffled many of his friends for many years and nobody managed to come up with the definitive answer to the riddle of why he left a city and a country where he had been idolised.

Despite concern over a knee problem which prompted Juve to send him to a clinic in Lyons for a surgical cure, he recovered, only to be kicked up hill and down dale by Real Madrid during a European

Cup quarter-final play-off at Parc des Princes in Paris. In renewing his contract for that 1961–62 season, which ended with an abject surrender of their domestic crown, Charles told Agnelli that he would not be staying. Juve spared no expense in trying to make him change his mind.

They offered him another five-figure signing-on fee, a larger one than for his first contract five years earlier, plus a hike in his basic wage. They offered to pay for his children's education at an English-speaking school in Milan, and they sent the faithful Colombo to intercede on their behalf with a personal plea.

'Juventus asked me to speak to John about staying and I left Bergamo to go and see him in Turin,' Colombo said in Mario Risoli's fascinating book, *John Charles: Gentle Giant*. 'All he said was: "I want to go home." He was having problems at home. He wanted to keep his family together and he thought getting away from Italy was the best way of doing that. He wanted to start afresh, but once the cracks appear it's difficult to put them back together again.'

The first time Leeds signed Charles, it cost them £10 and a new overcoat. The second time, in the summer of 1962, they had to fork out a club-record transfer fee of £53,000. Charles was welcomed back in the fond hope that he would pick up where he had left off five years earlier and everyone would live happily ever after. It proved to be such a bad move that within a matter of months John and Peggy were pining for Italy.

There were problems before the season began, not least the fact that Big John was bigger still. He was overweight at 15 stone and overwrought by a tough new training regime installed by the new manager Don Revie and enforced with sergeant-major efficiency by his trainer, Les Cocker.

The new regime came as a culture shock to a bronzed but out-of-condition Charles whose response, or lack of it, became part of Elland Road folklore. Willie Bell, a Scottish defender whom Leeds had signed from Queen's Park, has told the story of what happened when Cocker selected Charles for one of the new-fangled pre-training warm-up routines.

'Les would select different players and on this day he picked John,' Bell told Risoli. 'They went outside and John just stood there, put his two arms out in front of him and started flopping his wrists while the other players were stretching and working. "What are you playing at?" said Les.

'And John just said: "Three championship medals."

'Les had no answer to that.'

Leeds, then back in the Second Division, alienated the majority of their customers by more than doubling admission charges in a clumsy attempt to pay for a player whose messianic-like qualities of yesteryear they hoped would soon lead them back to the promised land.

The reality was very different. Leeds, like many other sports teams before and since, had deluded themselves into believing they could recreate what they had had in the mid-'50s, while ignoring the most remorseless old foe of all – Father Time. For the first time in his life, the man himself spent many a sleepless night tortured by the onset of self-doubt and his persisting inability to make any kind of impact.

Leeds decided to cut their losses, resigned as they must have been to off-loading their Welsh heavyweight for a good deal less than they had paid for him. They could hardly have believed their luck when Roma came in with a bid of £70,000. And so, for the second time, they had made a handsome profit from an Italian club. Charles's second stay at Elland Road lasted 91 days.

The late Jimmy Dunn, a Scot who had been a permanent fixture in the Leeds defence for more than ten years before becoming a milkman, summed it up best. 'Leaving Leeds was the best thing he [Charles] ever did,' said Dunn, who died at the age of 83 in January 2005, almost exactly a year after his old Welsh teammate. 'The silliest thing he ever did was to come back.'

His second coming in Serie A did not last much longer than 91 days. Roma found out to their cost that the Gentle Giant was no longer the supreme athlete of old. Charles still had his seaside refuge in Diano Marina but, more worryingly, the move to the Eternal City did nothing for his disintegrating marriage. Having chosen barely six months earlier to relocate abroad, he made a complete U-turn and decided the family's future lay back in the UK after all.

Cardiff City's opening bid of £22,000 illustrated the steep depreciation in his value. They raised it by £500, a long way short of Roma's price, and with his old friend Gigi Peronace oiling the wheels behind the scenes, the finest all-round footballer ever produced in Wales got the transfer he wanted. The contract details, as drawn up on 6 August 1963 between Cardiff City and the Roma president, Conte Franco Marini Dettina, can be revealed for the first time as follows:

> Cardiff City Association Football Club Limited pay to A.S. Roma the sum of £22,000 sterling.
> Payable:
> £8,000 on 31st August, 1963.
> £6,000 on 16th October, 1963.
> £6,000 on 31st December, 1963
> £2,000 not later than 1st May, 1964.
> A.S. Roma agree to play Cardiff City at home early in May, 1964 on a date to be arranged. A.S. Roma to take the full gate. A.S. Roma to pay all travelling expenses Cardiff-Rome-Cardiff and first-class hotel accommodation there for a party of maxim twenty two persons, together with other sundry expenses incurred by Cardiff in fulfilling this fixture.

When a copy of the agreement dropped through the post at Football League headquarters on the Lancashire coast, they promptly blocked it, for reasons spelt out by their autocratic secretary, Alan Hardaker, in a letter sent to his opposite number at Ninian Park, Graham Keenor:

> The Football League Limited
> Lytham St. Anne's,
> Lancs.
> AH/LD/496. 22 August 1963

The Secretary,
Cardiff City F.C. Ltd.,
Ninian Park,
Cardiff.
Dear Sir,
Re: – William John Charles

I have to refer to my letter of the 12th instant, and to inform you that the Management Committee, at their last Meeting, have decided that in view of the fact that a sum of £10,000 is still owing by Roma F.C. to Leeds United, they cannot accept The League Registration of the above Player, for the time being.

Yours faithfully,

A. Hardaker,

Secretary.

Once Roma coughed up, the League withdrew their objection. Cardiff had tried to buy Charles from Leeds before he went to Italy the first time, when the bidding went as high as £40,000. Now that they had got him at half the price, they had also got half the player he used to be. In retrospect, of course, it is easy to be wise after the event, but the Bluebirds' chairman, Ron Beecher, a local butcher, knew they were taking a gamble on Charles's fitness, never mind his waning power.

Mr Dillwyn Evans, an orthopaedic specialist who acted for the club, could not have been clearer in his medical report on the prospective new signing. This is the letter he sent Beecher, dated 30 July 1963, before the terms of the transfer were agreed:

Mr R.Beecher,
Chairman,
Cardiff City Football Club
Ninian Park,
Cardiff.

Dear Ron,

Re: – John Charles.

Orthopaedically speaking, he is by no means out of the top drawer – a cartilage removed from each knee twelve years ago with recurrence of trouble in the left knee two years ago and a pulled muscle on the front of the right thigh a year ago.

The ruptured muscle is visible on the front of the thigh and there are osteoarthritic changes on the inner side of the left knee. These produced a 'piece of gristle' which had to be removed in Lyons two years ago and there may be more to come.

It is always very difficult to know what to say under such circumstances and I hope that at some time you will send me a chap with two normal knees. Quite clearly, there is a possibility of a breakdown on the front of the right thigh or on the inner side of the left knee but this is only a possibility.

His brother, with much worse knees, has lost only one game in the last two years and, for all I know, John may do just as well. As I said on the phone, I can't advise against signing him because there is a very good chance that he has two or three years of good football left in him and, indeed, it may be some part which is now normal that will give him trouble before either of the parts that are vulnerable. We can only keep our fingers crossed and hope for the best.

Kindest regards,

Yours sincerely,

Dillwyn.

The gamble failed on every count. Far from accelerating Cardiff as serious promotion contenders, it could be argued that the signing contributed to their demise as a team much more likely to disappear into the Third Division than return to the First. To help pay for Charles, the Bluebirds sold one of their more promising local players, Alan Durban, to Derby County, where he won a League champions' medal under Brian Clough.

The manager, George Swindin, concerned that he had too many ageing players at Ninian Park, now found himself with another, despite having counselled his board against spending any more than £10,000 on Charles. Within 12 months of his coming, Swindin had been sacked and replaced by Jimmy Scoular, whose resentment of Charles as a spent force led to a fractious relationship.

The players loved Charlo and they loved his stories about his former life of glamour, about leaving tickets at the door of the Stadio Comunale for Sophia Loren. He was far too affable ever to be the least bit affected by his fame and was always willing to answer a few questions from a young reporter representing the local paper, the *South Wales Echo* – willing, that is, on one condition.

He liked a smoke, did John, which made a packet of cigarettes more essential than a notebook or, for those unwilling to trust their shorthand, a dictaphone. Any attempt to engage him in conversation on the issue of the day, invariably elicited the same answer: 'Got a fag, Pete?'

Charles lasted two and a bit seasons at Cardiff and started the last one in the Football League in August 1965 with a flew flashes of the old genius. A clutch of four goals in the first four games brought Cardiff fleeting hope, a last sparkle before the light went out and the old knee trouble brought the curtain down on his final season when it still had eight months to run. Standard Liege away in the first round of the European Cup-Winners' Cup proved to be the end of the road in senior football for Charles after 627 matches and 288 goals.

The 'club news' section of the programme for the first match of the following season, Ipswich Town on 20 August 1966, buried the reference to his exit on a free transfer halfway down the page in no more than a sentence: 'As you probably know, two popular personalities will be missing this term, Barrie Hole, who has now settled down well with his new club, Blackburn Rovers, and John Charles, who now joins former Wales star Ray Daniel at Hereford United.'

During his time there as manager, he signed Ricky George from Barnet and instructed the newcomer that he was to call him 'John' or 'Charlo', never 'Boss'. Charles left Hereford shortly before their famous FA Cup run in 1972 and George recalled bumping into him outside the ground before their fourth-round tie against West Ham.

'There was Charlo, camelhair coat, steely-grey hair, permanent suntan and wearing that broad grin,' George said. 'He was resting against the bonnet of his car and showed us an envelope. It read: "Mr John Charles, two tickets, £2 to pay."

'"I wouldn't mind," he said, as we stared at him in disbelief. "But I've only got 30 bob on me."'

He was running Merthyr, then in the Southern League, and when the football jobs ran out, he went into the licensed trade back in Leeds. By then, he had been hit by another failed business venture, a sports shop in one of Cardiff's northern suburbs, and as the money ran out, old friends rallied round to bring Leeds, then a force in the land under Revie, to Ninian Park for his benefit.

It got worse. In March 1988, unemployed and living on nothing more than a state pension, he hit rock-bottom, detained at a police station in Huddersfield pending 60 days in prison over non-payment of £943 in rates arrears.

Huddersfield magistrates sent him down for 60 days, a punishment that Charles acknowledged as 'the ultimate shame'. No sooner had the cell door slammed shut behind him than his partner, Glenda Vero, came to the rescue. The woman who would become the second Mrs Charles following John's divorce in 1982, arrived with the money, understood to have been a gift from the Leeds United chairman Leslie Silver.

A second testimonial match put him back on an even keel, helped by donations from members of the public saddened to read of his plight. One came from a London barrister who sent a cheque for £2,000 for the *Daily Mail*'s inimitable columnist, Ian Wooldridge, to pass on as 'grateful thanks for so many happy memories'.

Peronace, the agent who had sworn that Charles would never have to work again after Juventus, would have been spinning in his grave. The 55-year-old Calabrian died from a heart attack on 29 December 1980 in Montevideo, where he had been on duty with the Italian national team as general manager, leaving behind a wife and five children.

No amount of domestic difficulty made the slightest difference to the adoration that the Italian football public held for Charles. They rolled the red carpet out whenever he went back for an old players' reunion and feted him like some long-lost conquering hero. There are many extraordinary examples of his fame and sportsmanship which have survived down the years, none more extraordinary than what happened one night in the medieval town of Bergamo during the summer of 1971.

Charles had been back to play for Old Juventus against Old Internazionale. Signor Agnelli put one of his more luxurious cars at the Welshman's disposal and the next day Charles set off from Turin for Bergamo with a lifelong friend from Cardiff, Glyn Potter, for a meal with the former Juve captain, Umberto Colombo.

'We were trying to find our way through the centre of the town when John drove down a one-way street the wrong way,' said Potter, who acted as secretary-manager of the John Charles International XI, a charitable team whose number included Bobby Moore and Johnny Haynes. 'An officious young policeman stopped him. John was never one to trade on his name, so he tried his best to answer the questions while the policeman got his notebook out.

'At that point, I saw another police car draw up on the other side of the road. A senior officer got out and ran across to our vehicle. He said to the young officer: "*Qe pasa? Qe pasa?*" The older policeman recognised Big John and gave him a salute. Then he took the other copper aside and slapped him across the face – not once, not twice, but three times. It was an unbelievable illustration of what John Charles meant to those who remembered his years at Juventus.'

In 1997, he was voted Juventus's best foreign player of all time. The ultimate accolade was a posthumous one: in 2009, Charles topped a newspaper poll of the greatest foreign players to have appeared in Serie A. In other words, he beat the likes of Diego Maradona, Zinedine Zidane, Ruud Gullitt, Marco van Basten, Michel Platini, Lothar Matthaus, Dennis Bergkamp, Ronaldinho, Kaka and so many more.

In October 2001, he received the CBE from the Prince of Wales at Buckingham Palace. The freedom of the city of Swansea was conferred on him the following year before he made his last journey to Turin. When the Juve fans spotted him at the Stadio delle Alpe, they rose as one, all 40,000 of them, to chant his name: 'John Charles' – an extraordinary response for someone who had not played for the club for 42 years.

The old chap reached for his handkerchief and wiped the tears away. Shortly afterwards, when he was in the early stages of Alzheimer's, he collapsed before he was to appear on Italian television. After successful heart surgery, a circulatory emergency resulted in the amputation of his right leg. Juve paid for the treatment and used their club jet to fly him back to Yorkshire, where he passed away on 21 February 2004.

The great and the good, headed by Sir Alex Ferguson, attended the funeral, which took place, with poignant timing, on St David's Day. The hearse took him on one last lap of honour round Elland Park; one of Leeds's finest, Eddie Gray, spoke of 'a great man, as well as a great footballer'; and they brought his ashes home to Swansea, where a memorial service was held in the Brangwyn Hall.

The Morriston Orpheus choir sang '*Cwm Rhondda*'; his old primary school did their own musical tribute, 'I'm Going Home to Swansea Town'. Those paying homage ranged from the First Minister, Rhodri Morgan, to the much-loved former England manager, Bobby Robson.

In the rush to extol his virtues as a footballer, it is easy to lose sight of Charles the human being, whose easy-going nature ensured that his name never entered a referee's notebook. Rare qualities do not come much rarer than that.

Umberto Agnelli, who died 12 months later, provided as worthy an epitaph as any about Charles the man: 'John liked everybody and everybody liked him.'

John Helm, the journalist and football commentator who delivered the eulogy in Leeds Parish Church, offered another perceptive observation about his old friend: 'A man of great humility. As his wife Glenda said, "He never knew how great he was."'

5

TIGER BAY CHAMPIONS

Billy Boston

Born: Cardiff, 6 August 1934

As soon as he could walk, Billy Boston discovered rapidly enough that it paid to be quick off the mark. Growing up slap bang in the middle of five brothers and five sisters meant running a daily risk of being crowded out at the breakfast table.

A big family in a small house on a street at the heart of Tiger Bay in Cardiff's dockland put an extra premium on space. Most of it had been spoken for by the time William John entered the world during the summer of 1934, the sixth of eleven children born to John Boston, a seaman from Freetown, Sierra Leone, and his Irish-Welsh wife, the red-headed Nellie.

Billy arrived at No. 7 Angelina Street in the Bay after Doris, Joe, Johnny, Delia and Helena, and before Herby, Patty, Jimmy, Joanie and Raymond. A family large enough to field its own cricket or football team generated enough competition for the middle Boston to accept his place in the pecking order. When it came to running, he was not, by his own admission, the quickest in his own house, never mind his own street.

In those early days, he couldn't catch his big sister, Doris – hardly a disgrace, considering she was fast enough to compete against international athletes such as Maureen Gardner, the English girl who was still in her teens when she won a silver medal in the 80-metre hurdles behind the all-conquering Dutch sprinter Fanny

Blankers-Koen at the 1948 Olympic Games in London.

Doris's little brother was not the only embryonic superstar in the neighbourhood in the last days before the outbreak of the Second World War. One was to be found three doors away from the Bostons at No. 4 Angelina Street. Joe Erskine would graduate from the same Cardiff schools rugby team as his neighbour and become heavyweight champion of Great Britain and the Empire. A short walk away, at the bottom of Bute Street, lived a girl who would make it to the top of the hit parade – Shirley Bassey.

Before the war ended, the middle member of the Boston XI had come close to losing his life in a way that had nothing to do with the global conflagration. He fell into Cardiff docks and almost drowned.

'I couldn't swim then and, luckily, someone heard me shout and fished me out, otherwise I'd have been a goner,' he remembered. 'I got home dripping wet without one of my daps. I'd lost it getting pulled out of the water and got a good hiding from my mother, which made me make sure I wouldn't lose another.'

In 1948, when they were both 14, the neighbours from Angelina Street won selection for the Cardiff schools team – Boston at full-back, Erskine at outside half. Two years later, they joined forces at a higher level, for Wales in a Boys' Clubs match against England. Shortly after that, they went their separate ways: Erskine to learn his craft as one of the outstanding stylists of heavyweight boxing, Boston to Neath and his first taste of Welsh Rugby Union hypocrisy.

Those who went to rugby league were made social outcasts at a time when the WRU ignored the rogue clubs who paid their players to remain 'amateur'. They did so while rigidly adhering to the archaic rulebook, which effectively ostracised those who went north by outlawing any sort of contact, as if they belonged to a leper colony. The stink of hypocrisy was never very far away.

'My sole ambition was to play for Wales. Looking back on my life, that is the one big regret. I'd have given up everything I ever did in rugby league, *everything*, for a Welsh cap. I don't think I would ever have been picked for Wales because there was a lot of colour prejudice in those days.

'Another ambition of mine was to play for Cardiff. I grew up watching players like Frank Trott, Billy Cleaver, Lloyd Williams,

Cliff Morgan and Bleddyn Williams. Cliff was absolutely brilliant. He sort of waddled past the opposition but he was a good waddler. For me, Bleddyn was the greatest rugby player I ever saw. As a Cardiff boy, I wanted to play for Cardiff, but I didn't achieve it. I never thought I was welcome. There you are . . .

'They didn't pick me and I think it was all to do with colour, which was why I wasn't welcome. I wasn't the only one. There were other terrific young black players in Cardiff around that time. They were all good enough to play professionally. So why weren't they good enough for Wales?'

Johnny Freeman was one of those terrific young black players. A wing contemporary of Boston's, he went north 12 months after his teammate at South Church Street School. Freeman lived round the corner in Sofia Street and has known Boston ever since they enrolled at school as five year olds in 1939. Their careers continued to run along parallel lines: to the CIACs (Cardiff International Athletic Club), into the army for national service and on to rugby league – in Freeman's case to Halifax for a fee roughly a third of Boston's, £1,050. In a one-club career at Halifax, Johnny, a cousin of Erskine's, scored 290 tries in 395 matches.

A third old boy from the South Church Street School made the same cross-code move a few years later. Colin Dixon played more than 650 times for Halifax and Salford at the same time as another black Cardiffian, Clive Sullivan, was doing famous things on Humberside.

It beggars belief that four players who amassed more than 1,200 tries between them in rugby league could leave their native city without being granted the opportunity to play a solitary match for the capital's major rugby union club.

Freeman, back in his native city, where he first worked as an errand boy for a ship's chandlers in the docks, has no doubt they were all victims of racial prejudice.

'You couldn't play for Cardiff in those days if you were black,' he said. 'Nobody ever said as much, but that was the way it was. We'd have loved to play for Cardiff. As lads, we used to watch them all the time and dream about playing at the Arms Park. Billy was out of this world when he was playing for the CIACs at 15. Why Cardiff didn't give him a trial was unbelievable. And that affected the rest of us, so I thought: "If they ignore Billy, what chance have the rest of us got?"

'They never even looked at him. There was only one reason and that was because of his colour. I knew that I was never going to play rugby union because of my colour. Remember, back in the early and mid-'50s, attitudes were very different, not like today. When Billy told me that he'd signed for Wigan, I said: "That's fantastic. You'll be a big star, Billy, and maybe one day I might go to league myself. You never know . . ."'

When they did go head-to-head, Boston on the right wing for Wigan, Freeman on the left for Halifax, Johnny socked it to Billy big time by running in a hat-trick of tries.

'That only ever happened to Billy twice in all his years in the game and I still pull his leg about it,' said Freeman, who would have been a Great Britain Lion in his own right but for a knee injury. 'Because we've known each other for over 70 years, we have a laugh about it. As he said after the match: "Of all the people in all the world to do that to me, it had to be you, Johnny. But you still lost the match."'

Boston has always been too much of a gentleman to make a fuss, but the cold shoulder he felt in his native city provided a sharp contrast to the warmth with which Wigan embraced him as one of their own, just as the other clubs embraced Freeman, Sullivan and Dixon, not just as players but as ambassadors of high calibre for Wales.

'We were all coloured,' Boston said. 'Clive was very good, Johnny exceptional, but not one of us was made welcome once we'd gone to league. We were getting paid, so the door was shut to us back home. Getting into the clubhouse at the Arms Park was like getting into the Kremlin, except that I probably would've had a better chance of getting into the Kremlin!

'But that just shows you how many hypocrites were running rugby union in Wales. Even then, some players were being paid and nothing was ever said about it. I know because I was one of them. I got a fiver every time I played for Neath and it only cost me three shillings and nine pence in old money, so that wasn't bad, was it?

'A white fiver was really something. I'd never seen one of those before. Mind you, I never got to spend it because I had to give it to my mother to help with the cost of running the house and buying the groceries. It made me think that if they were giving a fiver to me, a 17-year-old kid, what were they giving to other more senior players?'

He would not be at Neath long enough to find out.

Boston still wanted to play for Cardiff and Wales. Nothing else mattered. During the immediate post-war era, Cardiff could field a larger galaxy of stars than any other union team, many of whom, such as Bleddyn Williams, Jack Matthews and Cliff Morgan, achieved the ultimate in beating the All Blacks during the late autumn of 1953 before repeating the feat on behalf of Wales a few weeks later.

It wasn't as if they were unaware of Boston's existence on their own doorstep. He had played in the Cardiff schools team of 1948–49 that swept all before it, then had furthered his rugby education with the celebrated docks team, the CIACs. His burgeoning ability earned him a small form of early recognition, allowing him to realise his dream of playing at Cardiff Arms Park, for the combined Cardiff & District XV, in the home club's traditional opening match of the season in September 1951.

A landslide defeat hardly gave the young fellow much chance to show what he could do.

When he reappeared there in the same fixture at the start of the following season, he did so as captain of the District team drawn from all the junior clubs in and around the capital. They lost 22–0, cutting the margin by one-third on the previous year. Within a month of turning 18, Boston had played at the Arms Park for the last time.

The shameful form of apartheid imposed by the union establishment, which barred rugby league professionals from access to rugby union clubhouses, meant that he would never be allowed to set foot in the members' club at the Westgate Street end of the stadium.

Boston did his national service with the Royal Signals at Catterick Camp in North Yorkshire and his regular appearances for the army alerted every leading rugby league club to his potential. In next to no time, the more ambitious began beating a long path to Angelina Street. Their enthusiasm, fired by the Welsh teenager running in six tries during the 1953 Army Cup final, made Cardiff RFC's indifference all the more difficult to understand. Boston's explanation – a clear case of colour prejudice – cannot be contradicted for historical reasons, given that no black player appeared for the club until Billy Douglas, a shopkeeper from Butetown, who played thirty-nine matches in three seasons from the late 1940s.

Frank Wilson emerged a generation later and made a name for himself by scoring the try for East Wales when they held the All Blacks to a 3–3 draw at the Arms Park in December 1967, before the law-makers came to their senses and upgraded the try from its miserably undervalued three points, first to four, then five. The uncapped wing, born in Cardiff of West Indian extraction, went north the following year to St Helens as the successor to Tom van Vollenhoven, the legendary Springbok. Wilson rose magnificently to the challenge, touching down 196 tries in 301 games.

The unrelated Danny Wilson – father of Ryan Giggs – whose own father came from Sierra Leone, appeared briefly two decades later. It wasn't until the 1970s and the advent of Carl Smith, a West Indian who had arrived in South Wales as a boy from his native St Kitts, that Cardiff picked a black player who, at the very least, deserved Wales B recognition. It never came and Smith, a carpenter by trade, who played almost 250 matches for Cardiff between 1970 and 1978, believes he, too, suffered because of his colour.

That Boston had no wish to turn professional, certainly not at such a tender age, made his departure all the more unfortunate from a union perspective. In the end, he went almost by accident. Boston's reluctance to leave was such that it is no exaggeration to say that he ran away, literally, whenever he approached home and saw a car parked outside. They were few and far between in the area in those days, so it meant only one thing: someone was waiting for him, bearing gifts of northern gold.

Turning on his heel, he would seek refuge with a friend in a neighbouring street and, a few hours later, return in the hope the coast was clear. He knew he could not go on dodging them indefinitely, that it would be only a matter of time before one lucky club caught him at home. That club turned out to be Wigan, who showed they meant business by dispatching their chairman, Joe Taylor, and vice-chairman, Billy Gore, to Tiger Bay. The day in question – Friday, 13

March 1953 – turned out to be lucky. The northern raiding party must have felt like gold prospectors who had stumbled across a Klondyke of their own.

They were waiting for Boston when he got home on leave from his army training. For once, there was no hiding place. 'They told us who they were and that they would pay me £1,500 to sign for Wigan. The chairman opened up his briefcase and put the money on the table – £1,500 in white fivers. I'd never seen so many notes in all my life. My mother didn't bat an eyelid. I looked at her as if to say: "How are you going to get me out of this?"

'I took her out of the room and told her: "I don't want to go anywhere. Get rid of them." She said: "I'll get rid of them all right, son. Leave it to me."

'So my mother went back into the front room, where the Wigan directors were waiting. "Give me £3,000," she says. "And he'll sign right away."

'I thought that was a clever way of getting rid of them because there was no way they were going to stump up that much. I was a 19-year-old lad who had played very little senior football. I left the room because I wanted to stay in union and see how far I could go. Instead of picking up their briefcases and heading out the door, the men from Wigan said: "OK, we'll give you £3,000 – half of it in cash now, the other half over the period of Billy's contract."

'When they agreed to pay, they brought out a contract and I didn't know what to do. My mother said: "I've given my word. You sign that." I signed it.

'I thought: "Oh my God, what have I done?" I never saw any of the white fivers spread out on the table. My mother took them, and that was fair enough, because she'd brought me up and she had a big family to look after. I wasn't bothered about the money and I certainly wouldn't have paid three grand for someone like me – not for all the tea in China. What you don't have, you don't miss.

'Money didn't motivate me. When the Wigan people left the house late on that Friday night, I cried at what I'd done. I understood that my mother felt she had to keep her word, but I knew at the same time that I would never play for Wales. It turned out to be the best mistake I ever made and I've been saying that now for over 50 years. Wigan never treated me any differently to anyone else. There was no colour bar as far as they were concerned.'

Boston made his first-team debut on 21 November 1953 against Barrow at Central Park. A crowd of more than 18,000 were duly rewarded when he started as he meant to go on, and would do for the remainder of that season – and the 14 after that, through to his last match for Wigan, against Wakefield Trinity on 27 April 1968. By then, he had scored 478 tries in 488 matches, a Himalayan level of consistency that made him the highest British try-scorer in the Rugby Football League, smashing the record of 368 tries in 329 matches set by another Wigan Welshman from an earlier era, the former Aberavon wing Johnny Ring, from Port Talbot.

The 'Black Bomber' gave Wigan the sort of run for their money that Messrs Taylor and Gore could never have envisaged the night they left Angelina Street with his signature on a piece of paper. Based on the £3,000 signing-on fee, his 478 tries work out at fractionally more than six pence per touchdown. No wonder they were more than willing to grant him a testimonial. (By the time he ran out of steam – on 25 August 1970, at home to Huyton – at the end of a short stint with Blackpool Borough, Boston had scored fifty-five hat-tricks and thrown in five double hat-tricks for good measure.)

In the pantheon of try-scorers for the Cherry and Whites, in a town where rugby league matters more than Premier League soccer, a Welsh one-two rule the roost: Ring and Boston are followed by Brian Nordgren (316), Shaun Edwards (274), Jimmy Leytham (258), Ernie Ashcroft (241), Eric Ashton (231), Jack Morley (220), Ellery Hanley (189), Johnny Lawrenson (187), Martin Offiah (186) and Jason Robinson further down the list at 171.

Even now, when he's had the best part of half a century to find an answer, Boston is at a loss to understand where all the pace and all the power came from, although weighing in at more than a stone (2.2 kg) at birth gave him a flying start.

'My father was a small man, no more than 5 ft 4 in., and he had never been much of a sportsman,' he said. 'My mother was a buxom Irish woman. When she had me, I was such a whopper of a baby that she was told not to have any more children. She then had five more after me.

'So I had five older and five younger. Five brothers, five sisters, but we didn't want for anything and there was always food on the table. Sometimes, mind, you had to go a bit to make sure you got there on time, otherwise it would all be gone. The marvellous thing about the Bay when I was growing up there was that you had every nationality under the sun and everyone got on with everyone else.

'I never had any problems. I played cricket for Cardiff Boys, I swam for Wales, I played basketball and I ran in every race on sports day. There were ten in all, from the sprints all the way up to what felt like a marathon. I played rugby for Cardiff schoolboys and for Wales Youth, but I never got the chance to play for Cardiff. I didn't make the grade, which was why I went to play for Neath.'

The prejudice that Boston felt towards him at the Arms Park clearly did not apply at the Gnoll. They could hardly believe their luck at the young Boston landing in their midst because they had seen him for themselves. He had played at the Gnoll for Wales in a Boys' Clubs international against England, on which occasion the red number 10 belonged to Boston's neighbourhood pal, Joe Erskine.

By the time he was 19, Boston's physique had changed somewhat. At 5 ft 10 in. and not much more than 12 stone, the youngster hardly fitted into the identikit of the modern behemoth on the wing embodied by Jonah Lomu and all the other giants who followed the monstrous All Black onto the Test stage. During his first Lions trip to Australia, a stronger Boston emerged, reinforced by an extra two stone of muscle. Once he had the power to augment all the wing's basic skills, there was no stopping him, as one St Helens player readily testified. Unashamedly admitting that he had contrived to take himself out of the firing line when his teammates enquired in the dressing-room as to why he had not tackled Boston, the offending player said: 'Tackle him? Bloody hell, it was as much as I could do to get out of his way.'

Ray French, a dual international who played in the second row for England at Twickenham in 1961 before switching to his native St Helens, could empathise with the player in question. 'Billy was very difficult to stop,' said French, a commentator whose rich Lancastrian voice became synonymous with the game. 'He would cut inside, pirouette around on a sixpence and throw you off balance so you never stood much of a chance. You had to put two or three men to mark him. When Billy Boston moved north, Wales lost their greatest-ever union player.'

That is some statement about a player who won a place on Great Britain's tour of Australia in 1954, the first to be made by air, after six matches for Wigan.

'As a wing in rugby union, sometimes you can be waiting for something to happen,' he said. 'But in rugby league, the ball never seemed to be out of my hands. It was so entertaining, certainly for me, if not the crowd. I loved it and sometimes I didn't have to do anything, like the first try I got for Wigan. The fella inside me made a break, I ran alongside and he put me over. Before I went to Australia, they'd take me to one side and explain a few things because I was still learning the game.'

Boston's Wigan aggregate record will never be surpassed and yet, for all its towering quality, his figure falls a long way short of the skyscraping total amassed by the only player in the history of both codes to score more, the phenomenal Australian Brian Bevan. How a balding little fellow with knobbly knees and hollow cheeks did it remains one of the wonders of twentieth-century sport, but the facts, no matter how staggering, are indubitable.

The Australian with the slightly haunted look scored 740 tries in 620 matches for Warrington. He got fifty or more a season four times and sixty or more another four times, including a high of sixty-six in 1952–53, Boston's debut campaign. Billy's most prodigious season, four years later, when his tally included fourteen in ten matches for Great Britain, fell two short of Ring's sixty-two, which has stood the test of time since the 1920s.

Bevan, who died in Southport on 3 June 1991 at the age of 66, twice scored seven tries in a match. Boston did the same, against Dewsbury on 20 August 1955 and again at Salford on 30 April 1962, when he crossed the line eight times, only to have one disallowed for a foot in touch. Four times, Bevan scored six in one match; Boston did it three times. Five times, Bevan scored five in one match; Boston, twice. Bevan got four in a match on twenty occasions; Boston, on seventeen.

Not surprisingly, Bevan was the only non-Test player chosen for the Australian Rugby League's Team of the Century, alongside the likes of Mal Meninga, Wally Lewis and Andrew Johns. 'Brian looked at times as though a puff of wind would blow him over, but he was the greatest player I ever came up against,' Boston said. 'Nobody will ever get close to doing what he did. And he was a real gentleman.'

Apart from a handful of games for one of the clubs in his native Sydney, Bevan spent his entire career in England and suffered as a consequence when it came to Test football. In his case, there wasn't any. Boston, in marked contrast, required only ten matches in his debut season at Wigan, ending in April 1954, to convince the Great Britain selectors that the Lions could not leave for Australia the following month without him. He was the only non-white player in a squad captained by a Welshman from Mountain Ash, the Hunslet stand-off Dickie Williams. It also featured another Welshman of still mightier stature, Lewis Jones, four years after he had toured Australasia as an eighteen year old with the British and Irish Rugby Union Lions.

While still a teenager, Boston marked his Test debut by scoring twice against Australia in Brisbane at the start of a drawn series against the Kangaroos. In Auckland three weeks later, he lined up against New Zealand and marked the occasion by doubling his number of tries to four. When Boston returned there eight years later for his second Lions tour, he wondered whether the Kiwis – or, to be more accurate, the New Zealand immigration authorities – were holding those tries against him. Suddenly, with no warning, colour became an issue, embarrassingly so.

'When I first went to New Zealand on tour, I waltzed through without a question being asked,' he said. 'When I got to passport control on the second tour, they stopped me entering the country. I said: "You are joking, aren't you? You've got all these Maori people living here and you mean to tell me, you won't let me in?"

'Then all sorts of people got involved. Again I said: "Will somebody tell me what's going on? Why haven't you stopped any of the other players? Why am I the only one?" Anyway, it got itself sorted out, but it should never have happened in the first place.

'I'm the last person to kick up a fuss, but it's hard not to when the only reason they have for stopping you is the colour of your skin. I could not believe it. They must have felt as embarrassed by it as I was because in the end I had a letter of apology from the Prime Minister of New Zealand.'

South Africa, in the grip of apartheid, reared its ugly political head twice during the course of Boston's professional career. In 1957, two years after the historic drawn series between the union Lions and the Springboks, the Rugby Football League decided to send their Lions to the same place. They did so, knowing that one of them would not be allowed into the whites-only hotel with the rest of the players, nor the whites-only restaurants, because of the colour of his skin.

Boston had decided from the outset that he would give South Africa the widest of berths. He had no wish to put himself in a position to be humiliated by the so-called pass laws, which segregated every aspect of work and social life in South Africa.

Why the RFL put one of their greatest players in such a predicament – for a visit designed to promote league in a country where only union mattered – baffled those who had sworn they wouldn't touch South Africa with a barge pole.

Five years later, the RFL did it again and paid a second visit, despite the fact that South Africa had by now been expelled from the Olympic movement and from the governing body of world soccer, FIFA.

For a second time, the game Boston more than anyone else of his generation had done so much to popularise shamefully put its No. 1 box-office attraction in an unbelievable position, of having to subject himself to that country's rules regarding second-class citizenship for blacks, just to please the authorities on the off-chance of spreading the 13-a-side gospel. For the second time, Boston stood by his principles and went straight home once the New Zealand leg of the trip had been completed.

It left a sour taste. Not that the RFL ever apologised for failing to do the decent thing, which would have been to inform the South Africans that *all* their players had to be made welcome, regardless of colour. When the MCC chose the England cricket party for the tour of South Africa in 1968, they caused a scandal over the non-selection of Basil D'Oliveira, a Cape Coloured whose absence was seen as evidence of pressure from the racist South African government. The issue came to a head following the withdrawal through injury of the

Warwickshire all-rounder Tom Cartwright and the choice of D'Oliveira as his replacement. The South African government found this unacceptable and the tour never took place.

'The first time they agreed to play in South Africa, they told me that it was for three exhibition games,' Boston said. 'They told me I could go, but I'd have to stop in a different hotel to the rest of the players and that I couldn't play in any of the matches. So I said: "What's the point me going?" They flew off and left me in Australia. Nobody should tell you what team you can or can't bring into a country. They missed a big chance to strike a blow for every black player by saying they would have nothing to do with South Africa until they got rid of segregation.'

Wigan paid their part-time professionals £25 if they won and £15 if they lost, sums that put them roughly in the same bracket as their soccer counterparts.

By 1958, the Football League had enforced a maximum weekly wage of £20, provoking complaints from the players' trade union that they were then only £5 a week above the national average, whereas in 1939 their maximum pay of £8 a week had been double the national average. A strike threatened for January 1961 forced the abolition of the maximum wage, whereupon Fulham made their England inside-forward, Johnny Haynes, the game's first £100-a-week player. Manchester United reacted by imposing a maximum wage of £50 at Old Trafford, which goes to show how times have changed.

Boston, more than anyone, could be relied on to act as some sort of cash machine for the rest of the players. As Joe Egan, Wigan's coach from August 1956 to May 1961, put it: 'Having Billy in the team, we were quids in.'

With Boston terrorising opponents, Wigan went to Wembley six times for Challenge Cup finals, with a 50–50 success rate. The three wins began in 1958 (Workington Town, 13–9), continued in 1959 (Hull, 30–13) and finished in 1965 (Hunslet, 20–16). The three defeats were crammed into a five-year period: 1961 (St Helens, 6–12), 1963 (Wakefield Trinity, 10–25) and 1966 (St Helens, 2–21).

Two years later, it was all over and thereby hangs another tale. Boston's take on retirement is that he never intended to bring the curtain down on his time at Wigan when he was still only 33.

According to the man himself, a chance remark after one match to Eric Ashton created the momentum which, in the end, left him no option but to quit. Ashton and Boston had run arguably the most productive partnership in the history of the game, the English centre contributing more than 200 tries in his own right to the myriad of mayhem they generated in the Wigan cause.

The chain of events begin after they lost at Workington on 17 February 1968, which Ashton presided over in his role as player-coach. Boston considered himself to have been every bit as out of sorts as the team. 'In the dressing-room afterwards, I said to Eric Ashton: "I've had enough of this. I think I'll retire."'

The news got out shortly afterwards and, for once, Boston found himself caught off guard. 'I was only joking when I said what I said to Eric, but obviously I didn't make that clear. Anyway, the word got out and it was all over the papers. There were so many headlines that it was hard to try and make out that it wasn't true. I knew then that once the season finished, I had to go.

'I had fourteen years at Wigan and I enjoyed every minute of it. They gave me the chance to get paid to do something I loved and I'll always be grateful to them for that. They always treated me with respect. It's been wonderful and still is. People who weren't born when I was playing say hello in the street and that's nice. I was even lucky enough to get a lovely wife.'

He met Joan Rudd, a local lass then working in a grocery, on a blind date and by the time the final curtain came down on his time at Central Park, they were busy rearing five little Bostons – Christine, Lisa, Karen, Angela and Stephen. Blackpool Borough talked the head of the house out of retirement for a brief comeback that ended in April 1970 with a home defeat by Hunslet, witnessed by a gathering, as distinct from a crowd, of some 500.

By then Boston had become mine host at the Griffin Hotel and its location across the road from Central Park made it a perfect fit. He ran the pub for 16 years and throughout that time he never forgot his Cardiff roots, making frequent trips home, often for occasions to remind him that his exploits in the North-west had not gone unnoticed. As evidence of the enduring affection in which he was held in league, Wigan asked him, in his 70th year, to lead their team out at the 2004 Challenge Cup final against St Helens at the Millennium Stadium.

Not all the homecomings gave cause for celebration. One of the saddest, in February 1990, was to attend the funeral of his old pal from South Church Street School, Joe Erskine. Cardiff's requiem for the passing of their own heavyweight champion coincided with the passing of much of the Tiger Bay of the '50s, an observation memorably captured by Dan O'Neill in the *South Wales Echo*.

> When they took Peerless Jim Driscoll on his last sad journey from a numbed Newtown to Cathays Cemetery, one hundred thousand men, women and children braved the bleakness of that February day in 1925 to say farewell to a folk hero. When it was over, and old men still talked about it in the *Old Arcade* and *City Arms* fifty years on, they told each other there could never be another outpouring of grief to match it.
>
> Until the day they took Cardiff's own Joe on that same last, sad journey. The sense of loss was just as profound and in a way Joe's passing marked, as well, the passing of old Butetown, Tiger Bay. Joe died alone in his Adamsdown flat, his money gone, his health gone, his second marriage over. But what a legacy he left, what a credit he'd been to the hard old game he graced with such dignity.
>
> Joe was British and Empire boss when Britain was pretty well stocked in the beef brigade with Henry Cooper, Brian London, Dick Richardson and up-and-comers like Billy Walker battling each other. But, although he went to the top of the tree, he never forgot his roots and they went deep, those roots, all the way back to his beloved Bay.
>
> Which is why his coffin was carried back through that Bay, the old Bay, along Angelina Street, where he'd been born 56 years earlier, and Bute Street and Mount Stuart Square, before going on to Thornhill. That was how he wanted it.

Cooper, who died in May 2011 within 48 hours of his 77th birthday, did his national service with Erskine, whom he fought eight times, as an amateur and professional, winning five and losing three. One of those defeats, on points over ten rounds, came during a final eliminator for the vacant British title on 15 November 1955 at the Harringay Arena; another on points over fifteen for the British and Empire crowns at the same London venue on 17 September 1957.

'If Joe could have punched, he would have been world champion,' said 'Our 'Enery'. 'They all thought Willie Pastrano [the American light-heavyweight] was the best thing on two legs when he first came to London. I did fifty or sixty rounds of sparring with him and then they matched him with Joe. Some of the reporters asked me who would win and I told them straight: "Erskine will box his ears off. Joe has more boxing ability in his little finger than Willie has in his whole body."

'Joe was a lovely character. I fought them all. I fought Brian London three times, knocked out Dick Richardson twice, I beat Billy Walker . . . and Joe always gave me more bleedin' trouble than anyone else. He'd such a poker face and an ability to recover from a good punch in a split-second that I never knew if I'd hurt him.'

Cooper, for one, would not have complained had Joe stuck to rugby like Boston.

Shortly after his retirement from the licensed trade in February 1996, Boston was struck by a stolen car and suffered multiple injuries. 'I thought he was dead, I really did,' his wife, Joan, said. 'I looked down and found that he was alive. He was very lucky. You wouldn't have believed the number of get-well cards he got. They came by the boxful from all over the world.'

The car, as the man himself points out with a grin, was a write-off. Five months later he had recovered sufficiently to be in London for the ultimate recognition of his enduring popularity. For services to rugby league, the Queen presented William John Boston with the MBE at an investiture ceremony at Buckingham Palace. He went there with Joan and, in compliance with Palace protocol governing the size of the official party, two of their five children.

'Billy got more nervous that day than before any rugby match,' Joan said. 'He wanted to have a tot of whisky or vodka, but I wouldn't let him because he was going to meet the Queen. He perspired so much that his suit was wet. After the investiture, we went for a look round the Palace and then the official photographer came up to take a family picture.

'There was only one problem. We couldn't find Billy. We searched high and low – no sign of him. Then we found out that he'd gone outside the Palace for a smoke. Once you go out, you can't get back in, so we never got the photograph. You could say I was not impressed with him that day, not impressed at all . . .'

Joan Rudd met her husband shortly after he had signed for her home-town club. They married in 1956 and preside over a family that now extends to 14 grandchildren and 12 great-grandchildren, each and every one proud of what their grandfather and great-grandfather achieved.

Central Park and its Billy Boston stand may be long gone, a theatre reduced to nothing more than a supermarket car park, but the Boston years still burn brightly in Wigan and the rugby league heartlands of the north. They remember him as a smiling superstar, once described as combining the power of Martin Offiah with the guile of Gerald Davies.

One of the first inductees into the Welsh Sports Hall of Fame, he is also to be found in the Great Britain rugby league equivalent, alongside two other Welshmen honoured for careers built on the same monumental lines – Jim Sullivan and Gus Risman. Elsewhere, the honours keep piling up for the first black Welshman to follow the yellow brick road north. Phil Melling, emeritus professor of American literature at the University of Wales, Swansea, acclaimed Boston as 'the Oscar Peterson of rugby league'.

His feats inspired a local singer-songwriter, Georgie Fame, from neighbouring Leigh, to compose his own 'Ode to Billy B':

> Land of my fathers the land of the free,
> Land of my granddad and W.J.B.
> Bill to us and a legend to all,
> Miracles happened when he got the ball.
> Raised with tigers around Cardiff Bay,
> He headed up north to do things his own way.
> Wigan befriended him right from the start,

They knew he was special and what a big heart.
The fifties and sixties were Billy's hey days,
And wherever he played he would thrill and amaze.
From Barrow to Brisbane and Wembley to Leeds,
The opposition were brought to their knees.

His name having become as synonymous with the town as its pier, pie-eating world championships, George Formby, the comedian Ted Ray and the actor Roy Kinnear, Wigan has long made him a freeman of the borough. The only shame is that Billy Boston never got to play for Wales against England at Cardiff Arms Park. Mind you, had he done so, there might not have been enough white fivers in Wigan to buy him.

6

TENNIS REBEL

Mike Davies

Born: Swansea, 9 January 1936

Mike Davies picked up a tennis racquet for the first time on a municipal court in his native Swansea at the age of 12 during the early summer of 1946. Ten years later, the boy from Sketty had gone from nowhere to the best in Britain, from Cwmdonkin Park to the Centre Court at Wimbledon.

From there, he took off on another unprecedented leap of faith, across the Atlantic as a pioneer of professional tennis who would transform the game from its humble beginnings into a global business. At a time when the stuffed shirts running the amateur game considered professionalism to be the dirtiest of 15-letter words, Britain's No. 1 had to pay a hefty price for joining Jack Kramer's embryonic professional tour and blazing a gold-plated trail for future generations. The All England Club banned Davies and his fellow professionals from darkening their doors and by the time they reinstated the Welshman almost 30 years later, he had changed the landscape of the game beyond all recognition.

In the beginning, long before he started working on his game at Cwmdonkin Park, the Luftwaffe did their horrific worst to blow the whole of his home town to kingdom come. Glyn and Gertrude Davies' younger son had just turned five when the blitz of Swansea began in February 1941.

'I remember the air-raid warnings and rushing down into the

cellar many times,' he said. 'For a small boy, that was fun; something different from going to bed. I remember walking back from the cinema one day with my uncle when bombs were going off very near and my uncle picking me up and running home to Gwydr Crescent in Uplands. I was too young to understand what it all meant.'

Dylan Thomas found Cwmdonkin Park an inspirational place at roughly the time when the young Davies started hitting a few worn-out balls around the place with a racquet borrowed from his aunt. Thomas, who was born round the corner at Cwmdonkin Drive, was not the only gigantic figure from the literary world to be found in that part of Swansea after the war. Sir Kingsley Amis, acknowledged as one of Britain's most celebrated novelists of the second half of the twentieth century, also lived there from the late '40s, during his 12 years as lecturer in English at the University of Wales.

Davies was so smitten by the tennis bug that he was never going to scale any academic heights at Dynevor School. He had been enrolled there many years after Sir Harry Secombe – and a few before another notable old boy, Spencer Davis, of the eponymous rock band. Swansea, famous for its conveyor belt of footballers, cricketers and rugby players, had never produced a tennis player of renown before, nor has done so since.

'It certainly wasn't a game that everyone played. I guess it was seen as an elite sport, not like football, rugby or cricket. I played all those at school, and a lot of table tennis. It was a natural talent, something I was fortunate to have been born with. It's what you do with the talent that matters.'

Davies, whose father worked as an area representative for a biscuit firm, did not come from a privileged background. 'Far from it,' he said. 'My parents didn't have any money, so if I went off to play in a tennis tournament, I had to hitch-hike. If a string went in my racquet, buying a new one was out of the question because I couldn't afford it. We didn't even have the money to get it restrung. If a string went, you repaired it yourself.

'My brother Leighton was my inspiration. He played some tennis, but he wouldn't play with me because I was five years younger and he didn't think I could give him a game. I wanted to emulate him, so one day I borrowed my aunt's old racquet and I had a friend who said he wouldn't mind coming out for a game. There was no one else around when we started hitting a few balls, and that was it.

'I was hooked. I fell in love with the game there and then. I found I had a natural ability to play. I'd played a lot of table tennis, so I had the racquet–eye coordination. From that first experience, tennis was all I was interested in doing – stupidly so, because I completely ignored my schoolwork. Had I realised back then how daunting a task it would be to make a living out of tennis, I would have thought twice. Being young, that didn't occur to me. It was a classic case of a fool rushing in where the angels feared to tread. When you're young, you don't think about becoming rich.'

That was just as well because the concept of anyone being paid anything to play tennis anywhere in the world had not been dreamt up in 1947, when the young Davies reached the ripe old age of 13. Jack Kramer, a crew-cut all-American boy, the son of a Californian railroad worker, won the men's singles crown at Wimbledon that summer and promptly decided to run his own professional circus, severing all ties with the amateur game.

In those early days, the play-for-pay pioneers existed in a twilight world, excommunicated by the establishment whose 'open' events were a misnomer. Don Budge was one of the professionals' first headline acts, an American whose monopoly of the four Grand Slam singles – the Australian, French and US opens, plus Wimbledon – made him unquestionably the best player on the planet.

Frank Kovacs, the son of Hungarian immigrants, whose cousin Ernie made a bigger name for himself as a Hollywood comedian, was undeniably the most entertaining. Not for nothing did they call him 'the Clown Prince of Tennis'. Once, when serving at match point, he threw three balls into the air and hit the middle one for an ace.

When Kramer took charge, Bobby Riggs, best remembered when he came out of retirement at 55 during the mid-'70s for his 'Battle of the Sexes' match against Billie Jean King, was one of the pro tour's leading lights, along with the pigeon-toed Pancho Segura from Ecuador, who made his debut against Riggs at Madison Square Garden in New York before a crowd of 15,000.

Kramer picked off the best amateurs one by one. Pancho Gonzales, whose Mexican parents settled in Los Angeles, turned pro in 1950 and became one of the all-time greats. Frank Sedgman crossed the divide at the beginning of 1953, the Australian having won 22 Grand Slam titles in the previous four years. He would have left sooner had Harry Hopman, coach of the Australian Davis Cup team, not spearheaded a campaign to keep Sedgman out of Kramer's clutches. They raised enough to finance the purchase of a petrol station in his wife's name, which enabled him to play on a little longer as a supposedly bona fide amateur.

Tony Trabert, Wimbledon champion in 1955, followed, as did the electrifying young Australians Lew Hoad and Ken Rosewall. One by one, all the big names in Davies' boyhood scrapbook were being picked off.

'I used to read the *Evening Post* and the *Echo*, especially the sports editions every Saturday night,' he said. 'I'd cut out all the articles I could find on tennis and the pictures of the players, like Kramer, Trabert, Gonzales, Jaroslav Drobny, Vic Seixas, and have books made of them. As a kid, all I ever wanted was that one day I would be like them. There was no television then, so you didn't see Wimbledon – you read about it. I had my own Welsh heroes, such as Dill Jones, who was in the Welsh team, and that was a big deal.'

As an increasing number of cities came within the orbit of Kramer's pan-American tour by the dawn of the 1950s, Davies won his first tournament, the 1950 boys' singles at Langland Bay tennis club, where the Mayor of Swansea, no less, did the honours at the presentation ceremony. During his run of four successive wins as Welsh junior champion, he had begun to be noticed in wider Welsh circles as a boy of above-average talent who might go far. Not that anyone then had a clue how far he would go, least of all Davies himself.

'After winning at Langland Bay, my main objective was to see whether I could get out of school the following Monday so I could spend the day on the tennis court. I never thought about being a pioneer or anything as far-fetched as that.

'I played in a couple of junior tournaments in Wales, at places like Penarth and Llanelli, but I needed a break if I was to push on to a higher level. Fred Perry and Dan Maskell, the two biggest names in British tennis, were touring the country, looking for young talent.

They asked the Welsh Tennis Association to get some youngsters together who they thought had some ability.

'I was one of about fifteen or twenty people chosen for their visit. We went to Bristol for a day and played in front of Perry and Maskell. They must have seen some potential in me because the next thing I was enrolled in their school, which they ran for promising players. There I met other young players, like Bobby Wilson, Billy Knight and Roger Becker. That was the start.

'The biggest change in my tennis game came when I went to Australia, which was a lovely way of avoiding the Welsh winter. Australia had Harry Hopman, the coach of their Davis Cup team, and they had more outstanding players than anyone else – Lew Hoad, Ken Rosewall, Roy Emerson, Ashley Cooper, Rex Hartwig, Mervyn Rose and so on. Australia was the place to go in the winter.'

The experience put Davies on the fastest of tracks to the top of British men's tennis. By 1957, he was their official No. 1 player. He had got there at the age of 22, with ample time to do what no British player had done since the war – win the singles at one of the four Grand Slam tournaments, an opportunity he sacrificed to become one of Kramer's professional pioneers.

Four years later, he and Wilson reached the Wimbledon doubles final, the first British men to appear in a final at the All-England Championships since Perry won the singles in 1936.

The Anglo-Welsh partnership fell in straight sets to the 18-year-old Californian Dennis Ralston and the Mexican Rafael Osuna, who lost his life at the age of 30 in a plane crash in June 1969. Davies and Wilson went down fighting, 5-7, 3-6, 8-10, each consoling the other with the belief that there was always next year and the year after that. Events would rapidly prove that, for one half of the double act, the chance had gone and gone for good.

'I had a hope that one day I would be good enough to win Wimbledon,' Davies said. 'That was everyone's dream. Then, after that doubles final, I was offered the chance to turn professional. It changed the course of my life. I knew I would be ostracised by the tennis authorities.

'Pros were barred from competing with amateurs in tournaments like the Davis Cup or any of the Grand Slams. On the other hand, I had the chance to play against the best in the world – Gonzales, Trabert, Hoad, Rosewall, Segura. That was my prime motivation. I was also tired of the hypocrisy of getting money under the table. It wasn't a great deal, but it paid for the hotels and travel.

'I didn't want to be part of the sham. I knew for a fact that some players were taken aside by their amateur federations when they heard they'd been approached to turn pro. "Don't worry," they told them. "We'll take care of you. We'll get you a 'job' so you can keep playing 'amateur' tennis and you'll still be eligible for the Davis Cup."'

There were times when Davies could not afford even the cheapest bed and breakfast. He slept in a hedge before one tournament, and at another event in Australia he crouched all night long in a doorway to escape the pelting rain. 'I hitch-hiked all over Great Britain and I did a fair bit in Australia too, because I couldn't afford to get around any other way,' he said. 'I guess it's good for the character.'

When he wrote a piece for a tennis magazine mentioning the name of a certain restaurant, the Lawn Tennis Association gave him a rollicking. 'They reprimanded me because I'd written an article about diet,' he said. 'A friend ran a steakhouse and in the article I mentioned his steakhouse and got ticked off by the LTA for promoting my friend's business.'

As a professional, he became *persona non grata*, his membership of the All England Club cancelled at a stroke. 'Once you'd turned pro, there was no question of being allowed to play tennis there or use the facilities for practice,' he said. 'If I'd tried, I'd have been stopped. It was almost as if they felt I was going to foul the grass.

'The International Tennis Federation controlled the Grand Slam competitions and ran the game, so I knew the score. What mattered most to me was the opportunity to play against the very best, and the very best were increasingly with Jack Kramer. I was keen to look beyond the day-to-day tour and see if professional tennis could be a major sport, which was a tall order because amateur tennis dominated everything through the ITF.'

He discovered all too soon that life on the fledgling US professional tour bore none of the perks taken for granted by the multimillionaire superstars of the twenty-first century. There was no business-class travel, no five-star hotels and, at some venues, no dressing-room.

Davies found that out for himself when Kramer's entourage pitched their not-so-big-top in Marseille for an indoor event at a convention centre. The Welshman made up a quartet, alongside Trabert, the Spaniard Andres Gimeno and Kurt Nielsen, the Dane who still holds a unique place at Wimbledon as the only unseeded player to reach two finals – losing to Seixas in 1953 and Trabert in 1955.

'At Wimbledon, everything was done for you,' he said. 'After a match, there was always someone there to ask whether you wanted a bath or a shower. I had my own locker and, in terms of facilities, we lacked for nothing. The first match I ever played as a pro was very different.

'We got there and they led us into a place with four walls and nothing else. I turned to Tony and said: "Trabe, where's the locker room?" With that, he took a six-inch nail out of his bag and hammered it into the wall with the sole of one of his training shoes. "There's your locker, rookie," he said, pointing to his handiwork on the wall. "Get used to it."'

Davies had only a hazy idea of what he was letting himself in for when he took the money, a guaranteed £4,500-a-year for two years. It may not sound much now, but in 1960 it amounted to almost 20 times the annual wage for tens of thousands of British workers. The prospect of getting in on the ground floor and building something of lasting value appealed to Davies every bit as much as the cash.

'I knew I was taking a big chance of maybe being part of a new era of creating open tennis,' he said. 'What Jack offered me wasn't a fortune, but it was enough for me to turn pro and take the chance to make more. I was involved in the professionalising of the sport and I've been in it all my life. I've never been afraid to try something different. Maybe it's stupidity because, if you knew all the problems, you wouldn't have got into them in the first place. I look back sometimes and question why I got involved because some aspects were so tough. Maybe I didn't think it all through. Some decisions turned out well, some not so well.

'What I did, I did because I believed it was good for the game. I'd never do anything to hurt it because I love it so much. I wanted to help the game, not hinder it. In the beginning, there were very few places where pro tennis players could play. We had to create our own venues.'

Once they'd found one, they then had to go out and find a crowd, which they often did by enlisting the help of tennis-friendly film stars, such as Charlton Heston. The success of *Ben Hur*, a $70-million box-office hit, meant that the main actor in William Wilder's biblical epic was just about as big as anyone in Tinsel Town. As a tennis aficionado, Heston would turn up, minus the chariot, whenever he could and stop the traffic.

'Charlton was a great friend of ours,' Davies said. 'He loved the sport and he came to various cities to hit a few balls with us, and of course the crowds would come. He did a lot of that and he did it all for nothing because he wanted to see it succeed as a professional sport.

'In the early days, it was very hard to get people interested. As we looked to expand our tour, we'd go to new cities, and to let them know we were coming we'd get permission from the local mayor to cut the traffic off for an hour or so. That gave us enough time to put a net across one of the main streets and play matches with stars like Charlton Heston.'

Soon Davies found himself doubling up as the tour's spokesman, selling the upcoming event, thereby taking his first steps towards a flourishing career as Mr Big in the promotion of tennis as a business. 'We realised the importance right at the outset that the sponsor had to be given value for money and that meant getting publicity,' he said. 'I found myself pushed into the role of promoter.

'The rest of the players chose me to sell the show because apparently I was talkative enough. We'd arrive in places like Albuquerque, New Mexico, and someone would be needed to do a radio show. They'd have two slots – one at six in the morning, the other at midnight.

'I kept doing that and the more I did, the better I got. I learnt by trial and error in a school of hard knocks. The reality at the time was that tennis had never been sold on television there and nobody had any idea how much a 30-second advert was worth. We were learning all the time.'

The brave new world came at a price. When he raised his game to its peak in the early '60s, Davies had no way of knowing how close he might have gone to winning a Grand Slam title, such as Wimbledon. 'Probably not, but it's impossible to tell for sure,' he said. 'There is no question that I learnt how to play better tennis when I turned professional. Until then I didn't know how to play in a professional way. I didn't know anything about playing the percentages and I didn't know much about tactics.

'The best tennis I ever played was two or three years after signing up with Kramer. If I'd stayed in the so-called amateur ranks, who knows? I might have got to the semi-finals at Wimbledon, possibly the final, but it wasn't to be. Looking back on my life, I'm glad I made that decision when I did. I made plenty of bad decisions, but that was a good one.'

Tennis existed in its them-and-us state until the All England Club, under the enlightened chairmanship of Herman David, declared Wimbledon an open championship with effect from 1968. They did so having staged the Wimbledon World Professional Championships, won by Rod Laver, the previous August, a bold initiative driven by David and his disenchantment with the so-called amateur game, which he described as 'a living lie'.

The timing could scarcely have been crueller for Davies. He had retired the year before at the age of 33, a frustrating state of affairs made all the more so considering how close tennis came to embracing professionalism in 1960 and providing Davies with the best of both worlds.

When delegates converged on Paris for the annual meeting of the International Tennis Federation, the proponents of an open game, headed by the perceptive Herman David, needed a two-thirds majority, which worked out at 139 of the 209 votes. According to one of the sport's most authoritative journalists, Richard Evans, they went desperately close in somewhat farcical circumstances.

In his book *Open Tennis*, Evans revealed that the vote in favour of an open game fell three short of the required number. One delegate had fallen asleep, another was in the toilet and a third was absent, arranging the entertainment for that evening. Pancho Gonzales was fated to be arguably the best player never to win Wimbledon and young Davies to spend his best years on the outside when he would otherwise have been flying the flag for Wales and Britain.

'All 140 nations were represented and the result went against us by a whisker,' Davies recalled. 'We heard rumours that a few people were not there when the motion was put to the vote and they, if you believe what people were saying at the time, could have made all the difference. So we were kept waiting for eight years. During that time, players like Hoad and Rosewall missed 32 Grand Slam tournaments because they were banned like the rest of us. I missed 28.'

As one door closed on Davies the player, another opened for Davies the tennis entrepreneur, which coincided with the creation of World Championship Tennis, bankrolled by its co-founder, Lamar Hunt. The son of an oil tycoon whose father was once considered to be the eighth-richest American, Hunt had such a flair for sports promotion that everything he touched seemed to turn to gold, most notably the American Football League and the Chicago Bulls basketball franchise, of both of which he was a founding father.

Davies set about the task of building WCT into a major force by learning from Hunt. 'We started off with eight contracted players and we promoted them as the Handsome Eight because they were all good-looking guys – Dennis Ralston, Butch Buchholz, Pierre Barthes, John Newcombe, Tony Roche, Niki Pilic, Roger Taylor and Cliff Drysdale,' Davies said. 'My job was to sell them to the public.

'Lamar Hunt and our company had guaranteed each a certain amount of money, but it wasn't as simple as that. It was down to me to find venues all over the world for them to play so we could recoup the money. We had to find a sponsor, then find a promoter. That's how we got going.

'As we grew, we realised we needed to do it on a bigger scale. We signed up more players and then I came up with something that was a major turning point – the first million-dollar tour. It was a rainy day in London when I conceived the idea, on a notepad, putting down my thoughts. Twenty tournaments throughout the world. I'd have 32 players under contract and they'd play in 20 cities, each paying $50,000, which was huge money in those days. A rising tide floats all the boats.

'The eight with the best record would qualify for the finals in Dallas, the WCT shoot-out, as we called it. I got hold of Lamar Hunt and told him my idea. We had a two to three-hour meeting. He asked all kinds of questions and I said: "I think I can sell this, but I cannot guarantee it. What I need you to do is to guarantee the money."

'He said "OK." We went ahead and put it all together.

'I learnt everything from Lamar. My knowledge of business was very raw. I learnt the hard way and I learnt that without a sound business plan, there could be no show. There's a show and there's business. Lamar Hunt taught me how to be a businessman.

'I'll always remember one piece of advice he gave me: "Mike, just remember that the money runs out long before the deals. There are always deals, there isn't always the money to pay for them."'

It helped having a few aces up his sleeve, even if time was fast catching up on the man whose absence from the Grand Slam stage for so long merely increased the mystique swirling around his name: Pancho Gonzales. He was still good enough at 40 in the first major open event, the French championships in Paris, to knock out the holder, Emerson, and lose in the semi-finals to Laver.

The respect his fellow professionals held for Gonzales rarely extended to friendship. Trabert never made any secret of his dislike of him. 'I appreciated his tennis ability, but I never came to respect him as a person,' he said. 'Pancho Gonzales was a loner, sullen most of the time, with a big chip on his shoulder, and he rarely associated with us on the road.'

Gonzales, who died from cancer in 1995 at the age of 67, married six times and every one ended in divorce. Kramer once said of him: 'Gonzales never seemed to get along with his various wives, although this never stopped him from getting married.'

Another Latin American player, Pancho Segura, said once: 'You know the nicest thing "Gorg" [Gonzales] ever says to his wives is: "Shut up."'

Davies ran the WCT as executive director for 13 years, his innovative quality making the sport much more viewer-friendly for an expanding television audience. Under his supervision, the game's expansion, particularly in eastern Europe, went a long way towards changing its image as an elitist sport. In 1981, he started work for the Association of Tennis Professionals (ATP), first as marketing director, then executive director.

'I'm not a wealthy man,' he said recently. 'A Warren Buffet I am not, but I am comfortable. I'd like to be remembered as someone whose passion for the game helped bring it up to where it is today from where it was 50 years ago. Today players have their entourages, trainers, coaches, lawyers . . .

'Changing the colour of the ball was unthinkable until we did it in 1972. Wimbledon certainly didn't thank me for introducing the yellow ball, but five years later they did the same. Coloured clothing was another departure from tradition. The public in America sat down, saw two players dressed in white and complained that they didn't always know who was who. So we made sure that the players wore different colours.

'We pushed ahead for 30 seconds between points. The rules of the game stipulated that play had to be continuous. Ilie Nastase used to take two minutes for arguments. Television wanted time for commercials. We decided we would allow a maximum of 30 seconds between points and 90 seconds between games.

'I once asked Rod Laver to play at a tournament in Hawaii and he said: "I'm not sure. I'm fed up playing Nastase. Every time he's losing, he starts arguing with the umpire for five minutes. It's no fun."

'I said: "If I find a way of stopping that, will you play?" He said he would and so we had 30-second clocks installed courtside. If they didn't play within the allotted time, they lost the point. When we played in the old days, we'd be serving in ten or fifteen seconds of the previous point.'

After presiding over the ATP tour as executive director, Davies served as general manager of the International Tennis Federation, which meant relocating from Arlington, Texas, to London. He did so at the behest of Philippe Chatrier, a former player and journalist who became the federation's president in 1977.

'Back in 1972 when I was at the ATP, we sued the ITF over various "illegal practices",' Davies said. 'They did not like the competition we were giving them. Many years later, when I was out of a job, Philippe Chatrier called me and asked me to work for the ITF. I guess I'd been forgiven!'

The All England Lawn Tennis and Croquet Club also forgave Davies, reinstating him as a member almost 30 years after putting him out of bounds.

He and his lifetime buddy, Butch Buchholz, are still active beyond staging their own tour event once a year, in Connecticut, more recently at their own cost because of the global recession. 'We're trying to make it work financially,' Davies said, a trifle ruefully. 'At least it works artistically.'

They are in the protracted process of devising a World Cup, an extension of the Davis Cup, which would feature the eight top countries each picking a four-strong team, two men, two women.

'The Davis Cup is fine on its own,' Davies said. 'We are trying to put something together which can be played from start to finish in no more than eight days. It will be based strictly on merit. There won't be any wildcard stuff. If a big name or a big country doesn't qualify, they won't be coming.'

Sadly, whatever the format, there will be no place for Great Britain, unless they discover another Andy Murray and a couple of latter-day Virginia Wades. Davies has his own views on why no British player has won the men's singles at Wimbledon since Fred Perry in 1936.

'My theory is that tennis associations don't make tennis players. Take Germany as a classic example. All of a sudden they produced two world-beaters at roughly the same time, Boris Becker and Steffi Graf. How long will it take a country like Germany to produce another two players of that calibre? It may not happen for 50 years. The level of competition is fantastically high and getting higher all the time. The 100th best player in the world today is very good. Fifty years ago, the 50th best player in the world wasn't very good.

'Before the war, Britain and France dominated. After the war, it was Australia and America. Tennis is now a global sport. There have never been so many good players from so many countries competing for the Grand Slams because they realise that tennis brings great rewards.

'You have to have that certain drive, that certain talent, a hard work ethic and hunger to succeed. Tim Henman did a great job for British tennis. Four times a semi-finalist is some record. Andy Murray has a real chance to go one better. He has the talent, he has the discipline and he has a better temperament now than he did a few years back. Winning a Grand Slam takes a lot. In addition to all the other qualities, you need to have a bit of luck.'

Davies, it could be argued, succeeded in spite of the system rather than because of it. 'Well, I wasn't exactly the LTA's favourite poster boy. I was a bit of a rebel because I liked to make my own way and do my own thing. I made it because I desired it. The work I put into it got me as far as I did. I wish I'd had some really good mentors and coaches when I was 15, 16, 17, 18, 19, 20 and beyond.

'Coaching from people who knew what the game was all about, like Jack Kramer or Pancho Segura, would have been brilliant. Instead we had to do it the hard way because there was nobody to teach us. Tony Trabert was a great mentor of mine. I just wish I'd had that kind of sage advice when I was a whole lot younger.

'Jack was a great figure in the game, a major figure in making tennis what it is today. He was also a great promoter. He wanted to see the best play for the prize money and the best man won the most. It was very simple with Jack. He did everything he could to push pro tennis.

'One thing I have learnt is that you take your chances when you can because you may not get that chance again. When I walked out onto the Centre Court for the men's doubles final with Bobby Wilson in 1960, it never occurred to me that I would never be back there. I thought I had another five or six years at Wimbledon, but that doubles final was the last I ever played because we were banned for the next eight years. I didn't know I was going to turn professional.

'So don't think: "My day will come again." Take your chance right now. This is your moment. It may not come again. Fate, luck, injuries – all play their part. We all knew the consequences when we signed up with Kramer. That was it. You didn't play in the Grand Slams and you didn't play Davis Cup.'

Davies now lives in Sarasota, Florida, where the climate enables him to play at his local club whenever he likes, while promoting Wales whenever the opportunity arises.

'Tennis is a wonderful way of keeping healthy,' he said. 'I've had a hip replacement, but I'm still able to play three times a week and that's essential to maintaining my quality of life.

'You'd be surprised how many people in America know about Wales because of Dylan Thomas and Richard Burton. They may not have been there, but they know where it is and they know a bit about *How Green Was My Valley* and they know about the coalmines.'

In a career stretching back over 60 years to his first match in the rustic surrounds of Cwmdonkin Park, Davies has seen all the finest exponents of the art, first as a player in his own right, then as one of the pioneers of the professional game. Asked to pick one great amongst all the other greats, he chose an Australian from the inner Sydney suburb of Glebe whose father drove a tram.

Lew Hoad's domination of the amateur game in the mid-'50s can be gauged by the fact that he collected eleven Grand Slam titles in four years before joining Kramer's circus at the age of 22. 'If I had to pick one person to win a match and my life depended on the result, it would be Hoad,' Davies said. 'Others like Ken Rosewall, Rod Laver, Tony Trabert and Pancho Gonzales achieved better results over a longer period, but nobody could match Lew for sheer brilliance when the mood took him. He was an incredible player. I liken him to Roger Federer because he could do anything. Hoad had the strongest forearm I have ever seen. He also had tremendous desire, fitness and speed.'

Hoad, who died at his tennis ranch in Spain in July 1994, a few months before his 60th birthday, has long since been enshrined in the International Tennis Hall of Fame. Davies, nominated for his central role behind the transformation of the sport into a worldwide going concern, came very close at the end of 2010 to winning his place in the pantheon. He polled 73 per cent of the requisite 75 per cent of the votes, a clear indication that his induction would be but a matter of time.

Trabert, his lifelong friend – even before showing the Welshman how to carry his own do-it-yourself locker room at the Les Champions du Monde tournament in Marseilles in 1960 – pays his own tribute: 'Mike Davies is a true trailblazer of the sport without whom people would not be able to enjoy tennis on today's global scale.'

During all the years it took him to make the long haul from Swansea to Sarasota, Welsh tennis has failed to produce another British No. 1. Gerald Battrick from Bridgend came closest, climbing to third in the national rankings behind Mark Cox and Roger Taylor. A British junior champion – like another Bridgend boy who went on to do famous things in a different sphere of sport, JPR Williams – Battrick never got beyond the last 32 in the singles at Wimbledon despite winning the British Hard Court championship in 1971.

He played Davis Cup, followed Davies' path into the professional game in 1972 and made his last exit from Wimbledon against former champion Stan Smith in the second round four years later, by which time the game had been declared open. Battrick, who began coaching in Germany, then in Wales, died in November 1998 at the age of 51.

Davies' advice to any young boy or girl wanting to give it a crack is typically enthusiastic. 'My message would be: "Live your passion." That's all I did. I was never going to let anything stop me from being a tennis player. But make sure you get an education first. I was stupid enough to think I would be a tennis player. I may not have been the best, but I've made a career out of it.'

7

BABE OF THE BUSBY BABES

Ken Morgans

Born: Swansea, 16 March 1939

Sebastopol Street rolls steeply down towards the docks in the east end of Swansea, the name of its Victorian terraced houses an enduring memorial to the Crimean War, a besieged port on the Black Sea and the British Empire.

As Swansea extended its boundaries to cope with the bulging population boom post-Industrial Revolution, the new street was built in the shadow of St Thomas' Parish Church, the spiritual centre of the community, where a blue plaque erected by the Heritage Foundation stands as a permanent memorial to a happy-go-lucky boy from the neighbourhood:

Sir Harry Secombe, CBE (1921–2001)
Goon comedian and singer, served here as a boy chorister.

The church is at least still standing, unlike the pre-war docks and the hundreds who perished there and in other areas of the blazing city during the Nazi bombing.

Over the course of three nights from 19 February 1941, the Luftwaffe dropped some 800 high-explosive bombs, as well as an estimated 35,000 incendiaries on the city, creating a firestorm which, they reckoned, could be seen at Fishguard, all of 70 miles away on the north Pembrokeshire coast.

That Sebastopol Street survived intact was little short of miraculous given its proximity to the docks literally across the road. It would only have taken one bomber to have been a fraction off-beam on any of those three nights of the blitz for the street, or parts of it, to have been blown to kingdom come.

No. 63, down towards the bottom, on the left-hand side, was closer than most to the docks. Kenneth Godfrey Morgans was born there on 16 March 1939, blissfully unaware of the impending Armageddon, which began five months, two weeks and two days later with the outbreak of the Second World War. How cruelly ironic that, having emerged unscathed from a three-night pulverising by the German war machine, he should be aboard an Elizabethan aircraft chartered from British European Airways that crashed during its third attempt to take off from German soil, the plane having stopped to refuel after Manchester United's European Cup tie in Belgrade the previous day.

Physically unimpaired, Morgans, alone of those who eventually returned to the football field, was never able to find a way out of the emotional wreckage left in the wake of the crash and back to his pre-disaster form. A dashing right-winger who began forging a reputation for himself in schools football, the steelworker's son had the big clubs beating a path to Sebastopol Street. United sent Jimmy Murphy, the Welshman then engaged as the architect-in-chief of the Busby Babes, to sign the 15 year old, who had given an eye-opening performance for Wales in a schoolboy international against England at Maine Road in Manchester.

'Jimmy Greaves played for England and we beat them 2–0,' Morgans said. 'I played against Denis Law in the match against Scotland and, shortly after, about five First Division clubs came to the house. One club representative would be in the back room, another in the kitchen and someone else in the living room – all at the same time.

'Arsenal were the first. Tom Whittaker, the manager, came down and he brought their goalkeeper, Jack Kelsey, a local boy from down the road in Llansamlet, to help sign me. They put me in digs in North London. I didn't like it. I stuck it for a fortnight and then I came home.

'I remember Jimmy coming to the house and asking my mum and

dad if they wanted to go to United to have a look around. Jimmy was so persuasive that I can remember him helping my mother pack her overnight bag.'

Morgans signed forms for United shortly after his 15th birthday in 1954 without any way of knowing that, before long, he would be part of a new phenomenon. Within three years, Busby's embryonic Babes, having grown into the youngest champions of England, were beginning to conquer new frontiers in Europe, with Morgans the youngest of them all. As part of a privileged apprenticeship, he achieved the rare distinction of winning three FA Youth Cup finals in a row, initially under the captaincy of Duncan Edwards, in teams that included Bobby Charlton and a local lad who would one day succeed Busby as manager, Wilf McGuinness.

'For a while they got me a job at a joinery works near Old Trafford in Stretford,' he said. 'It was very difficult at the beginning, being so far from home and not having many friends. In one of my first matches for the United youth team, we beat a Manchester schools side 13–0. Then, before I knew it, I was playing in the first of those FA Youth Cup finals in the same team as Duncan Edwards and Bobby Charlton. I worked at the joinery until I signed professional forms with United in 1956 when I was 17 and I went straight onto £20 a week, which was big money back then.'

In that same year, he helped the Babes win the fourth of their five successive FA Youth Cup finals at the expense of unlikely opponents in Chesterfield, whose last line of defence would become a byword for the excellence of English goalkeepers: Gordon Banks.

Morgans made such light work of learning his craft that it took him less than half his first full season as a professional to roll off Murphy's conveyor belt into the first team.

A home defeat by Chelsea at the end of a four-match run without a win convinced Matt Busby that changes had to be made and that, after thirteen appearances for the second team in the Central League, Morgans could not be held in reserve a moment longer. Busby dropped Johnny Berry from the right wing and replaced him with the 18 year old from Swansea, starting against Leicester City at Old Trafford on 21 December 1957. United, spearheaded by the England centre-forward Tommy Taylor, won 4–0.

'My fiancée Stephanie Lloyd and her father, Tommy, always said: "When you make your debut in the first team, we will be there,"' Morgans said. 'I phoned him as soon as the team sheet went up. Only a few weeks earlier I'd been sitting in the stand watching Tommy Taylor win another match for United and thinking to myself: "Will I ever get the chance to put the ball on Tommy's head?"

'Tommy lived three doors away from me and Duncan lived in the same vicinity. The three of us used to go down for training together every morning. The boss always said there wasn't a player living worth £30,000, so when he bought Tommy from Barnsley, he only paid £29,999, which was still a transfer record. Tommy used to say to me: "Dai, you hit those crosses as hard as you like, but just remember this – make sure they're nine feet high." So every time I beat my full-back, I'd look up to see where Tommy was and put it where he wanted – on his head.'

He did that to spectacular effect, his first nine matches bringing seven wins, two draws and a grand total of thirty-two goals, five of them against Arsenal at Highbury. His centres that day gave Taylor his last goals in England, the Babes turning their last domestic engagement into an all-time classic before the fateful trip to Yugoslavia and the return European Cup quarter-final tie against Red Star Belgrade. At 19, Morgans had the world at his feet.

'I had a fantastic game the night we beat Bolton 7–2 in between the Red Star matches,' he said. 'Jimmy was managing Wales on a part-time basis and I'd just had my first game for the Under-23s. Before we went to Belgrade, he went to Cardiff for the play-off against Israel, which would put Wales into the finals of the World Cup for the one and only time that summer. The last thing he told me was that I'd be in the squad for the World Cup. Then the crash happened.'

On Thursday, 6 February 1958, the plane carrying the United team home from Belgrade aborted two attempts at take-off from Munich after refuelling. Twice, Morgans left the plane with everyone else and returned to the terminal. His teammate Bill Foulkes said: 'I was sitting about halfway down the aircraft next to a window on the right-hand side of the gangway. Our cards school consisted of Kenny Morgans, who was on my right, and facing David Pegg and Albert Scanlon.

'Matt Busby and Bert Whalley [United's coach] were sitting together behind us. There was another card school across the gangway from us made up of Ray Wood, Jackie Blanchflower, Roger Byrne, Billy Whelan and Dennis Viollet, with one seat empty. Mark Jones, Tommy Taylor, Duncan Edwards and Eddie Colman were all at the back.'

By the time they strapped themselves in for the third time, Pegg made a decision that proved as deadly as the take-off. He swapped his seat in the middle for one at the back, telling Foulkes it would be 'safer back there'. Morgans and Scanlon decided to stay put. A sense of foreboding enveloped the cabin, moving Whelan, a devoutly religious Dubliner, to say: 'If the worst happens, I am ready for death. I hope we all are.'

Berry, who made the trip as a reserve after losing his place to Morgans, captured the terror in one sentence: 'We're all going to be killed.'

Foulkes said: 'By this time everybody was feeling really scared. The plane was bouncing along and I thought: "How are we going to get off the ground?"'

Morgans has never forgotten climbing back on board for a third time. 'We used to sit in the middle of the plane so we could get the seats beside the tables,' he said. 'Every time we got back on board, I sat down in the same seat. The weather was really bad and there'd been some talk about us staying overnight, but the boss wanted us to get back and have a good night's sleep at home because we had a big match against Wolves on the Saturday.

'For the third attempt at take-off, it got so tense that the cards were put away. I can recall David Pegg saying something about moving to the back of the plane because he reckoned he'd be safer there. I sat where I was, although quite a few others moved to the back, thinking that if anything did go wrong they'd have a better chance of getting out in one piece. I think they were all killed. I remember Bill sitting next to me saying: "I'm ready for it."

'I think the majority of the players knew we were going to crash. It was terrifying. I can remember us going through the fences. I was by the window and I'll never forget the screeching noise as the plane ripped through the fencing. I can't remember anything after that.'

The screeching was one of the wings being torn off when the doomed aircraft hit a house beyond the runway. There were other terrifying sounds, most catastrophically that of an explosion when part of the starboard fuselage collided with a fuel-storage hut. Morgans never knew what kind of inferno engulfed the plane until he made a pilgrimage 50 years later to the scene of the crash. On the edge of the Bavarian village of Kirchtrudering, beyond the south-western end of the runway of the old airport, which has since been relocated some 20 miles away, stands a granite memorial.

There, he met a man called Georg Fischer, a retired airport fireman who showed him photographs of the blazing wreckage of Flight 609 Zulu Uniform. Morgans had never seen them before.

'How anyone came out of that alive, I will never know,' he said. 'I'd seen a lot of photographs of the accident at the time, but I'd never seen any like these. They were shocking. You couldn't recognise it as a plane, just so many bits and pieces of twisted metal. The flames were eight feet high, but they didn't stop Harry Gregg going back into the plane to rescue the injured. You needed a miracle to get anyone out of that.'

The Munich air disaster claimed the lives of eight Manchester United players: Roger Byrne, Mark Jones, Eddie Colman, Billy Whelan, Tommy Taylor, David Pegg, Geoff Bent and Duncan Edwards, their names enshrined forever in the pantheon of English football. All told, twenty-three of the forty-three on board perished, among them three club officials and eight journalists, including two who had been almost as celebrated as the players they wrote about, Henry Rose of the *Daily Express* and Frank Swift of the *News of the World*.

In the grim aftermath, the rescue services thought they had accounted for all those players who had got out alive, without realising that one was still missing. The roll call of the dead, the critically injured and the walking wounded made no mention of Morgans.

Back in Swansea, Stephanie, now his wife of almost 50 years following their marriage in 1959, was beside herself with anxiety. 'For five hours after the crash, I didn't know whether he was dead or alive,' she said. 'There was a list of the dead and a list of the survivors and Ken wasn't on either of them.'

Morgans was missing, trapped in an unconscious state in what had been the hold of the aircraft and left, unwittingly, to freeze to death. 'We took off for the third time at three minutes past three in the afternoon, British time,' he said. 'We crashed at four minutes past three. I was still there in the wreckage six hours later. They found me at half-past nine that night and they'd never have found me if it hadn't been for two German photographers. They'd put two canisters of film of the match on the flight for the BBC to pick up when the plane landed in Manchester.

'Luckily for me, the photographers decided to go back into the wreckage that night to see if they could find them. They were searching through some of the burnt suitcases when one of them moved some stuff and thought he saw something move. That's how they found me. I'd got caught underneath one of the wheels, which was why they couldn't account for me. I'd have died of hypothermia otherwise because nobody could have survived the cold for very long.

'They got me to hospital and I didn't wake up until the Sunday morning. I had a cut head and a lot of bruising and I'd lost ten pints of blood. The last thing I remembered was the plane hitting the fence at the end of the runway. Everything between then and waking up three days later was a complete blank. It's funny how trivial little things stick in your mind compared to the terrible loss of life, which, at that time, I knew nothing about.

'One of my first memories after regaining consciousness was being told that they had to cut my Italian suit to get me out ... my lovely Italian suit. I bought it specially for the match. It was my first in the European Cup and I had to get the same suit as the rest of the lads, all made to measure. I remember I had three fittings to make sure it was exactly right. Thirteen quid, it cost me.

'When I came round in hospital, Ray Wood, Albert Scanlon, Bobby Charlton and Dennis Viollet were in the ward. There were a few upstairs – Matt Busby, Johnny Berry and Duncan. I thought the rest of the boys were all in the next room. I thought that any minute they would come in and we'd all be together again. We could all go home and the nightmare would be over. They told us the names of those who died and then we realised there was nobody waiting in the next room. It upset me for a very long time. Terrible, just terrible ...'

For their first match after the crash, an FA Cup fifth-round tie against Sheffield Wednesday at Old Trafford, the club programme, *United Review*, had been turned into a series of obituaries. Amid the tributes to the fallen, they published a piece entitled 'A Message to Munich from Old Trafford':

> Our thoughts are constantly with those who still lie in the Rechts der Isar Hospital, Munich. All of them have been through a terrible ordeal and now face a long period of convalescence during which they will need the prayers of everyone.
>
> Amongst them is our dear manager, Matt Busby, and we know that his first concern is always for his players. Even in the first moment after regaining consciousness we recall his words to Jimmy Murphy. 'Glad to see you, Jimmy. How are the lads? Look after them for me.'
>
> We will certainly do that for you, Matt, and wait eagerly for the day when we can welcome you back to the helm at Old Trafford.
>
> To the lads still with you – Ray Wood, Albert Scanlon, Ken Morgans, Dennis Viollet, Johnny Berry, Jackie Blanchflower and Duncan Edwards – we say: 'Get well soon – United needs you.'
>
> Mercifully a few of our players escaped serious injury. These were Harry Gregg and Bill Foulkes, who have since arrived safely home. We hope to welcome Bobby Charlton within the next few days and look forward to the time when they will be able to take their place in the team once more.

For some who pulled through, like Blanchflower and Berry, that would be a physical impossibility. Neither played again. The remaining few fortunate enough to be able to pick up the pieces included three who returned to ensure the phoenix would rise from the ashes – Gregg, Foulkes and Charlton. In marked contrast, their teenage Welsh friend never recovered, at least not in a professional sense.

The babe of the Babes at 18, Morgans' fate was to be the one survivor who, possibly more than any other, would be short-changed by history.

He was detained at the Rechts der Isar Hospital for six weeks while he recovered from a crushed skull, but what nobody knew back then was that Morgans would never manage to put the pieces together again; while superficially unmarked by the crash, his appearance masked inner scars that effectively destroyed him as a Busby Babe. Morgans, alone of the survivors, would discover all too soon that while he had indeed escaped with his life, the most traumatic of experiences had conspired to shatter his career as an electrifying winger. Life at Old Trafford was never the same again.

'When I left hospital, the physician said I should give the rest of the season a miss and not play again until the following season,' he said. 'But I was desperate to get playing again. I wanted to play for Duncan and Tommy and all the other boys who never came back. They'd played in the FA Cup final the year before and lost in controversial circumstances to Aston Villa. So when we reached the final again, against Bolton, a few months after Munich, I was prepared to play the game of my life.

'It broke my heart when they dropped me for the final. We'd beaten them 7–2 in the League earlier that season and I'd given their full-back the biggest runaround I ever gave any full-back. I was desperate to get at him again at Wembley. Instead, I was told on the morning of the match that I wouldn't be playing.

'Jimmy Murphy was in charge then, while Matt was recovering from his injuries, and he said he wasn't going to pick me because I'd lost weight and he thought the occasion would be too much for me, emotionally. Then, on the Tuesday after the final, he picked me for the European Cup semi-final against AC Milan and I was man of the match. I never understood why Jimmy left me out of the Cup final. After the Milan game, he called me into his office and said he should have played me at Wembley.'

Murphy then dealt Morgans another demoralising blow by leaving him behind when Wales went off to Sweden that summer for a World Cup campaign that would take them closer to the semi-finals than the three other home countries, with England and Scotland having fallen by the wayside before the last eight. Northern Ireland went as far as

Wales but lost all hope of going any further after finishing up on the wrong end of a four-goal beating by France. Despite the crippling handicap of confronting Brazil without an injured John Charles, Wales ran the eventual winners all the way in the quarter-final, only to lose to a solitary goal from the 17-year-old Pele. Another teenager, back home in Swansea for the summer break, would realise all too soon that his career had become jammed in reverse gear.

'I stayed at United for two more seasons but, hard as I tried, my heart wasn't in it,' Morgans said. 'I missed the boys so much. Because of what had happened to them, I just didn't seem to care. I did try, but there was something missing. Because they weren't there, I didn't have the same desire to play in the first team. I've no doubt that if it hadn't been for the crash, I'd have played for United for years.

'Before the crash, we used to have two dressing-rooms, one for the first team, the other for the reserves. You never went into the first-team dressing-room unless you were an established member of the side. When I came back after the crash, all the reserves were allowed into the first-team dressing-room. Some of them were never good enough to have been there. The Babes were the best team there'd ever been. The first team were like gods.'

Had it not been for Munich, Morgans might well have been one of them, a winger with the speed and trickery to have held the fort for five years until United discovered an even faster and trickier one in Belfast by the name of George Best.

By the end of the calamitous 1957–58 season, Morgans had chalked up nineteen first-team appearances, thirteen in the League, two in the FA Cup and four in the European Cup.

As evidence of the post-Munich trauma, he was permitted only four more First Division matches during the next three seasons before they sold him in March 1961 to Swansea Town, as they were then, for a cut-price £3,000. United reduced the fee as a favour to the player after he told them he wanted to return home. Morgans played fifty-four matches and scored eight goals before the emergence of a younger local rival, Barrie Jones, prompted the Swans to offload their Busby Babe in June 1964 to Fourth Division Newport County.

Three years there and three more in the Welsh League as player-manager of Cwmbran Town brought his career to an anticlimactic end at the early age of 31, whereupon he ran a pub at New Inn, near Pontypool, for ten years and finished the remainder of his working life as a ship's chandler.

On Morgans' calendar, 6 February has always been the saddest day – and always will be. For more than half a century, he has kept in touch with the club in general and the other Munich survivors in particular, a shrinking list whittled down at the start of 2011 to Foulkes, Gregg and Charlton following Albert Scanlon's death in December 2009 at the age of 74. He had been living in sheltered accommodation and left £41,000 in his will.

A left-winger who recovered from a fractured skull, broken leg and kidney damage, Scanlon reclaimed his place all too briefly before his career went rapidly downhill after United sold him to Newcastle for a transfer fee of £18,000.

'To my mind, Munich killed not only a lot of the players who were on that flight but some of the survivors, too,' Scanlon said. 'At least I played 40 games for them after the crash. Matt basically cut us off and I thought he was getting rid of what was left from Munich. He told me that financially I would be all right. He told me it was best I had a break and left Manchester: "Don't worry, I'll fix all the financial things for you." Five years later I saw him outside the ground and he didn't want to know me.'

Compensation for the Munich victims, or, to be more accurate, the lack of it, festered like a running sore down the years until United finally agreed to a testimonial match, in August 1998, fully 40 years after the disaster. The club chose to combine it with an official farewell for Eric Cantona, the exotic Frenchman who had retired rather abruptly the previous year to launch himself as an actor.

Inevitably, the Cantona factor hijacked the occasion, just as the survivors and their families feared it would. The subsequent revelation, as disclosed by Jeff Connor in *The Lost Babes*, that Cantona's agent sent an invoice on behalf of his client for £90,000, which came out of the Munich Memorial Fund, not Manchester United FC, did nothing to improve their mood. Once other expenses had been paid on top of those incurred by Cantona and friends, the survivors and relatives of those who perished 40 years earlier each received a sum of slightly more than £47,000.

For some, it was far too little far too late, literally so in the cases of Berry, who died in September 1994 at the age of 68, and Blanchflower, whose death from cancer at 65 a few weeks after the Cantona match added a poignant postscript to an issue that had dragged on far too long for those involved to ever forget.

Blanchflower, whose elder brother, Danny, captained the celebrated Tottenham Hotspur double-winning team of the early 1960s, did return to Munich, as a guest of Manchester United, for a Champions League match towards the end of his life. It inspired a story that captured Jackie's sharp Ulster humour: how he made a point of going to the left luggage office at the airport and enquiring if anyone had handed in his suitcase.

'When was it lost, sir?' the attendant asked.

'About 39 years ago . . .'

By then, the Babe always remembered by his teammates as 'young Kenny' had begun planning for retirement. 'Ken didn't come out of the crash very well financially, but we were always capable of looking after ourselves,' his wife Stephanie said. 'But more could have been done for others who were badly injured, like Jackie and Johnny. The crash impacted on them every day for the rest of their lives. We've gone through a lot over the years, but it's no good feeling bitter.'

Not one anniversary of the disaster has gone by without Morgans making the pilgrimage from Swansea to attend the annual memorial service. The old players never forget, as the Welshman found at a reunion dinner when he bumped into Bert Trautmann, the former German prisoner of war who had a distinguished 15-year career keeping goal for Manchester City on more than 500 occasions, including one against Morgans during the 1957–58 season.

'Ken, that was only your third game for United,' Trautmann told his old opponent. 'And that was over 50 years ago . . . the Busby Babes.'

A large colour photograph of them lining up for the start of their last match has long held pride of place in Morgans' home on a hill in Swansea, a cherished reminder of those who never came back, eight players forever fixed in their youth. If he looks at it for any length of time and thinks about the pals he lost all those years ago, the tears well in his eyes.

For 'young Kenny', the Babes have always stood united and shall remain so to his dying day. In his mind, they are all still there, lined up around him, as they were in the capital of what was then Yugoslavia before they fired three goals past the ballet dancer-cum-international goalkeeper Vladimir Beara to book their passage into the semi-finals of the European Cup.

Age may not have wearied, nor the years condemned, them but neither has time eased one Welshman's pain of a crash that brought the nation to a standstill.

'The sadness never goes away,' he says. 'It's there every time I look at that picture, and that's every day of my life when I'm at home. Such a young team. Eddie and Duncan were only 21. I was a baby of 18 and Bobby was only 18 months older. Duncan had another 13 years, at least. They rave about Bobby Moore, but he wouldn't have held a candle to Duncan Edwards.

'Had they all lived, they would have been the best club team in the world. People laugh at me when I say that, but the Babes were so good that they hardly ever made mistakes. If it hadn't been for Munich, they'd have been unbeatable.

'You know, I never lost a game with the old team . . .'

8

NOTHING BUT GOLD

Lynn Davies

Born: Nantymoel, 20 May 1942

They grew up at different times in different villages on opposite sides of the foaming Atlantic – one in the cotton fields of Oakville in Alabama shortly before the Great Depression, the other in the coalmining community of Nantymoel during the austerity of immediate post-war Britain.

Jesse Owens, the seventh of eleven children born to a share-cropper in the then segregated South of the United States, won four Olympic gold medals in front of Adolf Hitler at the Nazi Games of Berlin in 1936. Lynn Davies, the only son of a miner whose family knew all about the tragic consequences of digging for coal, wrote his name in letters of gold alongside Owens' 28 years later as the first, and so far only, Welshman to win a track or field Olympic title.

Owens started out picking cotton until his mother moved the family to Cleveland. There the 18-year-old 'Buckeye Bullet' won admission to Ohio State University.

At the same age, Davies, in his last year at Ogmore Vale Grammar School, competed for Wales against England at a schoolboy meeting in Cardiff. It turned out to be one of the most fortuitous events in his career.

Just as Owens found a coach to make the most of his natural ability – in his case, to run very quickly – so did Davies, rather by accident than design. England sent their finest teenage athletes to Wales that day in the care of a man who would become a household name as a coach and television commentator – Ron Pickering.

'The patron saint of national coaches must have been sitting on my shoulders that day in 1961,' Pickering said. 'I'd just been appointed national coach for Wales and the south-west of England. I travelled down from London to Cardiff to take a look at my new house and to accompany the England schools athletics team. I had two boys from my London school in the English team, one in the long jump and one in the triple jump.

'And the boy who was against them, representing Wales, was a shy, slim 18 year old called Davies. Well, he jumped appallingly. He hardly knew which foot to jump off. But he won the long jump against a boy who, technically, was vastly superior. As far as natural ability went, there was no question who had the greater potential. The other two English boys weren't in the same street as Davies.'

Pickering had seen enough during that Anglo-Welsh meeting at Maindy Stadium to pick the embryonic long jumper for his first Wales team. Davies responded by winning his event, shattering the Welsh national record with a jump of 23 ft 5 in. 'Lynn the Leap' was up and running. Even then, right at the very outset, he inspired comparison, however unfavourably, with the wondrous Owens.

Once the reporters had finished finding out about the new boy, Pickering made his approach.

'Everybody's telling you what great jumping that was,' he told Davies. 'But I'm telling you that was very ordinary jumping. Do you know that Jesse Owens jumped 25 ft 6 in. when he was only 15?

'Don't start thinking you've arrived, because you haven't. But I'll tell you this. If you want to be the greatest long jumper Britain's ever seen, and if you're prepared to work harder than any other Welsh sportsman in history, I'd like to coach you because I think you're capable of doing it.'

While Owens had gone some distance at 15 towards striking gold four times a few years later, Davies at the same age knew nothing of the concept of taking a running jump into a sandpit. All that changed during the summer of 1958, when he went to watch the British Empire and Commonwealth Games at Cardiff Arms Park and began to realise there was a lot more to sport than a round ball and an oval one.

'Until then, I played rugby and soccer,' he said. 'I'd been on Cardiff City's books as a right-winger. My heroes were footballers like Stanley Matthews and John Charles, and rugby players like Cliff Morgan and Bleddyn Williams. I don't think I could have named one British athlete.

'Ron was a charismatic character with great motivational skills. Nobody had ever made the effort to tell me that I had the potential to be any good. If I hadn't met Ron that day, I'd have played rugby and football and never taken athletics seriously. Watching the incredible spectacle of the Empire Games opened my eyes to a whole new world. What made the deepest impression on me was the six-mile race and how close John Merriman came to winning the first Welsh track gold of the championship.

'As I remember it, John was leading going into the last lap only for Dave Power of Australia to go past him. I waited for John to come out of the dressing-room and got his autograph just before I caught the bus home. John became my new hero. And if anyone had told me then that I'd be sharing a room with him as a member of the Welsh team at the next Games, in Perth in 1962, I'd have had him certified.'

Davies worked so hard under Pickering's motivational supervision that in three years he went from winning the Glamorgan county title to a creditable fourth in Perth. From there, he went on to take Olympic gold at 22, the same age as Owens when he won amidst the swastikas of Berlin. The newly appointed physical education master at Bridgend Grammar arrived in Tokyo for the XVIII Olympiad in the autumn of 1964 thinking he might have a chance of taking bronze behind the defending champion, Ralph Boston, and Igor Ter-Ovanesyan of the Soviet Union.

Superseding Owens in the record book made Boston famous even before his victory in Rome – so famous, in fact, that during a break in the US team's journey to the Eternal City, another young competitor approached the long jumper.

'He's got a camera and he says: "Ralph Boston. I want to take your picture" and he snaps it. I said: "Who are you?" And he said: "You don't know me now, but you will. My name is Cassius Clay."'

Boston took an immediate lead in the 1964 qualifying competition and, before Davies knew it, a 'dreadful' opening jump followed by a foul left him with one last shot at redemption. He never felt lonelier than he did on the long walk back to the end of the runway. 'Those were the toughest two minutes of my life,' he said. 'I was out on my own with nobody to lean on for a bit of support. Ron was on the other side of the arena in the main stand, watching and, so he said, having kittens.'

A misunderstanding between Davies and another British athlete, Fred Allsop, had pushed him to the brink of elimination without registering a single jump. 'After the second no-jump, I said to myself: "What the hell's going on?" All long jumpers use a check mark, the point on the runway where you start accelerating. I asked Fred to put it 54 feet from the take-off board. For the first jump, I was halfway over the check mark. The second time my stride pattern was still way out. I re-measured the run-up with a tape. The check mark was at 50 feet not 54. Fred had misheard me and thought I'd said 50 feet.

'Everything has to be spot-on because you're running flat out but with the handbrake slightly on to make sure you hit the board. Now I had one jump left.

'I knew it was make or break. I can remember standing there, thinking about my family and all the people watching at home. I reminded myself of all the hard work I'd put in, all the training on cold, wet nights, all that running up and down the sand dunes at Merthyr Mawr.

'I could either fail again and go home a flop or I could do something about it. I told myself: "You haven't come thousands of miles not to qualify." I reminded myself that I'd come to win the bronze medal. Somehow, I got the strength from somewhere to keep going and find a little belief. My nerves were jangling like hell, so I took a deep breath.

'I hit the check mark and accelerated. I still had to endure another horrible five or six seconds before I saw a white flag instead of a red one. My last jump turned out to be the second best of the day, behind Boston. I'd made the final and passed one of the toughest tests of my life.'

Still the rain pelted down. Davies, one of the first to report to the officials in charge of the pit, sat on a bench wondering what was keeping the others. Within minutes, Boston took a seat to his left, followed by Ter-Ovanesyan to the right.

In his apprehension, Davies tried to engage both in conversation, a ploy that in hindsight enabled him to strike a psychological blow. 'All the finalists go to the call-up room and I found myself sitting with two of my heroes,' he said. 'It was very quiet because everyone was concentrating on the final. I'd never been in that position before, so I didn't know any better.

'I felt I ought to talk to them, a little chat more out of politeness than anything. I tried to make some small talk about the weather, first with Ter-Ovanesyan. He grunted. I did the same with Boston and he just nodded. I kept chattering and they kept looking at me as if to say: "Why don't you shut up?" Eventually, I took the hint. They didn't see me as a threat. I'm sure they reckoned that I should have been overawed, that I should have been shaking and quivering. They were intent on trying to build up their concentration and here was this new boy trying to make conversation. As I say, I didn't know any better.'

Then they rose from the bench and walked, Indian file, into the arena, the rain still coming down by the bucketful. A fleeting contretemps between his American and Soviet rivals gave Davies further encouragement that maybe he could beat them both. Ter-Ovanesyan scratched a mark on the runway, as he invariably did, whereupon Boston made a complaint and the officials duly obliterated the marks.

'Because of the wind and rain, Boston asked the judges to turn the competition round, so we'd be running with the wind and not into it. I could see from the look Ter-Ovanesyan gave Boston that the Russian really hated him at that precise moment,' Davies said. 'I suddenly realised that these great athletes were no longer unbeatable. There was a vulnerability about them that I had not noticed before. They showed they could be beaten. I sensed this was my big chance.

'Boston was the world-record holder, but I knew I could beat him from what was said and not said during the minutes before the competition began. There was another reason why I knew I could beat him and that was the weather. An Olympic gold is a very elusive prize because it comes to who's the best on the day once every four years. I was the best in the wind and rain at Tokyo that afternoon.'

With two jumps left, Davies found himself exactly where he thought he would finish: third behind Boston (25 ft 9 in.) and Ter-Ovanesyan (25 ft 6¼ in.). At the end of the runway for the penultimate round, he looked up at the flags fluttering at the top of the stadium and remembered a little tip Boston had given him at a meeting in New York earlier in the year.

'The wind was gusting from two to five metres per second, which meant it hit you at take off,' Davies said. 'Then it dropped. Ralph told me once that if the flag dropped, it was a good sign that the wind was about to fade inside the stadium. I looked up at the flags and they were hardly moving. I sensed an opportunity and I grabbed it. I must have gone down that runway faster than at any time in my life and once I'd taken off I knew it was going to be one of the best jumps of the final.'

When they eventually finished measuring it to everyone's satisfaction, the distance put Davies out on his own at 26 ft 5¾ in., more than a few inches further than Boston. The American, his generosity unaffected by the heat of the competition, told the new leader: 'That's going to be the best one of all.'

Davies said: 'I wanted to believe him, but I knew Boston was the kind of guy who could respond on the big occasion. I couldn't bring myself to watch his last jump. I put a towel over my head.'

The entire British camp still had to endure frantic moments of anxiety once Boston had saved his best for last. It fell less than two inches short; Ter-Ovanesyan's last effort missed by almost a foot. Davies had won the gold four years ahead of his time.

The next morning, the Olympic champion at the last pre-war Games went out of his way to shake hands with the new one.

'Mr Dav-eez,' he said, striding into the cafeteria in the Games Village. 'I'm Jesse Owens.'

'I know who you are, Mr Owens,' Dav-eez said. 'It's wonderful to meet you.'

After their meeting, Owens gave the Welshman a glowing reference. 'I cannot recall any Olympic Games when the conditions were as bad as they were here,' he told BBC Radio in Tokyo. 'Give credit where it's due. In the wind and rain, Dav-eez proved he was the best broad-jumper in the world. I've had a chance to meet him.

He is a wonderful chap, with a wonderful personality. He will wear the gold medal really well.'

The interview brought tears of pride to Davies' eyes when he heard it for the first time 45 years later, thanks to producer Steve Groves digging it out of the archive for a BBC Wales programme. 'To hear Jesse say that is incredible,' he said. 'As a schoolboy, I read about Jesse Owens in the history books and meeting him has long been one of my most treasured memories.'

Back in Wales, they were preparing to roll out every stretch of red carpet they could find. 'I had no idea what sort of impact the win had made at home,' he said. 'The first inkling I had was when the train stopped at Cardiff. There were 3,000 people at the railway station and I had to make a speech standing on a porter's trolley. They'd given the kids the day off from school and there was bunting everywhere.'

The clamour to greet the new champion was so overpowering that Davies found his way blocked to the entrance of his home, No. 14 Commercial Street, Nantymoel, where the local choir sang 'We'll Keep a Welcome'.

'I couldn't get in because the whole valley was there, or so it seemed,' he said. 'The welcome was incredible. We had some champagne and then we went to the Miners' Institute in the village and there must have been another 500 people there.'

Davies only made one miscalculation during his meticulous preparation for the 1964 Games: the probable time and place of his winning an Olympic gold. He thought it was going to be Mexico City in 1968 instead of Japan four years earlier, a projection that failed to take into account Bob Beamon's launch as a human meteor. In retrospect, it was just as well 'the Leap' struck early.

As a result, he had all sorts of opportunities to cash in on his fame, not least a cheque for £7,500 to sign for Wakefield Trinity. It was unquestionably the most audacious bid ever made by any rugby league club – all the more so because the directors of Wakefield sent it to a slightly posher address than Commercial Street, Nantymoel.

'While I was waiting at Buckingham Palace to be presented to Her Majesty, a butler came up and handed me a telegram. It was addressed to Lynn Davies, c/o Buckingham Palace, London. Just looking at it made me even more nervous. I opened it and found that it was from Wakefield Trinity rugby league club. Before I could think about it, I'd been called to meet Her Majesty. So there I was, with the telegram in my pocket, a glass of champagne in my hand, talking to the Queen about long jumping.'

Davies was still in the first year of his reign when a skinny black kid won an athletics scholarship to the University of Texas, near the Mexican border in El Paso. Beamon, four years younger than Davies, had had a troubled upbringing. His mother died in the spring of 1947, eight months after his birth. A native New Yorker from a suburb of Queens – the borough whose other notable citizens include John McEnroe, Art Garfunkel and Paul Simon – Beamon was brought up by his grandmother.

His first summer on the circuit, 1965, coincided with the Davies– Boston rematch at the Welsh Games. The local council forked out for a fancy new landing pit in front of the main stand at the old Maindy Stadium in Cardiff and, for the first and only time, a British athletics meeting came to a complete standstill for a duel of Olympic long- jump champions before an outsized, five-figure crowd. What they saw, alas, turned out to be a non-event.

According to Pickering, Davies was in less than perfect condition due to his having only just recovered from glandular fever. Whatever the reason, he went down virtually without a fight. 'Boston slaughtered me in front of 10,000 Welshmen,' Davies said. 'It was so quiet when I jumped that I could hear my own footsteps on the cinders. I'd never cracked before, but I did that day, and I still can't understand why. I felt absolutely humiliated.'

It was all too bad to be true, as subsequent events proved. In August 1966, Davies added two more golds to his collection, in Kingston, Jamaica, at the beginning of the month, then in Budapest, Hungary, at the end of it, beating his old foe Ter-Ovanesyan into second place. It brought him the unique achievement of being the first long jumper in athletics history to hold the Olympic, European and Commonwealth titles in the same year.

Before leaving for the first Olympiad in Latin America, Davies knew that defending his precious title in Mexico would be infinitely more hazardous than winning it in Tokyo, even though he had beaten the world record held jointly by Boston and Ter-Ovanesyan at a training camp in Mexico the previous year. He could not take them all by surprise a second time. The unpredictable Beamon would see to that by disappearing into the blue yonder.

Davies went to Mexico to win another gold. Nothing else interested him, an attitude for which he felt no need to apologise either then or since. 'Nobody had ever jumped 28 feet before, not even Boston,' Davies said. 'I thought it might take 28 feet to win the gold. It was like the four-minute mile used to be, a barrier that nobody could break, although I'd gone very close to it in training.

'I went in as the Olympic champion and I didn't want to be introduced at future events as the Olympic silver medallist. I hadn't as much to lose as either Boston or Ter-Ovanesyan. It was going to be Boston's last Olympics and probably Ter-Ovanesyan's as well. Boston wanted to get his title back from me. Ter-Ovanesyan had done many great things, but he'd never won an Olympic gold medal.'

And Beamon? Davies expressed his thoughts before the event. One comment proved to be among the most strikingly prophetic in the history of sport. 'It only needs Bob Beamon to hit the board right once and we can all go home,' he said.

'I'd seen him jump nearly 27 feet off either foot. He could jump a long way, but could he jump off the board? He was so undisciplined that you never could be sure. He'd never competed in the Olympics before, so how would he react to the pressure?'

Before the event, Davies was in bullish mood. 'I've beaten them in major competitions before,' he said before leaving Wales. 'I'm every bit as good a competitor and they know it. The prize goes to the best man on the day. I've got a feeling that I'm going to win and that's what keeps me going.'

For all the champion's bravado, Pickering was never one to miss a trick. In his quest for any extra motivational crumb to help renew Davies' Olympic reign for four more years, he called his protégé's wife, Meriel, back home in Cardiff. 'Tell me something, Meriel, that will really anger Lynn,' he pleaded. 'I want to make sure we can get him fired up for the competition.'

Mrs Davies, remembering that her husband had planted a row of trees in the garden a few weeks earlier, told Pickering: 'Tell him one of the trees has died. That'll make him angry.'

As Davies ruefully acknowledged, no amount of anger could have prevented Beamon from hijacking the entire competition.

When the supposed novice took his chance along with the rest of the world's elite, he was written off by some of the alleged experts. They questioned his form, criticised his technique and derided his landing as 'terrible'. According to some, the demon Beamon was so confused he didn't know whether he was going to take off on the left foot or the right. That, they contended, explained why he had a tendency to miss the board twice in every three attempts and register a non-jump.

There must have been some knowing winks around the stadium when Beamon got the red flag for landing on the wrong side of the board on each of his first two jumps of the qualifying competition. Nobody will ever know whether he would have disappeared without trace had it not been for Boston's generosity of spirit in helping the younger American iron out a few wrinkles between the start of his run and the point of take-off.

Those in the know dismissed Beamon as a potential Olympic champion on the grounds of his inconsistency. His progress that summer had been disrupted by his suspension from the University of Texas athletics team for refusing to compete against Brigham Young University in protest against alleged racism. In retrospect, it can be seen as the luckiest of breaks because it left him without a coach.

Boston filled the void in terms of technical assistance and encouragement whenever the opportunity presented itself, as it did in Mexico City. In a sense, history was about to repeat itself.

During the 1936 Olympiad in Berlin, Owens began with two fouls and only managed to stay in the competition after a friendly tip from his German rival, Luz Long, a 23-year-old law student from Leipzig. He placed a towel on the ground to mark a new starting point for Owens' run in the belief that it afforded him the best chance of avoiding imminent disqualification.

'Ralph Boston did the same for me,' Beamon said. 'He told me: "Bob, you won't foul if you take off a foot behind the foul line. You can't miss." Basically, that's what Luz Long told Jesse. I took Ralph's advice.'

His place secured for the final the following afternoon, Beamon did not create the impression that he was about to fly, unaided, further than any human being since the creation of the universe. Just before he did so, Boston again showed his generosity of spirit with a last-minute pep talk almost identical to the one Long gave a nervous Owens.

'Now, come on, Bob,' the old champion told his compatriot. 'Make sure it's a good one.'

What happened next would destroy Boston's mission to regain the gold he had won in Rome in 1960 and lost to Davies on that rainy night in Tokyo four years later. If only the crowd had caught the whiff of history, they might have paid some attention instead of diverting their gaze away from the long jumpers to a counter-attraction on the track.

'Spectators were not even watching the long-jump pit because runners were getting into their blocks for the 400 metres,' reported the *Texas Monthly* magazine, continuing:

> Beamon's gangling 160-pound frame loped down the runway, hands and arms flapping as usual, and lifted off on a trajectory that he described as feeling 'just like a regular jump'.
>
> Sitting on the bench, watching as he left the ground, were the three men regarded at that time as the greatest jumpers in the world – Lynn Davies, the English [*sic*] gold medallist in the 1964 Olympiad; Ralph Boston, the American who broke Jesse Owens' record after it had stood for 25 years; and Igor Ter-Ovanesyan, the great Soviet theoretician who had battled Boston for eight years and currently shared the world record with him.

And who should be watching from the press box? None other than Jesse Owens.

What Boston did for Beamon evoked Owens' fond memories of his German rival Long, who died seven years after the Berlin Games at the age of 30 from wounds during the Allied invasion of Sicily in the summer of 1943.

'It took a lot of courage for him to befriend me in front of Hitler,' Owens said some years later. 'You can melt down all the medals and cups I have and they wouldn't be a plating on the 24-carat friendship I felt for Luz Long at that moment.'

One of the enduring mysteries of Olympic history revolved around Owens' quadruple success in Berlin and whether Adolf Hitler deliberately ignored the black American. Baldur von Schirach, the Nazi Youth leader, went on record claiming that the Führer told him in respect of Owens and other black athletes: 'These Americans should have been ashamed of themselves for allowing their medals to be won by Negroes.'

According to David Clay Large in his book *The Nazi Games*, von Schirach also related that when he suggested that the dictator be photographed with Owens, Hitler screamed in indignation: 'Do you really think I'd allow myself to be photographed shaking hands with a Negro?'

Back home, Owens told a large assembly in Kansas City: 'Hitler didn't snub me. It was our President [Franklin Roosevelt] who snubbed me. The President didn't even send me a telegram.'

When Beamon landed, Ter-Ovanesyan turned to Davies and said: 'Compared to that jump, the rest of us are children.'

The Olympic long-jump final was over before it began, before the majority of the finalists could get to the end of the runway for the first time. The defending champion was among them. The Welshman knew that his Olympic future had been wiped out there and then by a human flying machine with a supposedly 'terrible' technique.

As the watching world dropped its jaw in disbelief, the entire Olympic movement went into a state of near-panic over recording exactly how far Beamon had flown. Up in the commentary box, Ron Pickering sounded as awestruck as everyone else. 'Oh, it's an enormous one,' he said, in one of the classic 'Colemanballs' loved by the satirical magazine *Private Eye*. 'My goodness me, it is an *enormous* one.'

In those pre-electronic days, the stewards relied on an optical device to track each jump, being not the least bit concerned about what would happen in the event of a competitor virtually jumping out of the pit. In almost doing so, Beamon had landed beyond the range of the tracking system. After a suitably lengthy amount of head scratching, officials reverted to the almost prehistoric tape measure. The competitors, the 68,000 inside the stadium and countless millions across the world had to wait four minutes before learning exactly how far Beamon had jumped.

From Owens in 1935 to Boston in 1965, the world record had increased by fractionally less than nine inches. Owens' pre-war distance of 26 ft 8¹⁄₁₆ in. had been lengthened to 27 ft 4¾ in. by Boston and equalled by Ter-Ovanesyan two years after that, a total improvement of 8¹³⁄₁₆ in.

At his very first attempt, Beamon extended the world record almost three times as far in one afternoon as the rest had managed in more than three decades. He obliterated the record of 27 ft 4¾ in. and took it to a stratospheric 29 ft 2½ in., an increase of almost 22 inches.

'I heard some of the guys saying things like 8.90 metres or something,' Beamon said. 'Outside the United States, everything is in metres, so I wasn't sure how far I'd jumped. Then Ralph Boston came over and said: "Bob, I think it's over 29 feet," which was almost two feet farther than the world record.

'I said to Ralph: "What happened to 28 feet?"

Davies was as dumbfounded as Boston.

'We're sitting there and Ralph says to me: "That's over 29 feet," remembered Davies. 'I said: "No, it can't be. It's just not possible. Nobody's done 28 feet."

'Bruce Tulloh, the British middle-distance runner, was sitting behind me. When the scoreboard showed 8.90 metres, I asked him: "Bruce, what's 8.90?" He said: "Lynn, my conversion table doesn't go that far. It's over 29 feet." Then Bob came back to where we're sitting and he said to me: "Do you think I'll have to jump again."

'I said: "Bob, it's all over. Nobody's going to beat what you've just done if we all stay here for the rest of the century."'

According to *Texas Monthly*, another issue prolonged the delivery of the results.

The jump was so far they had difficulty converting it from metres to feet. Beamon collapsed on the track and prayed.

Was it a fluke, caused by the most favourable atmospheric conditions and the chance timing of an erratic athlete? Or was it a genuine feat of human strength and agility that would have occurred in any atmosphere any time?

Sports Illustrated consulted a professor of applied science and commissioned him to analyse all the variable factors affecting Beamon's jump. They wanted no stone left unturned in trying to reach a scientific explanation for the apparently inexplicable. In other words, how much of his monstrous leap was down to altitude, humidity, temperature, air density and gravitational pull.

Nobody can be too sure what formulae were used, but, by the time the professor had worked it all out, the answer detracted precious little from the freakish nature of Beamon's flight. The atmospheric conditions in Mexico City that afternoon accounted for no more than 11 inches of the jump, which meant that the New Yorker had shattered the world record by a foot, thanks entirely to his athleticism and ability to defy gravity longer than any other human being on the planet at that time.

Beamon, they said, was a man way ahead of his time, which set mathematicians the challenge of calculating exactly how far ahead. Working on the basis that the world record increased over thirty years by twenty centimetres (about eight inches under the pre-metric system), and allowing for technical improvements, they concluded that nobody had a right to jump as far as Beamon until 1994, which put Bob at least twenty-six years ahead of his time.

Other boffins devised a stratagem that told them that the world record set in 1968 would not be broken until 2016, which put Beamon almost half a century ahead of his time.

Subsequent events proved the 1994 theorists reasonably close to the mark, in that the record survived until another American, Mike Powell, a 27 year old from Philadelphia, broke it during the 1991 World Championships in Tokyo.

In Mexico City that afternoon, Davies immediately gave up the ghost. Mentally, the ex-Olympic champion quit there and then at what he saw as the utter futility of trying to get anywhere close to Beamon. Two other medals were still to be won. Davies, to the annoyance of many of his admirers, decided neither was worth the candle.

'Winning is the only thing that matters,' Davies said. 'When you've finished first, second and third are nowhere. It was very unusual for such a big sporting event to be over in the first round. The gold had gone and after that nothing else really mattered. I'd have needed wings to have got anywhere near Beamon. The competition was over, so what was the point of going on? I wasn't interested in finishing second.

'I was accused of quitting and giving up. What Bob did was so outrageous that it's like being all-square after 18 holes of golf. You go to the first play-off hole, a par four, and your opponent holes in one. If Bob had jumped 28 feet, which was still pretty outrageous, I would still have given myself a chance. If I had known Bob was going to jump 29 feet before I left for Mexico, I'd have thought very hard about staying at home.'

An East German, Klaus Beer, took silver with 26 ft 10½ in. (8.19 m), with Boston an inch and a quarter back in bronze position, which gave him a complete set of Olympic medals. Davies finished a long way back, joint eighth, more than three feet adrift of Beamon, who sounded more surprised than anyone. Either that, or he was merely being polite to his rivals.

'I thought the record would probably have been broken that day by Lynn Davies, Ralph Boston or Igor Ter-Ovanesyan,' he said. 'Like Ralph [Rome, 1960], I was extremely fortunate to have had the opportunity of being Olympic champion and the world record-holder at the same Games.'

In the excitement over Beamon, everything else was ignored or pushed aside, including the fact that Davies had been wrongly eliminated from the final three jumps after finishing joint eighth. 'I sat on the bench and tried to help Igor as best I could,' Davies said. 'Then I went under the stadium for a shower and about half an hour after the competition had finished, the chief marshal approached me looking a bit worried.

'"Davies, Davies," he said. "We've made a mistake. You should have been in the final. You want to take your last three jumps now?" I could have gone back out into the wind and rain and tried to beat the unbeatable. I thought about it for a second or two and said: "No, thank you."

'When I met Bob at the Beijing Olympics in 2008, we were reminiscing and I told him about that. He said to me: "You must go to the IOC [International Olympic Committee] and sue them. When I got to Mexico City 40 years ago, I thought you were going to win."'

Davies' gold-or-nothing philosophy provoked widespread public criticism, which, in turn, prompted Chris Brasher, an Olympian in his own right and the creator of the London Marathon, to mount a spirited defence of the pilloried Welshman.

'I have never heard more ridiculous criticism in my life,' Brasher said in his autobiography, *Winner Takes All*:

> Those who [criticise] do not realise the competitive spirit this man has. Nothing less than the gold would satisfy him. He was prepared to jump further than he has ever jumped before, but when Beamon shattered the bounds of possibility by jumping two feet further than Lynn had ever jumped before, there was nothing he could do but accept the facts. Instead of criticising him, I admire him for his attitude. It had to be another gold medal or nothing. Lynn Davies plays only for big stakes.

Boston, born in Laurel, Mississippi, celebrated his 72nd birthday on 3 May 2011. A great-grandfather and retired television sports commentator, he once said: 'You would always like to end up with a truckload of medals, but I learned a lot about life and made just a whole parcel of friends.'

He summed up his philosophy – that life itself was a far more important test than any duel in the sandpit or on the track – in two striking sentences: 'Being first to cross the finish line makes you a winner in only one phase of life. It's what you do after you cross the line that really counts.'

Beamon, born 29 August 1946, works for the Chicago State University as assistant athletics director. *Sports Illustrated* acclaimed his Olympic flight as one of the five greatest sporting events of the twentieth century, a list topped, in the view of America's iconic magazine, by the 'Miracle on Ice' during the winter Games at Lake Placid in 1980 when the USA came from behind to beat the USSR.

Davies retired in 1973 at the age of 31, finishing on home ground for Cardiff Athletic Club in a British League match at Cwmbran Stadium. Eleven years of international competition, spanning thirteen major games, brought him three golds, umpteen other prizes and more than forty records, including the UK one, which stood for thirty-three years.

Upon retirement, he remained on the global stage in a new guise, as Canada's technical athletics director for three years, climaxing with the Montreal Olympics in 1976. He captained the Great Britain men's team from 1979 to 1984, the golden era of Olympians such as Sebastian Coe, Steve Ovett and Daley Thompson. Another celebrated Olympian, Mary Peters, captained the women's team at the same time.

A man of many parts, Davies returned home to take up a new post, as technical officer for the Sports Council of Wales, before branching out into broadcasting as a sports producer for BBC Wales. He succeeded David Hemery as President of UK Athletics in 2002 and received the CBE four years later for his services to sport.

Welsh sportsmen and women have been to the four corners of the Earth in pursuit of global excellence. For all their periodic ability to beat the best, be it on the football and rugby fields, in the boxing ring, on the fairways of Augusta or over the most fearsome steeplechase course of all, at Aintree, Wales has produced one solitary Olympic track-and-field gold medallist.

London 2012 could possibly change that. Until then, a coalminer's son from Nantymoel stands alone in the Welsh pantheon – the one and only Lynn Davies.

9

WINNING THE WORLD CUP

Clive Sullivan

Born: Cardiff, 9 April 1943
Died: Hull, 8 October 1985, aged 42

For a city of its size, Kingston-upon-Hull has bred more than its share of the great and the good. Movie moguls and musicians, poets and politicians, aviators and actors, authors and comedians – the old seaport on the Humber has produced them all.

The who's who makes impressive reading: from J. Arthur Rank of motion picture renown to the guitarist Mick Ronson of *Ziggy Stardust* fame; from Sir Andrew Motion, a recent poet laureate, to former Deputy Prime Minister John 'Two Jags' Prescott; from Amy Johnson the aviator to Sir Tom Courtenay, John Alderton, Ian Carmichael, Alan Plater and Maureen Lipman. For all their achievements, none is as synonymous with Hull as William Wilberforce and Clive Sullivan.

As one of the great moral crusaders of nineteenth-century British history, Wilberforce stands more than 100 feet up in the air astride a stone column, a monumental tribute to his contribution towards humanity in abolishing the slave trade.

Sullivan, a Welsh rugby player from one of Cardiff's blue-collar inner suburbs, whose charm enabled him to cross the rubicon from one bank of the Humber to the other without making a single enemy, earned himself a slightly lower-level but no less enduring tribute. Upon his cruel early passing, they named the A63 dual carriageway

151

out of the city, heading east to the Humber Bridge, the Clive Sullivan Way.

Wilberforce would have loved it because Sullivan, as the first black man to captain Great Britain in an international sporting event, became a shining symbol of what the visionary politician had fought to make possible some 140 years earlier.

He would have been doubly proud to learn that the Sullivans have traced their ancestors back to the slave ships.

The British had been involved in the slave trade since the sixteenth century. Towards the end of the 1700s, their ships were taking up to 40,000 people from west Africa to work as slaves in the West Indies, primarily in the production of sugar, tobacco and cotton. An estimated 11 million had been enslaved by the time Wilberforce won his crusade after devoting more than 40 years of his life to the abolition of slavery in the British Empire.

A wealthy merchant's son who became Member of Parliament for Hull at the age of twenty-one in 1780, Wilberforce introduced the first parliamentary bill to abolish the slave trade eleven years later, with a four-hour speech in the House of Commons, which included the following:

> Let us not despair. It is a blessed cause and success, ere long, will crown our exertions. Already we have gained one victory. We have obtained for these poor creatures the recognition of their human nature which, for a while, was most shamefully denied. This is the first fruit of our efforts.
>
> Let us persevere and our triumph will be complete. Never, never will we desist till we have wiped away this scandal from the Christian name, relieved ourselves from the load of guilt, under which we at present labour, and extinguished every trace of this bloody traffic of which our posterity, looking back on the history of these enlightened times, will scarce believe that it has been suffered to exist so long a disgrace and dishonour to this country.

A two-hour debate resulted in a hefty defeat of 163 votes to 88. Wilberforce persisted, fired by his unshakeable belief that God and

Sir Matt Busby, right, and Jimmy Murphy – architect and chief engineer of Manchester United's European empire.

Jimmy Murphy jnr and a happy Nobby Stiles at Pentre in the Rhondda Valley, birthplace of United's post-Munich saviour.

South Africa v. England, Durban, 16 December 1948: an acrobatic Allan Watkins flat out in his floppy sun hat, catching South Africa's captain Dudley Nourse.
Inset: Allan Watkins. (Glamorgan Cricket Archive)

Don Shepherd's classic bowling action, in the nets at St Helens, Swansea, *c*.1955. (Glamorgan Cricket Archive)

Skipper Shepherd, left, and wicketkeeper Eifion Jones brandishing the spoils of victory at St Helens in August 1968 after Glamorgan's second successive win over Australia. (Glamorgan Cricket Archive)

John Charles, arrowed, at 14, with the Swansea schoolboy team of 1945–46.

The Gentle Giant after his homecoming from Italy in 1963, playing for Cardiff City at Ninian Park.

Cardiff schoolboy rugby team, 1948–49: Fourteen-year-old Billy Boston (first right, middle row), standing alongside the future heavyweight champion of Great Britain, Joe Erskine.

Boston at Central Park during his debut season, 1953–54, scoring one of the earliest of his 478 tries for Wigan.

Mike Davies (back row, fifth from left) with some of the pioneers of professional tennis as a global sport. Among the all-time greats are Rod Laver (second right, back row) and Ken Rosewall (second right, front row).

Lynn Davies leaping to Olympic gold, Tokyo, October 1964.

Eighteen-year-old Ken Morgans, left, in his first Manchester derby, Maine Road, 28 December 1957: City 2 United 2. The City goalkeeper – ex-German prisoner of war Bert Trautmann – clears from a soaring Dennis Viollet.

Morgans and his bosom pal England centre-forward Tommy Taylor immediately before the Busby Babes' last domestic appearance before the crash, 1 February 1958, Highbury, where they beat Arsenal 5–4.

Lining up four days later in Belgrade for the European Cup tie against Red Star. From left: Duncan Edwards, Eddie Colman, Mark Jones, Morgans, Bobby Charlton, Dennis Viollet, Taylor, Bill Foulkes, Harry Gregg, Albert Scanlon, Roger Byrne. The air crash at Munich twenty-four hours later claimed the lives of eight players, including five of the team above.

Clive Sullivan, as the fans of Hull, Hull Kingston Rovers and Wales remember him, giving another opponent the runaround. (Hull Football Club)

Mervyn Davies, leading from the front as usual: white headband, ball in one hand, on the charge, winning the Grand Slam against France at Cardiff Arms Park. Three weeks later, he was fighting for his life.

Gareth Edwards in classic pose, launching the Lions backs during their invincible tour of South Africa in 1974. (*Daily Mail*)

Keith Jarrett lining up the touchline conversion of his stupendous solo try for Wales against England at Cardiff Arms Park, April 1967. (BBC Wales)

Tom Pryce, the only Welshman to win a Formula One Grand Prix, revving up in the early stages of his career.
(Tony Vlassopulos)

Ian Woosnam after finishing two shots clear of a stellar field to win the 1997 PGA championship at Wentworth.
(*Daily Mail*)

'Woosie' as Ryder Cup captain after Europe's landslide win over the USA in 2006
(*Daily Mail*)

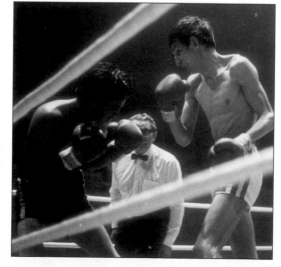

Johnny Owen on his way to stopping the Mexican Jose Martinez Garcia at Ebbw Vale in April 1979 – 18 months before his fatal shot at the world title.
(Huw Evans Picture Agency)

Carl Llewellyn showing them all the way home at Aintree on Earth Summit in April 1998, the second of his Grand National victories. (*Daily Mail*)

Ryan Giggs using his head to provide Manchester United with a late equaliser against Celtic in their Champions League tie in Glasgow, November 2008. (*Daily Mail*)

human decency were on his side. The Slave Trade Act received Royal Assent 16 years later; another 26 years elapsed before the Slavery Abolition Act was finally passed in July 1833. Wilberforce, after a long struggle with ill health, died three days later, almost as if he had fought to stay alive just long enough to win justice for his fellow man.

Considering there were 11 million slaves, it is hardly surprising that Sullivan's forebears were among them. By the time of his birth, more than a century after the emancipation granted by Wilberforce and his dogged campaigners, they had retraced some of their steps and gone eastwards back across the Atlantic in search of a better life in the Land of Hope and Glory.

Dorothy Green, whose father emigrated to England from Antigua at the turn of the twentieth century, moved from her native Bristol to Cardiff when she married Charles Sullivan, a Jamaican whose family had joined the transatlantic migration before the Second World War. They lived in the heart of Splott, or 'God's Plot', as the locals call it, in the shadow of the old East Moors Steelworks, which smoked and belched over the Sullivan family home in Wimbourne Street just as it smoked and belched over every other street in the neighbourhood.

Clive Sullivan was born there on 9 April 1943, the second of four children. To say his was a difficult childhood is an understatement, not because his father walked out never to be seen again but because of abnormalities in his knees and feet that made walking a hazardous proposition. After one of several operations, a surgeon warned the family that the boy would be lucky to walk properly. The boy responded to the prophecy of doom by turning himself into a sprinter.

The spectacular manner in which he defied one specialist's prognosis might have had something to do with events in the playground at Herbert Thompson Primary School. The family having outgrown their small home in Splott, Mrs Sullivan moved her four children – Brian, Clive, Yvonne and Elmyria – to Ronald Place in Ely, on the western side of Cardiff.

At school, the family's monopoly of the sprints for boys and girls earned them suitable recognition as 'the Four Flying Sullivans'. By then, the second of the four had recovered from surgery on his legs to prove himself too fast for the rest, especially one of the bigger boys, who happened to be another embryonic Great Britain rugby league professional.

Jim Mills, or 'Big Bad Jim', as he has occasionally been referred to down the years, was one year younger but a whole lot bigger when he first came across Sullivan in the schoolyard. 'Clive lived round the corner from me,' Mills said. 'I was born in Aberdare, but we'd moved to Cardiff when I was one year old and I used to go to the school once a week for woodwork.

'I was big for my age and one day this kid shouted out, with a big grin on his face: "Hey, lanky." I'd chase him around the playground, but I could never catch him. He'd say the same again the following week and the week after that and the week after that, knowing full well that he was too quick for me.'

He also proved too quick for any of the leading Welsh clubs, although it may be more accurate to state that they were far too slow. They were still stuck in the starting blocks when the young Sullivan joined the army, played for their rugby union team in between square-bashing, and impressed a scout for Bradford Northern, as they were then. They invited him along to Odsal for a trial and, according to his widow, sent the teenager off again with instructions to 'come back when you've learnt how to play rugby'.

Bradford might have been less dismissive if only they had known that another scout, acting for Hull, thought the triallist had learnt a fair bit about the game and intercepted him at the railway station with an offer to try his luck on Humberside.

Appearing on the team sheet against Bramley on 9 December 1961 as 'A.N. Other' – the time-honoured, albeit wonderfully naive pseudonym designed to protect anonymity and spare the individual from losing his amateur status as a bona fide union player – Sullivan scored three tries in his first trial match.

A complete stranger had upstaged Hull's expensive international signing from South Africa, Wilf Rosenberg, who had starred for the Springboks during the drawn Test series against the Lions in 1955.

'All the talk after the match was about this amazing young Welshman and the brilliance of his three tries,' said David Doyle-Davidson, a teammate of 'Sully' throughout his time there. 'The

154

buzz around the city really was something very special.'

The Hull directors had struck gold and they went on striking it for the next 12 years. The kid from Cardiff with the knobbly knees and spindly legs had taken his first step towards captaining Great Britain's only World Cup-winning rugby league team in stirring defiance of his boyhood physical afflictions.

He could beat opponents on the outside and inside, and he had the upper-body strength to pull his weight defensively. He had a gearbox that gave him more than one change of pace and the footwork to find a shaft of space where, to the untutored eye, none existed – all the tools of a wing's trade except one.

'The only thing Clive couldn't do was side-step,' Doyle-Davidson, who later coached Hull, said. 'We used to practise for hours on end under Roy Francis, but the side-step was the only bit to elude him. It didn't matter much because he'd just rely on his swerve and blistering pace, and the results were there for all to see.

'From 60 metres out, Clive was like a gazelle. But from about 20 metres out, he was like a wild bull – very, very strong. The other great thing about him, which a lot of other wingers at that time didn't have, was that he had a great defence. He was a wonderful man and a superb ambassador for rugby league.'

At the Boulevard, he came under the influence of another pioneering Welshman from Cardiff, Roy Francis, who after a distinguished playing career became the first black coach of any professional sports team in Britain when Hull created the role for him in 1954. Those who played under him remember Francis as an innovator whose methods made him a man way ahead of his time.

Sullivan's status as a part-time professional meant he could stay in the army until 1964, when the 21-year-old apprentice Hull legend met Rosalyn Byron, the girl from the East Riding village of Welton who would become his wife. Their 'love at first sight' introductions took place at the Duke of Cumberland public house in Welton.

'I was only 17 and on a night out with a few girl friends,' Rosalyn said. 'I would be allowed in on the strict understanding that I didn't drink. So I'd buy a bag of sweets and offer them around in between sipping a lemonade. That's how I met Clive, by offering him a sweet in a pub.

'I didn't know anything about him. My English teacher at school was a Welshman and he always used to go on about rugby and what a great game it was. If you played sport, then as far as I was concerned you were either a flannelled fool or a muddied oaf. I once wrote an essay about these silly men chasing funny-shaped balls, which shows you how much I knew about it.

'Then I started going to the Boulevard to watch him play. His mother was so nervous that she couldn't bring herself to watch because she'd be worried that Clive was going to get hurt. She'd say to me: "Rosalyn, I don't know how you can watch him."

'Clive wasn't the tallest of men. Six foot may seem tall, but not in rugby league. He wasn't what you'd call beefy, what with his spindly legs.

'As a child, he had a lot of trouble caused by the calcification of muscles in his thighs and legs. He had a scar from the top of his thigh to his knee, where they had operated to scrape away a lot of stuff. That's why, at the age of 11, he was told he wouldn't walk again.'

When they first met, Sullivan had enrolled at technical college to start an apprenticeship as a motor mechanic and spent most of his playing career doing a semi-skilled job for Hawker Siddeley. Hull paid him £16 for a win before tax and £8 for a defeat, on a no-play, no-pay basis, which meant he could never afford to be injured.

Rarely a man to do anything by half, Hull's new wing came close to losing his life in a car crash within two years of his debut hat-trick. Despite multiple injuries, he was playing again three months later. Once again, Sullivan had triumphed over adversity, and for the next 20 years the rugby gods gave him a long enough break to make a famous name for himself, his adopted city and the whole of Great Britain.

He and Rosalyn married in 1966. 'I knew from that very first meeting that I'd marry him,' his widow said. 'It really was love at first sight. Clive was a bit of a nine-day wonder when I took him home to meet my parents, although I had told my mum beforehand. He was black, after all, and I lived in such a small village that I don't think they'd ever seen a black person there before.

'Everyone was so fascinated by Clive that they wanted to touch his hair, my mum being the first. There was never any trouble or embarrassment. He won everyone over because he had a lovely personality – always very polite, with a lovely smile. Everyone loved him. All I can say is that his mum did a really good job bringing him up the right way after his dad had left. Clive never said he missed his father.

'He was always very comfortable with his colour. He always said to me that it was an asset because it made him stand out.

'He very quickly identified with the people of Hull. They'd had tough lives, especially the fishermen, and, coming from a humble background himself, he understood that. He was loved by everyone in Hull, which was a great tribute to him because there's such fierce rivalry between the two rugby clubs.'

Sully won his first Test cap in 1967 at the age of 23, by which time he and the big boy who could never catch him in the playground had renewed acquaintances. 'I was playing for Widnes and I managed to collar Clive as he was about to go in at the corner,' Jim Mills said, remembering what Sullivan had said to him in the playground years before. 'I got hold of him on the ground and said: "Now, who did you call 'lanky'?"'

For Sullivan, the crowning glory came five years later: the World Cup final against Australia on neutral territory at Lyon in France. None of the 405 other tries he'd scored could match the historic significance of the one that he ran in against the Kangaroos over a distance of 80 metres in the final.

It helped secure a 10–10 draw, after extra time – good enough for the British underdogs to clinch the trophy by virtue of a 27–21 win earlier in the tournament at Perpignan. The unexpected triumph under Sullivan's captaincy never won the universal acclamation it deserved.

The players responsible could have been forgiven for thinking that their success had fallen foul of the Official Secrets Act, certainly in comparison with the national celebration of the England football team's victory over West Germany in the football World Cup six years earlier. For a start, the attendance for the final at the Stade de Gerland was roughly what Stockport County would expect on a bad day: 4,231. The fact that no British team has regained the trophy during the four decades since has turned it into a once-in-a-lifetime event.

It did not change his lifestyle, but it did make Mrs Sullivan's life as a housewife with a young family a little more bearable. 'We were able to buy a washing machine with the bonus he made from winning the World Cup,' she said. 'It cost about £80 and that was the money all gone. Clive loved the game so much that I always reckoned he would have played it for nothing and there were times when that almost seemed to be the case.'

In Hull, more than anywhere else in the British Isles, East is East, West is West and never, according to Rudyard Kipling, the twain shall meet. Hull FC, alias the Airlie Birds, play in black and white and reside on the west bank of the Humber. Hull Kingston Rovers, alias the Robins, play in red and white and are located on the east bank. Lord Prescott, a Welshman by birth who spent most of his working life in the Yorkshire city as the MP for Hull East, once explained the rivalry in his capacity as a director of Hull KR, claiming that the Foreign Office had granted he and his fellow directors special visas to attend a local derby on the west bank.

Imagine, then, the consternation when, in 1974, Sullivan left Hull and joined the opposition; the same year in which he went to Buckingham Palace for his investiture as a Member of the Order of the British Empire for services to rugby league. They should also have made it clear that the gong was in recognition of his services to humanity as well. The Airlie Birds could hardly complain that he had short-changed them in any way, not after scoring 250 tries in 352 matches, when nobody had ever scored 100 or more for *both* Hull clubs, largely because it wasn't really the done thing to play for both.

Each club has always generated a deep passion among its devotees and none, on either side of the river, can have taken that innate devotion quite as far as the late Arthur Fletcher, alias 'Mad Fletch'. His love of Hull FC was such that, according to local legend, he would never allow anything, or anyone, to darken his door in red and white, the colours of his nearest and not dearest, Hull Kingston Rovers. Bacon fell into that category and no more reliable a witness than Fletcher's wife Mary once confirmed that he never touched a rasher of the stuff. Cigarette packets in red and white were excluded, along with anyone daft enough to knock on his door in a white shirt and a red tie.

It gets worse. Mad Fletch had bought a cat, black and white of course, whom he called 'Sully'. When his Welsh hero switched allegiance, Fletcher lost all affection for the animal until 'the cat got the message'. Rumours that he had it put down remain unsubstantiated.

Dick Tingle covered the black-and-white part of the city for the *Hull Daily Mail* for 36 years. 'I'd have got less for murder, but there was rarely a dull moment,' he said. 'There were Rovers fans living in east Hull who would go 25 miles out of their way to avoid going through black-and-white enemy territory. For all I know, they probably still do. The rivalry was phenomenally intense, every bit as much as Liverpool–Everton, Arsenal–Tottenham, Rangers–Celtic . . . except for one big difference. There was hardly ever any trouble.'

Rovers, beaten in the Challenge Cup finals of 1925 and 1964, had never won the trophy when Sullivan joined them. They had by the time he left, a victory made all the sweeter for having come at the expense of the club's local rivals. The first, and, 31 years later, the last all-Hull final took place on Saturday, 3 May 1980 in front of Her Majesty the Queen and 95,000 of her subjects.

Back on what is now Clive Sullivan Way, someone left a note asking one of the convoy of coaches and cars flooding south: 'Will the last one out switch the lights off?'

Sullivan, still untouchable on the left wing at 37, filled one of the few gaps in his rugby life with a winner's medal made possible, in no small way, by the never-say-die attitude personified by Rovers' stand-off, Roger Millward. He broke his jaw 15 minutes into the match, refused to leave the field and hurled himself about as though nothing had happened with a series of tackles, one of which proved most fortuitous in clicking his jawbone back into place.

Not for nothing did they call it the 'Hum-ber-dinger'.

Sullivan stayed for one more season, raising his try tally for Rovers to 118 in 213 matches. Nobody else had made as handsome a contribution to both the city's clubs, a suitable tribute to Sullivan given that only he could play for both and make himself a true folk hero for all the people of Hull, whatever their allegiance, without causing any permanent offence.

After a year at Oldham, he rejoined Hull on the coaching staff and proceeded to do for them what he had done for Rovers, playing his part in bringing the Challenge Cup back to Humberside in 1982. After playing out the first drawn final at Wembley (14–14 against Widnes), Sullivan left home for the replay at Elland Road never imagining that he would be required for any role other than as a coach. By the end of the night, he had cause to be mighty grateful to his wife's female intuition.

'Just before he left the house for the match, I said: "Take your boots," Rosalyn remembered.

'He said: "What on earth would I need them for?"

'I said: "Take your boots because I think you'll be needed."

'He said: "Don't be stupid."

'I said: "Don't be daft."

'Anyway, he wouldn't listen and went off without them. Then later in the day they had to send one of the kit men all the way back from Leeds, well over an hour by road, to get his boots.'

Hull beat the Merseysiders 18–9 in the replay at Elland Road, with Sullivan back in the old routine, playing from the start as an emergency wing replacement after Dane O'Hara had been ruled out at the eleventh hour by injury. Hull FC had not won the Challenge Cup since before the First World War, losing their five subsequent finals, to Rochdale in 1922, Leeds in 1923, Wigan in 1959, Wakefield Trinity in 1960 and, worst of all, to Hull Kingston Rovers in 1980. Hull KR had lost their only two previous finals, to Oldham in 1925 and Widnes in 1964. Now, in a matter of two years, Sullivan had united the city in unique fashion as the only player to have won the Challenge Cup with both Hull clubs.

Having come out of retirement once, he did so again, a few weeks after his 42nd birthday in May 1985. When injuries stretched Hull's resources to the limit, Sullivan came off the bench for his last match, ironically against the club responsible for showing him the door some 20 years earlier, Bradford Northern, at Odsal.

Nobody was to know then that Sullivan was not just in the twilight of his career but the twilight of his life. He had every reason to look forward to the rest of his days, to three score years and ten as a modest expectation for an athlete still at the acme of fitness. He had gone into business and had just started running his own version of a working men's social club when he began to feel unwell.

'He played in the May and two months later he went to see the doctor,' Rosalyn said. 'In July, round about the time when we'd just started the social club, he was getting a little acid in his stomach. We thought it was caused by the stress of getting the club up and running.

'The doctor asked him to come back in a week. Then the doctor said: "I think it best if I send you for a scan." After the scan, they called Clive back in and told him that they needed to carry out further investigation. He had a biopsy of the liver and that's where they found the cancer. I thought: "Oh, my God."

'They operated to take the tumour out of his liver, but then they found that the cancer was extensive. Because he was so fit, it had spread very quickly. Clive's sister, Elmyria, came up from Cardiff to stay with me. We went to see the surgeon at the hospital in Leeds and I asked: "How long?"

'The surgeon said: "Maybe six months to a year." I just could not take it in. I was so shocked. The surgeon said they were going to try chemotherapy and I could see that he was really upset.

'Before I left, I asked: "Will you tell Clive?"

'And he replied: "Only if he asks."

'I'm a medical secretary, so I knew a little about these things. My impression was that Clive knew. He said: "I'm going to fight this." He never said: "Why me? What have I done to deserve this?" There was never any self-pity.

'He belonged to that generation of men who believed that their main job in life was to look after their wife and family. He was being strong for me. Then one day he went out, saying he was going to make a will.

'They said he reacted really well to the first load of chemo. Then they gave him a second dose and he started to lose all his hair.'

He never lacked support from friends beyond the immediate family circle. Mills, his friend from their days at primary school in Cardiff, was among those who crossed the Pennines to see him. 'He wasn't too good by then, but he kept saying: "I'm going to beat this," which was typical Clive,' Mills said. 'We all hoped he would beat it, but we didn't know then how bad it was. He was a really brave lad and wonderfully positive. Sadly, there are some things you just can't beat, no matter how hard you try. He was one of those people you really looked up to. He never fell out with anyone and you can't say that about many people in this life.'

Nothing could weaken his spirit, and in the August of that fateful summer Sullivan went home to Cardiff for a family reunion and what would be a final visit to the city of his birth. His half-sister, Sharon Dixon, whose mother Dorothy remarried Bassey Esien, a steelworker from Nigeria, remembered it well.

'Clive gave me away when I got married and we were always close,' Sharon, now a business coach and consultant, said. 'I was a bridesmaid when Clive married Rosalyn and I used to spend a lot of my summers staying with them in Hull. I went back there after Clive was taken ill so I could take Rosalyn back and forth to the hospital in Leeds.

'It was a tragic time. When he came down to Cardiff for that last time, the whole family was there and Rosalyn had made Clive a little Afro wig because his hair had all fallen out. That was in the August and he was gone by the start of October. Sixteen weeks from diagnosis to his passing. Terrible . . .'

During a third course of chemotheraphy, Sullivan became so ill that he was taken back into hospital in Leeds. He died there on Tuesday, 8 October 1985 at the age of 42.

A service of thanksgiving for his life took place ten days later at Holy Trinity Parish Church, the largest in Hull, with room for a congregation of a thousand. Five times as many crammed the square outside, with loudspeakers relaying the service to the multitude.

The family asked Doyle-Davidson to deliver the eulogy, the same Doyle-Davidson who had been there in the Hull back line against Doncaster when Sully ran in seven tries, a club record that has stood since that Saturday in 1968. When the papers carried a report of Doyle-Davidson going 70 yards for a try against Keighley, a disbelieving fan told him: 'You couldn't have run that far, Doyle. You must have been on Sully's shoulders . . . That typified what they thought of him – and, I suppose, what they thought of me.'

A service of thanksgiving for his life on Friday afternoon, 18 October 1985 almost brought the city to a standstill, as the fans turned out in force, black-and-white and red-and-white united in grief. They came to pay their last respects to a humble Welshman who had been struck down in his prime. As Doyle-Davidson told the great congregation from the pulpit of Holy Trinity: 'I never met anyone who had a bad word to say about Clive Sullivan ... No matter who they were, whether a rugby league fan or not, there was something special about the man everyone loved.'

More than a quarter of a century later, his family reflect on that day and burst with pride. 'When I look back on his life, I realise what an impact he had on this city in his short time,' Rosalyn said. 'I'd love him to have been able to see the impact for himself. He would never have believed it. Even today people still talk about him and I think they always will. He will never ever be forgotten.'

Sullivan's innate humility would never have allowed him to imagine that his early passing could generate such affection from the people of a city some 250 miles from where he had been brought up. The award of the MBE and a surprise ambush by Eamonn Andrews with his red book as the subject of *This Is Your Life* were accolades that gave the Welshman an inkling of his popularity.

'I knew my brother was a star, but I had no idea how big a star he really was,' Sharon said. 'The outpouring of love from the people of Hull is something I shall never forget. It was hard for us all but particularly my mum. She was an absolute fighter, as she had to be to raise four children on her own before she met my dad. My mother was a very strong person who was always positive. She made sure we were all brought up in the right way. Good manners were very important to her and I would never have dreamt of answering her back. She was very fair and very loving, a wonderful role model, and Clive was exactly the same.'

The Four Flying Sullivans, alas, are no more. Brian, the eldest, who followed Clive into rugby league, also died young, from pancreatic cancer. Although the sisters, Yvonne and Elmyria, passed away in 2009, they had the satisfaction of seeing the family's success in the arena of international sport extend into a new generation.

Yvonne's son, Nathan Blake, played football for Wales and several Football League clubs, including Wolves. Elmyria's son, Matthew Robinson, won five caps on the wing for Wales in 1999, while Rosalyn's son, Anthony, kept the Sullivan flag flying high as a dual international in his own right in both league and union.

Before and after the service of thanksgiving, old friends paid tribute to the blood, sweat and tears that went into the creation of a true folk hero. It began with 'Cwm Rhondda' and ended in 'Abide With Me'. The chaplains of both Hull clubs led the prayers, the respective chairmen of Hull and Hull Kingston Rovers took it in turn to read the lessons, and David Oxley, for many years chief executive of the Rugby Football League, delivered his own eulogy, but nothing said that day fitted the occasion with quite the same poignancy as a poetic tribute from Doyle-Davidson, in his capacity as a BBC Radio Humberside broadcaster:

The life that I have
is all that I have
And the life that I have
Is yours.
The love that I have
Of the life that I have
Is yours and yours
And yours.
A rest I shall have
A sleep I shall have
Yet death will be but a pause.
For the peace of my years
In the long green grass
Will be yours and yours
And yours.

10

TRIUMPH AND TRAGEDY

Mervyn Davies

Born: Swansea, 9 December 1946

Sunday, 28 March 1976. Gerald Ford sits in the White House, albeit a trifle uncomfortably, as the unelected President of the United States, thrust into the hottest of seats vacated by Richard Nixon following his resignation over the Watergate scandal. On this side of the Atlantic, staff at Downing Street spend a second successive weekend with no Prime Minister at home, Harold Wilson having stood down 12 days earlier. His successor, James Callaghan, the honourable member for Cardiff South-East, is waiting in the wings.

Across the country, a few household names are celebrating birthdays, along with a few others who have not yet had the time to become famous in their own household, let alone anywhere else. Dame Flora Robson, the actress, is 74. Dirk Bogarde, the film star, 55. Michael Parkinson, chat-show king, is 41. Neil Kinnock, politician, 34. Steve Bull is 11 and still some way off scoring his first goal for Wolverhampton Wanderers, while Nasser Hussain, at eight, is even further away from starting his ascent to the captaincy of the England cricket team.

This particular weekend in March sees Liverpool locked in a three-cornered fight for the Football League title with Manchester United and the surprise team of the season, Queens Park Rangers, who would finish one point behind the Anfield Reds in second place.

Muhammad Ali is preparing for the next defence of his WBA-

WBC world heavyweight title after knocking the Belgian Jean-Pierre Coopman out in five rounds at San Juan in Puerto Rico.

In Wales, celebrations of another Grand Slam span a second weekend. Meanwhile, in a corner of suburban Swansea, the captain of the national team drags himself out of bed for the big match of the day, the All Whites' Welsh Cup semi-final against Pontypool at Cardiff Arms Park. Mervyn Davies clambers aboard the Swansea team coach and the fateful journey to the last match of his life. But for prompt emergency medical care and the surgeons' skill it would have been the last day of his life.

When it comes to putting their rugby greats on a pedestal, the Welsh public do so in a special way, revering them by the use of a single name. There was Cliff and Bleddyn, their surnames – Morgan and Williams – made redundant by their on-field brilliance. Then along came Clive, as in Rowlands; Barry, as in John; Benny, for Phil Bennett; Gareth, as in Edwards. Then there were JJ, JPR, Gerald (Davies), Pricey (Graham Price), Charlie (Tony Faulkner), 'Panther' (Allan Martin) and Merve. In the case of The Duke – Bobby Windsor – it was two words.

On that late spring Sunday morning, there was no limit to what Davies could achieve on top of his two Grand Slams, three Triple Crowns and four outright Five Nations titles. On the very highest level, as a Lion, he had been to New Zealand in 1971 and helped win the Test series there for the one and only time. Three years later he joined the tour to South Africa, retaining the back-row place he had held against the All Blacks throughout that invincible Lions tour.

In eight years as an ever-present member of the Welsh back row, Davies had played twenty internationals at the Arms Park and lost only one, to New Zealand. As captain he had won eight out of nine, with every reason to believe he would win considerably more at the helm of the best team in the northern hemisphere.

Three weeks earlier, during the championship denouement against France, Davies had endured the incessant pain from a damaged calf rather than leave his post. At the end, in what would be his last interview as captain of his country, he gave a straight-from-the-shoulder answer to the question of how Wales intended to follow their Five Nations clean sweep: by doing it again and again during the next two seasons.

'My aim now is to win three Grand Slams in a row,' he said without a trace of bombast. 'This team will get better. We are only at the beginning of what we can achieve. Nothing is impossible.'

Almost four decades later, he finds no difficulty justifying his words. 'I remember being asked the question and I remember thinking: "Let's be outspoken and say three Grand Slams in a row." It was a realistic thing to say and one which I believed was going to happen.

'Wales were the dominant force in northern hemisphere rugby at the time, with France the nearest competitor. France in Paris the following season would be the only problem, although I'd like to think my presence might have made some slight difference. The rest, I thought, would be a matter of course, as it proved.'

A hat-trick of Grand Slams in successive seasons had never been done. Wales lost one championship match over the next two seasons, to France in Paris, which they avenged in Cardiff the following year, a victory that ushered Gareth Edwards and Phil Bennett into Test retirement in suitable style. History, therefore, almost proved their stricken ex-captain right, except that nobody will ever know how different history might have been had the gangling number 8 in the white bandana still been in command.

As the Swansea coach cruised along the M4 towards a pre-match stop at the Bear Hotel in the market town of Cowbridge, Davies knew that he only had to avoid serious injury to reach the pinnacle for any British or Irish player, captaincy of the Lions. He had been informally offered the position by John Dawes, the honorary Wales coach who was appointed to a similarly honorary post with the Lions for their four-month odyssey around New Zealand at the end of the following season.

Davies had taken some persuading before being sworn to secrecy. The private tête-à-tête between the pair, whose friendship went back a long way to their early days as schoolteachers in London, took place on the Friday night before the first match of the Grand Slam campaign, against England on 17 January 1976.

'I was sitting alone in the team room at the hotel when John came in and said: "Can I have a quiet word?" As soon as we were on our own, he said: "How do you fancy going to play the All Blacks again next year?"

'My gut reaction was to say no, that I'd been on two Lions tours and I knew how bloody hard they were. So I said: "I'll have a think about it. I can't really think that far ahead. I'll let you know before the end of the season."

'Then he said: "You'd come as captain, wouldn't you?"

'That was the ultimate honour. I said yes, of course I'd be delighted to go as captain. We shook hands on it there and then.

'He said: "I know this won't go any further."'

When the Swansea players filed out of the bus for their pre-match meal, Davies had the world at his feet. He felt 'invincible'. At the zenith of his power, he had enough time left at twenty-nine for at least two more international seasons before Anno Domini could begin to take its toll. What nobody imagined as morning passed into afternoon that Sunday was that 'Merve the Swerve' had only 28 minutes of rugby left.

He felt as he had always felt going into a match.

Davies had shot from nowhere into the rugby stratosphere with a speed that made the average meteor look as though it needed a turbo-charger. As a schoolboy and student, his beanpole stature hardly suggested – even to the most educated eye – that he would grow into a colossus. There had been no representative recognition along the way, and when the 1968–69 season kicked off Davies, the newly qualified schoolteacher, began it in the depths of the English game, playing for a club so far down the pecking order that no self-respecting international had ever heard of Old Guildfordians. Within six months, he was playing for Wales against Scotland at Murrayfield.

'I still don't know to this day how I managed it,' he said. 'I won no rugby honours at school, mainly because I went to an unfashionable school [Penlan Comprehensive]. I played in the trials but never had a look-in, probably because our teachers were not on the selection committee. I played a bit of college rugby and one game for Swansea before going to London.

'I lived in Guildford for a few months and during that time a couple of mates came up with the idea of going to play for the local club, Old Guildfordians. The standard was desperately bad, almost to the point of being horrendous. So we decided to make the long journey in those non-motorway days from Guildford to London Welsh.

'I began in the third team, the London Welsh Dragons. The following Saturday, I was up to the second team, the London Welsh Druids. I thought: "This is a bit more like it – some half-decent rugby."

'The half-term holiday then intervened and I drove back to Swansea to see my parents. A telegram arrived a couple of days later to say I'd been chosen for the London Welsh first team to play Moseley. That was in the November and by the third week of January I was playing for Wales. I thought: "This is too easy." Nobody really knew who I was or where I'd come from. I felt it couldn't happen that quickly.'

How he found out about his first cap reinforced his sense of disbelief. 'I wasn't on the phone, so the selectors presumably couldn't get in touch with me,' he said. 'I'd played in the trial and was driving with a mate to school on the Monday morning. I knew the team was supposed to have been picked the day before, but I'd heard nothing.

'My friend said: "Well, let's get a paper and see if you're in." We stopped the car and I bought a copy of the *Daily Mirror*. At the bottom of one column, occupying about a quarter of an inch of space, there was the Welsh team and there, at the end of the list, was my name. We turned the car round, took the day off and went out to celebrate. The telegram from the Welsh selectors arrived three days later.'

His sheer athleticism at the tail of the lineout and around the field marked him out as a player ahead of his time, but even the most gifted need the odd lucky break. Perhaps one of Davies' luckiest came during the long approach to the 1971 Lions tour of New Zealand, when Ken Goodall, the Irish number 8 who had led the rout of the Welsh in Dublin that season, decided to cash in his union chips and sign for Workington rugby league club. In doing so, he cleared the way for his opposite number in the Wales team to claim the number 8 Lions Test jersey.

'My entire career had been a series of lucky breaks,' Davies said.

'Joining London Welsh at a time when they played such an exhilarating style of rugby was certainly one. That was a good example of being in the right place at the right time. Coming up against someone as good as Ken Goodall was a real eye-opener. There was no doubt he would have been on the '71 Lions tour if he hadn't gone north.'

In forty-six Tests for Wales and the Lions, Davies won thirty-one, drew six and lost nine. He played twenty internationals at the Arms Park and lost only once, to Ian Kirkpatrick's All Blacks in 1972, by a mere three points. Had such success not been built over a period of eight years, he might have been forgiven for thinking that it all seemed too good to last.

'Winning international matches was the norm, in the same way the Lions beating New Zealand and South Africa was the norm,' he said. 'Yes, there were fortunate circumstances, especially against South Africa. We played them at a time when they had been in the wilderness for many years and they made the mistake of underestimating the strength of British rugby at that time. When you're in the thick of it, I don't think you realise that you are making history, that there is something special about it.'

There were times, of course, when it did go wrong, when Wales came a cropper, like at Murrayfield in 1975 after the Big Five selectors had punished Phil Bennett for skipping the annual trial. The untouchable Lion of the previous summer suddenly found himself out in the cold, dropped from the squad, as well as the team, being demoted behind the Aberavon fly-half John Bevan and the uncapped 20-year-old David Richards from Swansea.

Bennett, half-reprieved by an injury to Richards, sat on the bench until the luckless Bevan fractured a cheekbone. When Steve Fenwick pulled up lame, Davies summoned Bennett to take a penalty that had been awarded in front of the Scottish posts.

'Phil had been on the field for three minutes and I said, in my domineering way: "Kick that goal."

'Phil said: "No, Merve. I've only just got onto the field."

'So I said: "Listen. You kick that goal."

'He did and he missed. And we lost by two points.'

Time has lent enchantment by the bucketful to the memory of Wales in the '70s as a team of all-singing, all-dancing showmen. They could also win an ugly war of attrition, if that was what was required to grind it out. Davies, nothing if not pragmatic, never lost sight of the three basic tenets that underpinned his leadership – confrontation, consolidation, domination.

'I was fortunate to play in a very successful period for Welsh rugby. As captain, I had the freedom to make my own choice. Once the coach had left the dressing-room before a match, I was in charge for the last 20 minutes before we went out. It was never a case of ignoring what my good friend Mr John Dawes had just said – heaven forbid – but I had my own views.

'You had a rough idea of what would happen after ten or fifteen minutes. It would either be a case of: "We're going to win this" or "This is going to be tough, but we should still win it." Shortly after losing in Scotland, we beat Ireland 32–4 at the Arms Park and Mr Dawes was most unhappy with our performance. I remember thinking: "What do you have to do to please this guy?"'

Courage at Test level is often taken for granted; the courage that drives the genuinely hard men through the pain of physical damage without allowing it to affect their contribution. For all his willowy appearance, Davies was as tough as old boots and never more so than in his last match for Wales, the Grand Slam decider against France at the Arms, on Saturday, 6 March 1976.

Wales won a ferocious duel, the match turning on an incident that showcased the indestructible JPR Williams. He saved them with a shoulder charge, which prevented Jean-Francois Gourdon from touching down at the Taff end and re-routed the French right wing towards the terracing beneath the North Stand, a tackle that under subsequent laws would have justified a penalty try for France and a red card for the Welsh full-back. Above all, Wales got home that day because their captain refused to leave the bridge and succumb to a collective French mugging.

'I remember being run over by the entire French pack in the first five minutes and thinking that I might have to go off,' he said. 'Someone's stud had gone through a muscle in the front of my shin and left a hole in my leg, which I've still got. That was fairly standard French practice. Pick on one player and give him the treatment. The ball was 20 yards away at the time.

'Gerry Lewis, the trainer, came on and said I'd have to come off. I said: "I'm not bloody well going off, mate." When the adrenalin is pumping, there is no pain, unless you start thinking about it. By the end of the game, I was struggling, but by then we had it pretty well sewn up. Winning for the Lions was an incredible experience but winning for Wales was that bit closer to my heart. If I had to single out one game, it would be that last one against France.'

At the end, an ecstatic group of fans carried him shoulder-high, like a conquering Roman general leaving the scene of battle for the last time. Davies really ought not to have been on the field that day, or any other day. Had his case history been delved into a little deeper, it would have revealed that Davies should probably have been advised to quit three years earlier, at the age of twenty-five. In April 1972, he had suffered a brain haemorrhage either during or immediately after a routine club match for London Welsh against London Irish. True to form, he went the distance despite suffering a headache that he likened to 'the entire All Black pack doing the Haka inside my skull'.

'I collapsed in the showers and was rushed to Roehampton Hospital. I was there for a few days and seemed to recover. Bright lights were affecting me and when I mentioned that, they said it was a minimal bleed, which had been caused by an inflammation of the nerve ends of the brain. Really, my career should have ended there and then. Other players, like Bill Beaumont and Keith Jarrett, had a similar sort of thing and had to retire. They were told: "That's it." From a personal perspective, therefore, I was fortunate to have four more years.'

The wrong diagnosis had long been forgotten when the Swansea team disembarked into familiar territory, the Wales captain back at his favourite stamping ground, to prepare for the unenviable task of shifting the one obstacle standing between them and the Welsh Cup final – Pontypool.

'I have only a vague recollection of being in the dressing-room prior to the game. People have told me since that they thought I was out of sorts, that I wasn't my normal self, but they put that down to the importance of the occasion. Before any match, I'd always go into a little corner of the dressing-room so I could think alone and get myself organised.

'My colleagues thought I looked a bit tense, more so than usual, quieter and more reserved. My memory of everything else that day has gone. I knew nothing about what had happened to me for six weeks. The world was my oyster in terms of rugby football. I felt that day, as I always felt going into any game, invincible.

'The season would finish and then I could look forward to the next one and being captain of the Lions in New Zealand. Then, in the blink of an eye, it was gone – and gone forever. I had been used to treading the hallowed turf of the great rugby grounds of the world. I went from doing that to not being able to beat my 12-month-old son at tiddlywinks. I'd gone from such a high to such a low that I found it very difficult to cope.'

The second, almost terminal haemorrhage struck 28 minutes into the match, causing Davies to collapse in open play with the ball nowhere near him and every Pontypool opponent otherwise engaged in pursuing it. Roy Woodward had scored the second of his first-half tries, which put Swansea through to the final when the captain went down in a heap. Baden Evans was the first Whites player to reach him.

'I couldn't get his gumshield out and I made a mess of his lips trying to rip it clear,' Evans said. 'It was obvious there was something seriously wrong. For a few seconds there was no breathing, then some heavy panting, then nothing. I was worried in case he had swallowed his tongue. Then the paramedics arrived, opened his mouth and cleared the airways.'

For more than a week, Davies lay 'seriously ill' in the neurological unit of the University of Wales Hospital in Cardiff. Neurosurgeon Robert Weekes admitted that yes, the captain of Wales was indeed fighting for his life. It wasn't until nine days had elapsed, nine days of tests and painstaking analyses of the results, that Mr Weekes operated. Davies admits he was lucky to survive.

'They cut along my hairline from the centre of my forehead to the tip of my ear, peeled back my skin, drilled a hole in my skull and got on with the job,' he said, unaware that he had very nearly died in the ambulance. 'The stakes were high. The slightest mistake could have caused irreparable damage or even death.'

Eventually, he recovered sufficiently to be removed from the danger list. Davies knew from that day he was lucky to be alive. He also knew that nothing would ever be the same again.

'It destroyed my life. But I was totally unaware that my life was in the balance,' he said on a sunny day at home in Swansea in May 2010. 'When I regained consciousness, there was no strength in the left side of my body. I was blind in one eye. Keeping any sort of balance was very difficult. The weakness in my limbs meant I had lost coordination. I knew that was it. There would be no more rugby.

'I told myself: "Be thankful that you've done everything you wanted to do, except for one." OK, the '77 Lions was not going to be, but at least I was alive. Hundreds of people were waiting to see me; there were telegrams and letters from all over the world. I had no idea that it was such a big thing and I shall forever be grateful for every single one of them.

'What do you do without rugby? Rugby, to me, was like a drug. Every Saturday, you turned up for the kick-off and you got rid of all your inhibitions and problems. It was a totally mind-clearing exercise. Without that outlet for the hassles of the week, what do you do? Suddenly, there was no way of releasing the tension.

'You have no escape. Without that, for a period of time I was lost. Inevitably, your family and friends suffer. You do things you shouldn't have done, like drink too much. There were other times when the lack of coordination made me look drunk when I wasn't. You ask yourself, why did it have to happen to me? I've asked myself that question many times. Fortunately, the last time was about 20 years ago.

'It took me a while to get myself back into some sort of normal way of life. There are certain problems that you learn to live with. The human body is an amazing piece of kit and I'm fine. Life's good.

'I've always acknowledged that I'm lucky to be alive because if it had happened somewhere else, I probably wouldn't have survived. They had doctors in attendance who were geared up for just such an emergency. I'd stopped breathing immediately after I went down and they gave me mouth-to-mouth resuscitation. The hospital being in close proximity was another big factor in my favour because I'd stopped breathing two or three times during the half-mile journey from the ground.

'Then they had to delay the operation and wait until I got stronger. When they realised that wasn't going to happen, they went ahead. Had it happened at home, sitting in my chair watching television, I would probably have been a goner.'

In the days and weeks that followed, the whole of Wales awaited every hospital bulletin with bated breath. Thanks to the skill and dedication of the medical team, Davies slowly recovered, by which time more than 3,000 letters from well-wishers had flooded into the hospital.

Inevitably, the trauma provoked speculation as to whether the blows of a violent, physical contact sport had caused his brain to haemorrhage. A few years later, in January 1982, another neurosurgeon advised another famous Lion, the England captain Bill Beaumont, to retire without further ado because of the cumulative effect of the blows he had taken.

'The wear and tear to my neck was causing me to have blackouts,' Beaumont said. 'I was warned that I could end up suffering permanent damage, which would affect the rest of my bodily functions. It could have affected the nerve ends of my brain and there was simply no point taking the risk.'

Six months later, Davies had recovered sufficiently from the sledgehammer blow to be back at work, representing the industrial clothing company owned by Len Blyth and subsequently run by his son Roger, both Welsh internationals in their own right. Davies still made the Lions tour in New Zealand the following summer, adopting a role very different from the one he had been promised.

In hindsight, Merve wished he had given it a swerve. An unhappy tour grew steadily unhappier, with coach Dawes and manager George Burrell breaking off diplomatic relations with journalists from Britain and Ireland, as well as New Zealand. It was Davies' misfortune to be caught in the crossfire through no fault of his own, having agreed to do a series of ghosted articles for the *Daily Mirror*.

Ludicrously, the Lions management refused to make an exception in Davies' case, a failure that resulted in an embarrassing bust-up between the former Wales captain and the former Wales coach who had offered him the captaincy in London less than 18 months earlier. Dawes also happened to be his 'great friend and mentor'.

Davies discovered all too rapidly that, whatever the special nature of his relationship with Dawes, it did not earn him any immunity from the coach's hostility towards those writing or commentating about the tour. Allan Martin, the lineout specialist who locked hundreds of Welsh scrums, with Davies packing down behind him, spotted his old skipper after one match and, being a friendly sort, the Aberavon second row invited him into the team room for a beer.

An embarrassing incident ensued. 'Who should walk past but George Burrell, the Lions manager,' Davies said. 'He said to Dawes: "What's he doing in here? Get him out."'

The balloon really went up at an end-of-tour party thrown by the New Zealand Rugby Union on the evening of the fourth and final Test.

'I was probably very unwise to have gone on the tour,' Davies said. 'Yes, I wrote a few articles for the *Mirror*, but I stayed away from the team.

'Our paths crossed occasionally and, when they did, I discovered how bad relations were between the Lions and the press. Players had been barred from talking to reporters and I was viewed as another reporter, even though I had been invited to that function as a guest of the New Zealand Rugby Union.

'I was at the bar with Clem Thomas, who was covering the tour for *The Observer*. John Dawes came up and said: "Merve, no press are allowed in here." I then had a fall-out, which cost me a friendship for the next three or four years.

'I said: "John, I'm leaving, but the only reason I'm leaving is that I don't want to cause any hassle. You haven't invited me here. The New Zealand Union have invited me. It's got f*** all to do with you."

'I walked out, but I'm happy to say that we resolved the issue in time and continue to be the best of friends.'

According to no less a judge than Willie John McBride, who has more than a rough idea of what it takes to lead a winning Lions squad, the miserable trek round the All Blacks' kingdom in 1977 would have been very different if only Davies had been at the helm, as had been planned. 'As a captain for Wales, he led like a Lion,' McBride said. 'I am sure he would have been the difference between success and failure on that tour of New Zealand.'

Roger Uttley, the outstanding captaincy candidate outside Wales, missed the honour of a lifetime because of injury. Another member of the invincibles from the previous Lions tour, to South Africa three years earlier, Phil Bennett, had the distinction of leading the team. The experience turned out to be a miserable one for a player who was honest enough to admit, with typical candour, that he was the wrong man for the job.

'I should never have accepted the captaincy of the Lions tour in 1977,' he said. 'I have spent many a wistful hour thinking what may have been achieved had the leadership gone to someone far better equipped than I to deal with the pressures of a three-month expedition.'

It is fair to say that Davies the international rugby player proved to be infinitely more successful than Davies the soothsayer. His autobiography, published in 2004, contained a classic prophecy of doom: 'I do not think we will win another Grand Slam. I hope and pray we will, but I cannot see it.'

'Wales had been so dreadful in the 1980s and '90s,' he said. 'Things went from bad to worse. I've had to eat my words many times.'

While not defending his ability as a clairvoyant, it has to be said that the two Grand Slams of the early twenty-first century defied the odds. The first in 2005, under Gareth Thomas's captaincy and Mike Ruddock's coaching, came out of the blue. The second, three years later, under Ryan Jones's captaincy and Warren Gatland's coaching, came from even further out of the blue. Considering that he's had to eat so many words over so long a period, Davies can count himself fortunate to have avoided a chronic case of indigestion.

There have been many outstanding captains during the last half-century of team sport, and a few great ones, from Richie Benaud to Franz Beckenbauer, Bobby Moore to Martin Johnson. Then there was the Welshman who might, just might, have gone down in rugby history as the winner of three Grand Slams and the only Lion to win successive Test series in New Zealand.

11
PLAYER OF THE CENTURY

Gareth Edwards

Born: Gwaun-cae-Gurwen, 12 July 1947

Just before the Americans and Europeans began to shoot it out over a thousand acres or so of rolling parkland in the Usk Valley on a soggy September in 2010, their respective teams had listened to speeches made by three people from very different backgrounds. Their presence on the eve of the biggest biennial sporting contest between the continents said everything about the significance of a duel named after a seed merchant from St Albans.

Samuel Ryder can never have envisaged that the eponymous event launched during the '20s would one day assume enough importance for the respective captains to have their players, multimillionaires one and all, addressed by inspirational speakers. In their quest for a little motivational magic at Celtic Manor, the Americans listened to a decorated war veteran from the state of Oklahoma, Major Dan Rooney.

'I am an F16 fighter pilot,' Rooney said, recalling his talk to the team the night before the first day of the first Ryder Cup in Wales. 'I've done a few tours of duty in Iraq, but I am also a PGA [Professional Golf Association] professional. That's a unique combination to be able to speak from. When we go into combat we become one unit. I was sharing a little of my background and inspiration about what it's like to come together as a team for a bigger cause.

'Among the specific stories I shared was the fact that in 2008 I was in Iraq watching that year's Ryder Cup at Valhalla and how the competition is much bigger than just about the team playing over here in Wales. It's also about what it means to the armed forces.

'I also shared the story of how in 2006 my life took a new direction when I was on [a] United Airlines flight waiting to fly to Michigan and there were the remains of a soldier killed in Iraq being taken home. This led me to set up the Folds of Honor foundation to help [those] who have had somebody killed or disabled in Iraq and Afghanistan. It's a continuation of what we do on the field of battle: we never leave a man behind.'

Major Rooney ended his speech by presenting each of the 12 players with a leather aviator jacket, as used by fighter pilots in the United States Air Force since the First World War. 'These had the Ryder Cup and their names on them,' he said. 'I handed them over to Corey [team captain, Corey Pavin], Tiger Woods, Phil Mickleson and everybody. It was a very spiritual, very special time we spent together.'

His final observation enhanced the idea of it being a military operation designed to ensure that Uncle Sam still had a grip on Old Sam's gold trophy at the conclusion of what was to be the longest Ryder Cup of all. 'There is a great warrior spirit,' Major Rooney said before a shot had been fired. 'And we certainly hope we pull it off on hostile territory.'

The European nerve centre, in the same hotel, had been specially soundproofed to ensure that whatever was said remained within its four walls and out of American earshot, presumably on the basis that careless talk could undermine the entire operation, as planned by captain Colin Montgomerie. While the Americans sat 'spellbound' by their fighter pilot, Europe treated their team to the thoughts of two sportsmen from similar working-class backgrounds.

Severiano Ballesteros was one, addressing a Ryder Cup team for the last time some seven months before his death in May 2011 at the age of 54. Unable to travel because of his terminal illness, the stricken champion spoke by telephone from his home in Spain. At the team dinner, Montgomerie turned to his second speaker, Gareth Edwards.

By then, he had already introduced him to a wider audience, briefing those American sports writers who looked a bit vacant at the mention of Edwards. 'Gareth Edwards is a legend in these parts,' he told them during a pre-tournament press conference. 'He has to be Wales' most famous sportsman of all time.'

And so, for the first time, an international sportsman made the quantum leap from the great stadia of the rugby world to help weld a team of individual golfing superstars from various countries, used to playing for nobody other than themselves, into a team with the collective backbone to beat the might of the Stars and Stripes.

The Europeans talked and chatted to the Spanish labourer's son who electrified golf with his attitude that no shot was impossible to craft. They listened to the indomitable Lion of a scrum-half from Gwaun-cae-Gurwen in the Swansea Valley, a place they could never have heard of let alone pronounce, and Montgomerie duly acclaimed both speeches 'fantastic'.

'We didn't need to be motivated,' he said. 'The motivation was from losing two years ago. I was after passion and, by God, I got it.'

Anxious to leave no stone unturned, he had also consulted others, notably Sir Alex Ferguson. 'Sir Alex and the likes of Gareth were the first on the list for me,' he said. 'To get advice from a former Lions player of Gareth's status, and Ferguson, who has brought big egos together over the years, would prove useful. We are rarely brought together in golf in a team competition and there are 12 large egos that I have to cope with. I have to make sure they are playing for each other.

'Gareth is someone I have got to know from pro-ams at the Wales Open. He was also a member of the steering committee to bring the Ryder Cup to Wales. He was a truly great team player and he offered a fascinating insight into how the Lions brought together players from Wales, England, Scotland and Ireland to conquer the world.'

Some of those he addressed, like Martin Kaymer from Germany, would have been hard pushed to know their rucks from their mauls, but Edwards knew a lot about what it took to bring a disparate group of sportsmen from four countries and put them under one banner. He had a few rib-tickling anecdotes up his sleeve, too, the funniest of them revolving around the inimitable Bobby Windsor, his Wales and Lions teammate.

'To be asked by Monty to address the European players was

something beyond my wildest dreams,' he said. 'During the dinner, he stood up and said: "Gareth, would you like to say a few words to the boys?"

'I had watched Ryder Cups in this country and in America for many years, never imagining for one minute that I'd ever be a part of it. So when I stood up, I touched on my experiences with the Lions as an example of players from different countries coming together in a common cause. I talked about Bobby and Willie John McBride in a light-hearted Lions context to get the message across.

'The whole point was that this was a team event. I said: "Like it or not, you guys really have to rely on one another in the coming days. That half-point which you will have to dig out against the odds could very easily be the half-point to make all the difference." The players were very receptive and they said afterwards that they'd enjoyed it.

'It was a very small contribution and if what I said provided a little bit of motivation that helped them on their way to victory, then that was great. The wonderful thing was that my wife Maureen and I were both given official badges that said "European team No. 9" and "European team No. 10". They allowed us to get inside the ropes and have the best seats in the house. It was a sheer delight, a unique experience.'

No slouch with a handicap as low as eight, there was rather more to Edwards than merely being the best rugby player of the twentieth century, as voted by readers of the monthly magazine *Rugby World*. To the European golfers, he knew what he was talking about, having negotiated his way around half of the hazardous Ryder Cup course earlier that week when, with more than a little help from Ian Woosnam, the all-Welsh pairing finished one-up on Sam Torrance and Sir Ian Botham before a gallery several thousand strong.

The mind boggles as to what Edwards might have achieved had someone confiscated the rugby ball and put a sawn-off golf club into his hand as a nine year old whose natural athleticism separated him from the common herd. He could, had he put his mind to it, have been an outstanding gymnast or a professional footballer.

Had fate not dictated otherwise, Edwards would have signed for Swansea Town, as they were then, in the spring of 1963. The 15-year-old left-winger had scored twice for Swansea in the final of the

Welsh Youth Cup and the club's manager, Trevor Morris, set out the next morning on the half-hour journey to the Edwards family home in the village of Gwaun-cae-Gurwen.

Swansea had long established itself as a cradle of international footballers, including the Charles brothers, John and Mel; the Allchurch brothers, Ivor and Len; Trevor Ford, Cliff Jones, Terry Medwin and the unrelated James boys, Leighton and Robbie, to name but a few. Morris had the gift of the gab to underpin the management skills that made him one of the finest soccer salesmen before the sport succumbed to the economics of the madhouse.

However, despite his considerable powers of persuasion, the Welsh-speaking Morris was getting nowhere at the Edwards home until he had the nous to shift from English to the native tongue. Morris, a pilot in the RAF's bomber command during the Second World War, recalled the moment several years before his death in February 2003 in his 83rd year.

'We met in his grandmother's house and the atmosphere was not all that convivial until I asked for a cup of tea in Welsh,' he said. 'We were sitting there talking about the virtues of soccer and rugby and not getting very far when that one request suddenly changed the whole atmosphere. The grandmother's eyes lit up and I even got an extra lump of sugar. I could sense that, like my own grandmother, she only trusted Welshmen. The rest were all foreigners.'

Morris duly left with a spring in his step – and a contract in his pocket. He had signed Gareth Edwards, on one condition: that the boy's education came first. Despite the risk of an academic stumbling block, Morris returned to his modest office at Vetch Field happy that he had done everything possible to secure the services of a highly promising youngster.

'Gareth was a special case,' Morris said. 'I realised he had something and all the reports bore that out. He had all the requisite skills. He was strong, he was fast, he had two good feet and he wasn't afraid. He would have made a really good professional soccer player but, at that time, he was undecided about furthering his education. So before he signed, we agreed to a condition that if he chose to stay at school, I would release him from the contract. When he changed his mind, we were very disappointed to lose him.'

Had Edwards not been offered a scholarship to one of Britain's most famous public schools, Millfield in Somerset, the course of Welsh footballing history in both codes would have taken two very different turns. Soccer's loss turned out to be rugby's gain, with a vengeance.

'I was just about to start a soccer career with the Swans when I got an 11th-hour reprieve to go to Millfield,' Edwards said. 'If that opportunity hadn't arisen, I'd have gone to the Vetch. I had the chance of trials at quite a number of bigger clubs, but I'd have been happy to start at the Vetch because they had such a good reputation for developing local players.'

Edwards owed a debt of gratitude to Bill Samuel, his mentor and coach since they first came across each other at Pontardawe Secondary Technical School when the pupil was 14. In his book, *Rugby: Body and Soul*, Samuel described how he discussed at length with Edwards' parents the prospects of his protégé pursuing a career in professional football.

'I had no objection to Gareth becoming a soccer apprentice,' Samuel had told Glan Edwards and his wife, Annie. 'It would suit Gareth perfectly. No more schooling. An idyllic existence. Ever since I have been in the Tech, I have seen excited boys going on trials to some of the top clubs in the country. Not one of them made the grade.

'I am a qualified soccer coach and referee. What would Manchester United do if I recommended a promising boy to them? Not only would they thank me, they'd send me a cheque as well, providing the boy was any good. Name your club, Gareth. I'll fix a trial period for you.'

When asked by Mrs Edwards what he would do if it were his son, Samuel said: 'I am sorry, Mrs Edwards. He must make that decision for himself. I can write on his behalf to Manchester United, Arsenal, Spurs, or he can work for his O-levels to become a PE teacher and play rugby for Wales.'

According to legend, the observation elicited a sharp riposte from Edwards' mother: 'Play rugby for Wales? He'll be lucky to play for Cwmgors [a neighbouring village with its own rugby club].'

It sounds baffling in retrospect but some fairly shrewd judges

183

viewed the schoolboy, pre-Millfield, as nothing more than an average scrum-half. He promised a great deal more as a gymnast and athlete, so much so that those who knew their onions believed he could have represented Great Britain at both.

His athletics prowess had earned him the Welsh national long-jump title before Samuel smoothed his path for the longest jump of all, one which took the coalminer's son from a council house in the Swansea Valley to an English public school in Somerset with a reputation for taking the privileged sporting elite and making them more elite. At the beginning, Millfield was somewhat less than impressed by the Welsh boy's personal best in the long jump, 21 ft 6 in. The school informed Samuel: 'We have a 12-year-old boy from Brazil who jumps 25 feet.'

Soon Edwards blossomed in the hothouse sporting environment – to such an extent that he rapidly developed into a British schoolboy track champion by winning the sprint hurdles. In doing so, he beat an English boy who recovered to become an Olympian of some repute before making it big in the field of sports marketing, Alan Pascoe.

Very soon, Edwards the rugby player would outpace Edwards the hurdler and Edwards the gymnast. Within a year of leaving Millfield and enrolling as a student teacher at what was then known as Cardiff Training College, now the University of Wales Institute, he was playing for Wales on the strength of a spectacularly short apprenticeship at club level.

Six months after his debut for Cardiff RFC, Edwards won his first Wales cap, against France at Stade Colombes, aged 19. He slept so soundly the night before that they had to wake him up at half-past nine the next morning, or so the story goes. If true, it was about the only time anyone ever caught him napping.

Far from being overawed by the rarefied atmosphere of Paris, or anywhere else, Edwards took to it with the composure of a seasoned campaigner who had it all, with the glaring exception of an adequate pass. He was still in the process of rectifying the weakness when, after four matches, Edwards found himself no longer one-fifteenth of the team but in charge of it. At 20, he was the youngest Wales captain of all time.

His reign may not have lasted that long, but his stratospheric consistency and apparent immunity from injury meant that throughout 11 years as the most automatic of automatic choices, he left the field just twice, the first against England at Twickenham on 28 February 1970. The only other instance of Edwards failing to go the distance followed three years later, against Australia.

Twickenham in 1970 turned out to be a unique occasion, the only one where Wales, losing 13–6 in the second half *with* Edwards, turned the match upside down and won 17–13 *without* him. That they did so was due largely to the impact of substitute scrum-half Ray 'Chicko' Hopkins of Maesteg. Edwards having broken the habit of a lifetime by succumbing to a hamstring problem, his long-suffering understudy had 20 minutes to make the most of a rare event.

Seldom can anyone in any sport have made so much from so little time. Hopkins – adamant that his nickname is 'Chicko', as in chicken, and has therefore been misspelled all these years as 'Chico' – announced himself by shooting down the blind side to make a try for JPR Williams before scoring the match-winner himself from an English overthrow into their lineout, which has long earned him a place in Welsh folklore.

Chicko, used to kicking his heels as the redundant reserve while the immovable Edwards reeled off game after game, took his seat near the royal box at Twickenham, having convinced himself that his day had come at last. 'I sat next to a young chap by the name of Phil Bennett and I said to him before the start: "I've got a funny feeling this is the day I get my cap. You mark my words."

'Phil shook his head. "Forget it, Chicko. Gareth never gets injured." When he did get injured, it wasn't clear that he was going to come off, but I didn't wait. I ripped off my tracksuit and shot down from the stand towards the touchline. Gareth was there, humming and hawing about the effect of the injury, and Jack Young, one of the selectors, was asking him whether he could carry on.

'I'd been sub to Gareth 19 times and I didn't hang about. I ran on and I heard Jack shouting after me: "Kick it up in the air." The first time I got the ball I did just that. From then on, everything fell into place for me. In the last minute, we had a scrum in our own 25 and I was praying that the ref wouldn't penalise me for a crooked feed. I kicked the ball, it went forty yards, bounced another ten yards into touch and everyone thought: "Christ, he's a good player."'

For all that, Hopkins never played for Wales again. The subsequent cheapening of the cap, as highlighted by the Welsh Rugby Union's shameful decision to award them for the friendly against the Barbarians in June 2011, has done nothing to ease his sense of grievance. Even after all these years, Hopkins still feels short-changed that Wales did him a disservice at crucial times during Edwards' unprecedented run of 53 consecutive Tests.

'Gareth was lucky because it was a great team,' he said. 'I filled in for him on three or four different occasions in non-Test matches for Wales and they didn't miss him. I should have been picked for the first Test in New Zealand the previous year, but Gareth walked in bandaged up from his knee to his belly and they still picked him.

'Clive Rowlands, then the coach, said to me years later: "That was the biggest mistake I made. You should have played."

'On his day, Gareth was great, but there were times when he wasn't great. I felt I should have been picked for the final match of the 1970 season against France. After beating England, we went to Ireland for the Triple Crown and lost 14–0. Gareth and Barry John were terrible that day. That was the time I felt he should have been dropped, but then he never was.'

Hopkins also came up trumps the only other time he took over from his compatriot, during the Lions' winning series in New Zealand in 1971.

By the time the Wales number 9 position became briefly vacant for the only other time during Edwards' rule, for all of 90 seconds against Australia in 1973, Hopkins had gone north to rugby league. Just as he had made his only Wales bow at Headquarters three years earlier, so another of Edwards' high-class number 2s, Clive Shell of Aberavon, made his against the Wallabies.

The bare facts of Edwards' Test record present incontrovertible proof of his success at home and abroad. In the 11 years from 1967 to 1978, Wales played 22 matches in the Five Nations at Cardiff Arms Park with their supreme scrum-half at the helm: they won 21, losing to France in 1968 when Les Bleus won their first Grand Slam.

'You'd hear all the singing and you knew they were on your side,' he said. 'When you came out of the dressing-room, you felt like Popeye after the spinach.'

In the finest showbiz tradition, he went out leaving them clamouring for more. A third Welsh Grand Slam, achieved against France on 18 March 1978, brought his career to a suitable climax. Two of his three tours as a Lion have a special place in history as the first, and hitherto only, series win in New Zealand (1971) followed by the invincible tour of South Africa (1974).

When *Rugby World* conducted a global poll of many world authorities on the game to rank the 100 greatest players of all time, the experts decided that Edwards was truly peerless. They put him first in a top ten that included Serge Blanco, Colin Meads, JPR Williams, Gerald Davies, Mike Gibson, Barry John, Philippe Sella, Frik du Preez and Willie John McBride.

Cliff Morgan, ranked a long way down that particular list at 69th, did not need anyone to tell him what he knew about Edwards all along. 'I've always said that, of all the players I've known during 50-odd years' involvement with the game, Edwards stood out head and shoulders above the rest. Not only was he a great gymnast, he also had all the physical attributes, not least a strong pair of shoulders and a strong neck. And he was fast.

'What Edwards also had, and it's one thing which I believe is essential to great sportsmen, was 250-degree vision. Even if he was looking straight ahead, he could sense when there were players on either side and what they were doing. He was unbelievable.'

Despite performing in an era when television coverage of Lions tours never amounted to more than the occasional highlights programme, Edwards' fame spread far and wide. On top of everything else, he had a penchant for scoring stupendous tries, like the long-range solo effort launched from almost 80 yards out against Scotland at the Arms Park in February 1972.

Perhaps only Edwards could have come up with something still more outrageous at the same venue 11 months later, for the Barbarians against the All Blacks, this time with more than a little help from his friends. The most celebrated try since William Webb Ellis picked up the football at Rugby School stemmed from Phil Bennett mesmerising the Kiwis in front of his own posts.

In his native Auckland, a nine-year-old boy sat transfixed in front of the television during the early hours of a Sunday morning. Despite unhappy family memories of the Welsh and their victory at Cardiff in 1953 over an All Black team that included the boy's father, Sean Fitzpatrick eliminated every single New Zealander from his imagination when Edwards finished the try with a hurtling dive over the line.

'My dad got me up in the middle of the night so I could watch the match with him and what I saw was just sensational,' he said. 'It made such an impression on me that from then on, whenever my brother and I played footie out in the backyard, I was always Gareth Edwards.'

The late Sir Terry McLean, the distinguished New Zealand journalist, who had seen them all come and go for most of the twentieth century, reported the final stage of the Baa-Baas' try as follows:

> At about 45 yards from the All Blacks' goal-line, [Tommy] David passed to Edwards. Kent Lambert, a Clydesdale type, gave chase to Edwards, who was Thousand Guineas stuff. Whether the try was the greatest ever, as is still contended, is unimportant. Simply, it was perfection.

The masterpiece, which required stitching from many hands once Bennett had delved into his magic box, surprised the Baa-Baas and their glittering array of Lions as much as anyone else. They went into the match fretting over their own sloppiness on the training field at Penarth in wintry conditions.

'We'd had the worst sort of preparation we'd had for any game,' Edwards said. 'We practised for two days on a sloping pitch and a muddy field. If I threw a decent pass to Phil, he dropped it. If he actually caught it and passed it to Mike Gibson, he fumbled it. JPR, of all people, actually dropped passes. No matter what we did, it was clumsy. Bloody awful.

'In the actual game, all I can remember was my energy being sapped. I was thinking: "The ball's got to go to touch so we can get our second wind." So when it went deep into the corner and Phil went scampering after it, I thought: "Thank God. He'll put it into touch."

'Then, all of a sudden, Phil had to run with it because he was surprised at how quickly their flanker had come up. So I had to let the players go past me. I thought I'd better follow up because, as a scrum-half, if the ball goes to ground and I'm not following up, they'd all say it was because I hadn't been training hard enough.

'By the time I turned around and started to go after them, I was generating some pace. So when Derek Quinnell went to pass to John Bevan, who was outside, I was picking up pace and their full-back was expecting the ball to go to Bevan. When I came into the line, I shouted to Derek: "Give it to me." I took the ball and that injection of pace took me round the full-back.

'I can remember seeing someone out of the corner of my eye closing on me and I can remember praying: "Don't let my hamstring go now." My PE master always told me to dive from five yards out because it is harder for them to tackle you. So I just dived into the corner.'

During his eleven years with Wales and the Lions, spanning sixty-three Tests, Edwards had only five outside halves – David Watkins (2 matches), Barry John (28), Phil Bennett (28), John Bevan of Aberavon – not John Bevan the ex-Cardiff wing – (4) and Mike Gibson (1).

Edwards' durability did not happen by accident. 'I don't think I've ever met anyone who worked as hard as Gareth did to perfect his game,' Watkins said. 'You would only have to mention once that some part wasn't quite right and it would be put right the next time you saw him. He was way ahead of his time. Very few players then had such a professional attitude. Second best was never good enough.'

Edwards was briefly partnered with Gibson, the distinguished Ulsterman, during the first of his three Lions tours, to South Africa in 1968. John, against whom he had first played during a regional schools trial as a 16 year old, broke his collarbone during the first Test of that series.

Gibson and Edwards were an item for only one match, a 6–6 draw at Port Elizabeth. They would have remained in harness for the rest of the trip had the Welshman not torn a hamstring during the week of the third Test, the only bad injury of his career – an astonishing fact, considering how he pushed himself to the limit of his physicality in the red jerseys of Wales and the Lions.

The range of Edwards' pass from the scrum, which gave John a few more atoms of space in which to work his magic, came about not by accident but through sheer dint of hard work. 'He would practise with a leather rugby ball filled with sand to develop distance,' Bill Samuel said. 'He used a car tyre attached by a rope to a hook in the ceiling to create a pendulum through whose centre he would pass the ball as it moved to and fro. He was pressure-trained for reflex action.'

Edwards and John, then college boys aged 19 and 20 respectively, first played together for the Probables in a Welsh trial in January 1967, a few weeks after the latter made his debut against Australia. A pairing made in heaven had begun in less than promising circumstances a few days earlier, when they arranged to meet on a rugby pitch at Johnstown on the outskirts of Carmarthen for a primitive introductory session.

'I'd been out with the boys the night before, with the result that Gareth had to knock for me at about half-past eleven on the Sunday morning,' John said. 'I thought: "Do we really have to?"'

'It was pouring with rain, but we went out and threw a few balls around. I was out there in a pair of gym shoes and slipping all over the place in the mud. At one point we had a discussion and I said: "Look, Gareth. You throw it, I'll catch it."'

'And he said: "Listen, I'll get passes out to you that nobody else would think of. So be prepared."'

'And with that we called it a day. We'd been out there for only fifteen minutes, but by then we were like two drowned rats.'

Edwards proved true to his word and John was never more grateful than against the All Blacks for the Lions in 1971. 'Some of the passes were so long and accurate that I felt a bit like the man at the counter of the post office, rubber-stamping each one as I moved it on,' he said. 'I could have played at times in a duffel coat and still done my job without any problem because he made it so easy.

'I had the greatest scrum-half on the inside, and arguably the greatest centre on the outside in Mike Gibson. People talk about Gareth's long pass but, in many cases, the shorter pass had an even greater impact. He had such terrific upper-body strength that even when he was badly off balance and his whole weight was in the wrong direction, he could still get the ball out to me. Some of those passes only travelled five yards, but they would take about ten players out of the game because nobody believed he could possibly get the ball out to me from such hopeless positions. He could flick it with his fingertips.'

He could also be relied on to lighten the grind of a training session with a little mischief, as happened during the course of Wales winning the Grand Slam in 1976. A sudden outbreak of 'mayhem' stemmed from Edwards calling a variation on the back-row moves for the flankers, Tommy David and Trefor Evans.

'We wanted to keep the signals simple,' Edwards explained. 'Tommy was from Pontypridd and Trefor from Swansea, so we based them around P and S. Anything with a P was for Tommy, anything with an S for Trevor. We had a few easy shouts like sugar and salt, play and pepper. Couldn't be simpler. Everything was going like clockwork. So, at the next set scrum, they waited for me to call the word.

'I shouted: "Psychology!" Well, talk about mayhem. Tommy ran smack into Trefor and ended up on the floor. Trefor was a bit sharper and avoided the worst of the contact. They weren't allowed to forget that one in a hurry.'

In addition to everything else, Edwards also had an uncanny knack of ensuring he never overstretched himself. The in-built alarm system rang when the Lions sounded him out for a fourth tour, to New Zealand in 1977, and Edwards, like JPR, chose to stay at home. Those who went will swear to their dying days that the Lions would have won a third successive series had two of the pillars of six years earlier revisited the scenes of their triumph.

Nor was there the remotest danger of Edwards going on too long with Wales. He took his final bow against France in March 1978 with a third Grand Slam at the age of 30, having decided to quit after a gruelling 80 minutes in Dublin a fortnight earlier, when Wales took care of a triple Triple Crown.

'Physically, they didn't come any tougher than that,' he said. 'I wasn't enjoying it as much as I used to, to the point where at one stage in that match in Dublin I thought to myself: "What am I doing here?" There had always been such a thrill every time I played for Wales, but by '77 it was no longer quite what it used to be. I came to the conclusion that after that there was nothing left to go for.'

In an era when the amateur reactionaries recoiled in horror at the thought of a World Cup and anything else that smacked of professionalism, Edwards had done it all. More to the point, he had done it so well that almost 30 years after hanging up his boots his towering status remains undimmed by the passing of time.

Will Carling, still in nappies when Edwards made his Cardiff debut at 19 against Coventry on 17 September 1966, named his 50 greatest players of all time, or at least as he thought they were, in August 2007. The England captain, who also won three Grand Slams, had no hesitation in putting Edwards at No. 1, with the rest of the top ten, in descending order: Michael Jones (New Zealand), David Campese (Australia), Jonah Lomu (New Zealand), Serge Blanco (France), Danie Gerber (South Africa), Hugo Porta (Argentina), Martin Johnson (England), Zinzan Brooke (New Zealand) and Brian O'Driscoll (Ireland).

'It's hard to compare generations, yet Edwards is the one guy I can say who would have been great whenever he played,' Carling said. 'He was a supreme athlete, with supreme skills; the complete package. He played in the 1970s but, if he played now, he would still be the best. He was outstanding at running, passing, kicking and reading the game. He sits astride the whole of rugby as the ultimate athlete on the pitch.'

That Carling found room for only one other Welshman in the first twenty, JPR Williams, at No. 20, puts his choice of Edwards into a steeper perspective. Only five other Welshmen made the fifty: Barry John (28), Gerald Davies (36), Phil Bennett (38), Rob Howley (39) and Graham Price (46).

As soon as he had finished one career, Edwards found more time to devote to another sport where the only combat element is to be found at the end of a fishing rod. In 1990, he claimed the British angling record for the biggest pike, a 45 lb 6 oz monster that he reeled in at Llandegfedd Reservoir in Monmouthshire.

Edwards, whose directorships include one for the Cardiff Blues regional team, was made a CBE in 1997, his 50th year. Shortly afterwards, Wales showed its appreciation of a unique player in a unique way. They commissioned a sculpture of him passing the ball and gave it a prime location in the middle of the St David's Centre in Cardiff, a large mall designed to cater for thousands of shoppers. It stands not far from Queen Street and the statue of another crusading Welshman, Aneurin Bevan, the creator of Britain's welfare state.

12

THE BOY WONDER

Keith Jarrett

Born: Newport, 18 May 1948

The ultimate accolade for any individual in a team sport is to have a match renamed in his or her memory. To capture the public imagination on such a scale demands a performance so far out of the ordinary that the player concerned becomes forever synonymous with the event which, by the very excellence of its nature, can be guaranteed to stand the test of time.

The Matthews Cup Final, for example, is still spoken of as precisely that by every generation since Sir Stanley wove his magic into football folklore during the final moments of the 1953 FA Cup final between Blackpool and Bolton Wanderers at Wembley a few weeks before the coronation of Queen Elizabeth II. Blackpool, losing 3–1 with time fast running out, won 4–3 and Matthews finally earned himself a winner's medal at the grand old age of 38.

Stan Mortensen made it possible by scoring a hat-trick and yet he scarcely warrants much more than a footnote in the record book. All very strange, and stranger still, given that nobody has managed a cup final hat-trick in more than half a century since the Matthews final.

Cricket's most astounding example of a single player monopolising a Test match occurred in the summer of 1956, during the third England–Australia match at Old Trafford, when Jim Laker took all ten Australian wickets in the first innings and nine more in the second, unheard of before or since. For a while, the Surrey off-spinner found that his name had become a verb, to Laker, as in to rout or to run through the opposition like a dose of salts.

And then, on a sunny spring Saturday, 15 April 1967, along came an 18-year-old boy from a background as colourfully improbable as his Test debut, a boy whose father had played county cricket for Warwickshire and Glamorgan and whose grandfather, a Polish Jew by the name of Jarewski, had moved from southern Africa to London between the wars to further his career as a concert pianist.

What transpired under a blazing sun has gone down in history from that day to this as the Keith Jarrett match – Wales 34 England 21, at Cardiff Arms Park, the last fixture of that year's Five Nations Championship. In the days leading up to the event itself there was not the faintest clue that a boy who had left school only four months earlier had it in him to take the rugby world by storm.

On the contrary, there were those who feared the worst, that the selectors, that august body of men revered in good times as 'the Big Five' and ridiculed in bad times as 'the Blundering Five', had taken leave of their senses. Wales, rock bottom of the Five Nations, had been beaten by Scotland, Ireland and France. England, the dreaded enemy, fancied their chances of rubbing it in, driven by the incentive of perhaps sharing the title with France.

The way some saw it back then, Wales's selection of a new full-back would prove to be every bit as pointless as the team's general predicament. The sum total of their endeavour over three matches amounted to two tries, by Stuart Watkins against Scotland at Murrayfield and Dewi Bebb against France at Stade Colombes.

Jarrett had not been around long enough to be considered a novice. Only a few months earlier, he had been lining up for Monmouth School at the national seven-a-side schools' championships at Rosslyn Park in London. On 17 December 1966, he played his last match for Monmouth, against Llandovery College. Seven days later, on Christmas Eve, he made his Newport debut at Ebbw Vale.

Now, barely 100 days later, the Welsh selectors were adamant about picking him in defiance of all conventional wisdom, or so it seemed. What few games Jarrett played for Newport's first team were all at outside centre, which meant the Big Five were not only going to pick a boy almost straight out of the classroom, they were going to play him in a position in which he had never played before. It was either going to be a stroke of genius or madness.

Twelve days before the England match, they asked Newport to pick Jarrett at full-back for their weekend derby at Newbridge. Newport found themselves on the horns of a dilemma, torn between doing something in the national interest, but at the same time not wishing to run the severe risk of paying a hefty price in terms of lost pride against local rivals.

With some reluctance, the Black and Ambers acceded to the request, making every effort to help Wales see the bigger picture, while privately unable to see it for themselves. Jarrett played at full-back for 40 minutes that Saturday before it was decided enough time had been wasted on the experiment that had been foisted upon them.

Jarrett may have been good enough to play full-back for Wales, but not for Newport. They decided they would lose unless they switched the fumbling teenager back into his natural midfield habitat and restored John Anthony, the specialist full-back who had been temporarily sacrificed, to normal service.

At half-time, the half-baked idea of Jarrett at full-back got short shrift. As luck would have it, who should find himself charged with the responsibility of flying in the face of the selectors but the captain of Wales and Newport, David Watkins. He knew he had to cut his club's losses while there was still time to do something about it before a precarious position deteriorated into an embarrassing defeat.

'Newbridge was a big game for us because of the incredible rivalry,' Watkins said. 'Keith made a few mistakes early on and we thought there was a danger that it would ruin him. He was having a bit of a nightmare. I then moved him from full-back to centre because I wanted to make sure we had the best chance of winning a game that we wanted to win badly.

'I was too engrossed in that to wonder what the Welsh selectors would make of it. To be perfectly honest, we didn't like them telling us where to pick him in the first place. In the old days when the national selectors told you to pick so-and-so in a certain position, you did it, but people at the club were peeved about it.

'My reaction to change things halfway through was an instinctive one. Walking off the pitch at the end, I did think to myself: has that ruined Keith's chance of playing for Wales? When I moved him to centre, where he was much more effective, I thought I'd thrown away his international cap, but I had to do what I thought was best for the team.

'Keith had been introduced to the club while he was still at Monmouth School and he had begun to make a reputation for himself right away. There was no doubting his potential to be an outstanding rugby player because he could do just about anything. Maybe that was why the selectors stuck to their guns and picked him at full-back in spite of his problems there at Newbridge.'

The change convinced more than a few at the Welfare Ground that some of the Welsh selectors had gone soft in the head, though it was better for Jarrett to have dropped a few clangers in a club match watched by a few thousand than at the Arms Park against England with millions watching him suffer a similar fate on television.

In their desire to pick a callow youth who was patently not a full-back, or so it seemed, they ignored another who most definitely was. John Peter Rhys Williams, a doctor's son from Bridgend who had begun to make a name for himself as a tennis player, had turned 18 at the start of the previous month and would have given his eye teeth for a crack at England. JPR would have to bide his time until the following year. Wales were going to pick Jarrett, come hell or high water.

'When the team to play England was announced, everyone was aghast,' Watkins said. 'We all thought: "Bloody hell . . ." From a personal point of view, as a Newport player, I was pleased that another Newport player had been picked, but I didn't know how he was going to cope.

'His selection came completely out of the blue. Nobody could understand where the idea came from. Fortunately, Keith was the sort of guy who was never fazed by anyone or anything. It all came easily to him, which was one reason why he was always hugely confident and laid-back. The only advice I gave him before the match was to stand a fair way back because they were bound to fire a few up-and-unders at him. I did my best to look after him, but I knew Keith was definitely not the type who would have lain awake all night thinking, what if?'

Watkins had more than enough on his plate without worrying unduly about the new boy. He had captained the Lions in two of their four Tests in New Zealand the previous summer only to find himself discarded by Wales against Australia before Christmas and superseded by a 20 year old from Cefneithin – Barry John. Restored for the England game, Watkins knew his future depended on a home win.

Apart from a younger rival who was being acclaimed as the next big thing in world rugby, and who would rapidly fulfil every prophecy, Watkins was confronted by the grim reality of a Five Nations whitewash. 'You lived from one game to the next, hoping you'd done enough to keep your place but without really knowing whether you had,' Watkins said. 'We all said we would do everything we could to help Keith out on every occasion. We shouldn't have worried because he was made for the big time. He listened to everything and took it all in, with the air of someone who looked as though he wanted to say: "Don't worry about me, fellas." Nerves never seemed to be part of his make-up.'

After the obligatory Friday night film, the Wales team returned to their central Cardiff hotel, the Angel on the corner of Westgate Street, for a few sandwiches, tea or coffee and bed. The newcomer may have given the impression of not suffering from nerves, but nothing could have been further from the truth that Friday night. Sharing a room with Newport teammate Stuart Watkins, Jarrett found himself in such a state of anxiety that the pair of them got out of bed, dressed and sneaked out of the hotel. Heads down, they walked a few hundred yards to a nightclub where, had they been spotted, the fairy tale later that same day might never have happened.

'I was never a good sleeper at the best of times,' Jarrett said. 'Five or six hours and I'd have done well. We'd watched the cowboy film, come back about half-past ten, had a cup of coffee, went to bed. I kept tossing and turning. Neither of us could get to sleep so Stuart said: "Come on. We'll get up."

'We got dressed and went out at what must have been about a quarter to midnight. Round the corner in St Mary Street there was this little nightclub and at the top there was a piano bar. We had a couple of pints up there and 45 minutes later we came back. I went straight to sleep and nobody was ever any the wiser. Luckily, nobody spotted us, but it certainly did the job in terms of relaxing me.'

The Monday morning after the climax to the 2011 US Masters golf tournament gave Jarrett a topical example of what jangling nerves can do to a sportsman, contributing at Augusta during the final round to Rory McIlroy's demise from potentially the second-youngest winner of the Green Jacket after Tiger Woods to a distraught also-ran.

'A lot of people have always said to me: "You're not showing any nerves,"' Jarrett said at his home in the Gwent countryside. 'I was so nervous, like that poor lad McIlroy. He looked as though he was bubbling over with the tension of the occasion and I was exactly the same. I knew what he was going through because I'd been through it myself.

'Yet people still say to me: "Oh, you handled that well." I was a very nervous type, whether it was cricket, athletics or rugby. The stomach was always heaving and that, with the rush of adrenalin, spurs you on to make occasions memorable. I didn't have a clue what was going to happen when I went out against England because I'd never been in a position like that before.

'Well, that's not quite true – since playing in the Wales trial in January of that year, I had been a reserve in the three matches before the English game. From that perspective, it wasn't new.'

Wales walked, as they did in those days, the 100 metres or so from their hotel to the other side of Westgate Street and down the ramp beneath the North Stand at the Arms Park. By the time they walked back up again a few hours later, Jarrett had been transformed from nervous teenager into national hero.

Before leaving the hotel, he checked to make sure he had enough cigarettes to last him until the end of the match. 'I smoked then, but I wouldn't smoke in the dressing-room – well, not before a match,' he said. 'We had a team meeting before lunch and at the end of it I'd go out for a quiet smoke. I remember Brian Price, who was in charge of the pack, saying to the forwards: "At the first lineout, I don't want any of you to jump. Let them have the ball and we go through and show them we're there."

'Basically, I'd just played schools rugby, apart from a few months with Newport, and I'd never heard tactics like that. There was nothing dirty done. It was just a way of letting England know what they were up against.'

Jarrett owed the most unexpected of opportunities to the fact that Terry Price had missed six shots at goal in Paris a fortnight earlier, when another teenager, Gareth Edwards, had won his first cap. Although nobody knew it then, Price had played his last match for Wales and within a matter of months had gone north to Bradford Northern for £10,000.

Wales needed a new goal-kicker and the selectors, headed by the pre-war fly-half Cliff Jones, made Jarrett the chosen one.

Jones called the new boy to a meeting at a few hours' notice four days before the match. What the chairman of selectors told him could not have been bettered, combining as it did the wisdom of Job and the foresight of Nostradamus.

'I knew they wanted me for my kicking,' Jarrett said. 'I would have thought they would have put me on the wing, as Monmouthshire did. Cliff Jones was the boss man. On the Tuesday of that week, he said: "I want to see you and David at Rodney Parade this afternoon."

'He said: "Keith, I could meet you every day for the next five years and I still wouldn't be able to teach you how to become a full-back because it would take too long. All I'm going to tell you to do against England on Saturday is this: stand at least 30–40 yards behind Dai Watkins' backside. Stand that far back and you will be running onto the ball as opposed to turning and going backwards." If he hadn't said that to me, I doubt whether I'd have been in the position to score that try.'

The selectors had nailed their colours to the Jarrett mast the night *before* his unhappy experience at Newbridge. The news came through during a birthday party for another Newport centre, John 'Dick' Uzzell, whose famous drop goal at Rodney Parade on 30 October 1963 sank Sir Wilson Whineray's All Blacks, their only defeat during a thirty-six-match tour spanning four months.

'Colette, Dick's wife, hasn't stopped telling me off to the present day because once the call came through, everyone forgot it was Dick's birthday,' Jarrett said.

The mountainous apprehension hanging over the game began to

disappear in the matter of minutes it took Jarrett to start performing his primary function by kicking the opening penalty. Despite it falling comfortably within his range, he still needed a friendly ricochet off the woodwork to help the ball on its way.

'It just crept over off the post, which shows you how nervous I was,' he said. 'It was on the left side of the field, on the English 25, about halfway to the touchline. I just had enough strength in my leg. The second penalty was much better and that helped settle me down.'

Despite England controlling chunks of the match, their bombardment never came to anything at any stage of a game that Wales led from start to finish. 'I saw little bits of the match over the next ten to twenty years, but I'd never seen it from start to finish. The BBC gave me a copy of the film, which I gave to Monmouth School. They had the huge projector and all the equipment. Whenever it rained on match days during the cricket season, they'd go into the assembly hall and watch that game.

'Years later, a friend of mine turned the old tape into a DVD, which enhanced the quality no end. So I sat in his front room and watched the whole game through. It changed my entire concept of the game. I'd been telling everyone that the Welsh pack were so on top that the English half-backs didn't have much chance to test me.

'The truth was that the English forwards were in control. Sitting there watching the match, I almost began to think that the result of the match on this film would be different to the one which I had played in. I was shocked at what I saw. England were so much on top, I could hardly believe it.

'I think I had to collect one early ball. If Dai Watkins had been playing outside half for them, he would have had me running from one touchline to the other. I never understood why England didn't do that.'

There are dream debuts and then there are debuts beyond dreams because they come straight out of a Hans Christian Andersen book of make-believe. Jarrett's belonged to the second category, his tally of 19 points including a 70-metre solo try, which he then converted from the touchline.

Yet England had filed into the Arms Park convinced they had the weaponry for the job. Of all their big guns, none proved bigger that day than John Barton, the Coventry second-row forward who would become the first Englishman to score two tries at the old shrine of Welsh rugby. He would also be the last – a feat that would be reduced largely to an irrelevance, vanishing like a puff of smoke from Jarrett's last drag of his fag before stubbing it out to light up the history books.

'We went onto the pitch that day feeling very confident,' Barton said. 'They had a kid at full-back who had never played there before and we talked beforehand about testing the new bloke. As far as we were concerned, that was an area of huge weakness that we reckoned we could exploit.'

So much for the theory: admirable in concept, utterly useless in practice. 'The kid' began by kicking two early penalties. Barton, lauded as the 'best forward on the field', pulled England back with the first of his tries, then worth a measly three points. Despite two more Jarrett goals, England had cut the deficit to four points when they unwittingly set Jarrett up for his *coup de grâce*, a long-range try straight out of the Boy Wonder textbook.

Nobody who was there that day will have ever forgotten it, how Jarrett seized a long punt from the Moseley centre Colin McFadyean and ran like the wind along the left-hand touchline, leaving every prospective English tackler in his slipstream. Jarrett, still waiting for the bombardment, could hardly believe his luck.

'[McFadyean] hoofed it, and I suppose it could have bounced into touch. Instead, it bounced straight up. I'd been in a situation like that once or twice in schoolboy matches, where, on a hot day and a dry pitch, the ball would sit straight up and hang there, almost as if it's waiting for you to catch it.

'You see the ball going up and you think: "I've got 20 or 30 yards to run. If I get a move on, I'll catch it before it bounces." That was about the only gamble I made that day and it came off. I'd been there before, so I knew what I had to do. Once you go for it, there's no time even for a split-second's hesitation while you wonder whether you've made the right decision.

'I went for it, hoped for the best and it came off. I was nearer the ten-yard line than the 25. I was running at an angle towards touch, which meant I had four or five yards to straighten up. Keith Savage, the Northampton winger, was there and it was only because of the angle of the run that I got past him.

'Then I looked up and couldn't see any English player between me and the line. I'm thinking: "Where are they?" I don't remember seeing anyone. All I had to do was get up the touchline as fast as I could, and I don't think anyone was close to me when I put the ball down.

'Because I was kicking the goal, you would assume I would have gone in as close to the post to make the conversion easier. I was so glad to reach the line that I forgot about doing that. It was a beautiful day from start to finish, not a cloud in the sky.'

Lining up behind the posts with the rest of a deflated England team, Barton knew the game was up and that two more Welsh points would be winging their way from the touchline. By then, he had been left with an indelible rear view of Jarrett, speeding away into the blue yonder.

'Everything Keith touched that day turned to gold,' Barton said. 'They ran us ragged and the new boy at full-back was responsible for most of it. I can still see him now, the ball popping up into his hands and him taking off for the corner. Someone tried to get across but missed his tackle. The try was a real last nail in the coffin for us. And then he hit the conversion from way out off the pinnacle of the post and over.'

Barton did get a little of his own back on England's behalf, even if by then it was hopelessly late, merely a matter of reducing the margin of defeat from 18 points to 13. 'I caught Jarrett with the ball. We grabbed him and I ripped it from his hands and went over for the try. Scoring two tries in an international made that match my fondest memory, irrespective of the result.'

Just as he had lit up the stadium, so Jarrett did likewise when he got back to the dressing-room. 'I had a fag,' he said. 'My concern was about seeing my father, who was at the game. Then someone came in and said I was wanted on *Grandstand*. I was still in my kit, so I had to walk quickly round the North Stand to the bottom of this 30-foot ladder to the studio.

'When I got to the top, the first person I saw was my headmaster from Monmouth School, Robert Glover. He used to watch the 1st

XV and he'd be walking up and down the touchline, barking this, that and the other.

'I went back, had a shower and got changed. I came out and bumped into my father about 40 yards from the Cardiff Athletic Club. There were thousands of people around and it was difficult to stay still, so we walked towards the clubhouse. He was very emotional and he passed that trait on to me.

'You're either emotional or you're not. Sometimes that can be a little embarrassing. When I first saw Dad, we looked at each other and neither of us could speak. There were a few tears. We weren't bawling, but it was very emotional. I didn't realise how big a deal it was until I had calls from all the newspapers and a couple from America, the *New York Times* and the *New York Post*.

'I had a few pints after the game at the banquet, where I was presented with my cap and after that a party. I was very pleased to have a lift back home to Newport.'

England lost despite some formidable support in the shape of a Test cricketer of ample girth, Colin Milburn, whose presence ensured that the night went with an extra swing and that, had it been an eating contest, England would have won hands down. 'I bumped into Colin in the players' lounge and, after the dinner, we headed out into the town with Gerald Davies,' Barton said.

'Colin and I finished up in a curry house. Now, I thought I could eat, but I've never seen anyone eat like Colin. I'd have needed a shovel to keep up with him and, even if I'd had one, I doubt whether it would have been enough. Everyone, of course, was talking about the star of the day, Keith Jarrett. He was in our company for part of the evening until he got dragged away. Everyone wanted to talk to him and no wonder. It was as if he'd said to himself that afternoon: "Right . . . I'm here, so I might as well have a go." He was absolutely tremendous.'

Jarrett woke up on Sunday morning to find he had become an overnight sensation. An old school friend, Trevor Williams, did his best to make Sunday as normal as possible.

'Trevor, who's now my next-door neighbour, knew what sort of state I'd be in on the Sunday morning,' Jarrett said. 'So he said: "We're going to lunch tomorrow. We'll go down to the Foresters Arms." I'm told there was quite a melee outside and that's when I began to realise that what I'd done was news.

'Yes, I did well that day and it made me. It changed my life. I bought my house in the early '70s from the money I got for turning professional. I had a couple of bad moments at the end of that year, 1967. It got so bad that I couldn't kick the ball. I wasn't playing badly in the centre, but my kicking went. I tried everything to get it right but nothing worked.'

To say the Jarretts took a roundabout route to Wales is to put it mildly. Harry Jarrett, born in Johannesburg in 1907, went to school in Nairobi, where he learnt to play cricket well enough to pursue a career as a professional during the '30s, first with Warwickshire, then with Glamorgan. His son also played for the county, if far too briefly for his liking.

Within six weeks of his heroics against England, Jarrett batted at number five for Glamorgan against India, a fixture that marked the official opening of the county's new headquarters at Sophia Gardens in Cardiff. Any prospect of another fairy-tale debut dissolved into a duck, which left him more time than he would have liked to look at the new surroundings.

His second match, against Pakistan at Swansea in August 1967 – when Majid Khan made the fastest 100 of the season in 61 minutes, and hit 13 sixes in his 147 – turned out to be his last. He made nine in the first innings, eighteen not out in the second and went for sixty-six in twelve overs without taking a wicket.

Jarrett's paternal grandparents had moved from their native Poland to South Africa at the turn of the twentieth century. 'My grandfather was a concert pianist and composer who came over to London in the late '20s or early '30s,' he said. 'Unfortunately, I didn't get any of that musical talent. My grandparents ended up in Bulawayo and not many people there wanted music lessons, which was why they moved to Highgate, North London, where he continued his music career. My ancestors were everything but English.'

Much to his surprise, Jarrett went to South Africa in 1968 as a privileged guest, a member of the British and Irish Lions. 'I didn't give the tour a second thought because I was struggling with aspects of my game,' he said. 'I got picked to play for the London Welsh

President's XV against London Welsh towards the end of that season never realising that it was doubling up as a late Lions trial.

'I didn't have a clue as to the significance of the match until one of the London reporters, Terry Godwin, rang me and said: "Congratulations, Keith. You played so well today, you're going on the Lions tour." That came as such a bombshell that it really took some believing. I didn't have a good tour, for one reason or another, but it was still a fantastic experience.'

By then, David Watkins had turned professional with Salford, cashing in his union chips to the tune of £16,000, a record for a union player. After his debut, Jarrett resisted all sorts of blandishments from rugby league, but it would be only a matter of time before the money talked.

'Suddenly, Keith had gone from nobody to being in great demand,' Watkins said. 'Barrow had seen him in action against England and their chairman, Bill Oxley, came down to South Wales to make him an offer. Barrow wasn't the place to go because it was so far out of the way.

'The only advice I gave Keith was to make sure he got as much as he could up front. Some players signed for, say, £6,000 without realising they had to play for four or five seasons to get their money. You were relinquishing your amateur status and you had to make sure you were being fairly compensated. The signing-on fee was regarded by the Inland Revenue as a tax-free gift. Wigan also made Keith an offer, but it wasn't as big as the one from Barrow.'

Barrow eventually got their man, in October 1969 for £14,000. 'I also had offers from Leeds and St Helens,' Jarrett said. 'The chairman of Salford, Brian Snape, said to me: "Why didn't you come to Salford?"

'I said: "Well, you didn't offer me any money."

'He replied: "What?"

'We never made a penny playing rugby union and we never expected to. Expenses were strictly controlled and I remember Gwilym Treharne, the London Welsh scrum-half who played for Newport while he was studying at Caerleon, claiming bus fares of two shillings, five and a halfpenny. Nick Carter, the Newport secretary, gave him 2s 5d one week and 2s 6d the next week, which shows you how amateur the game was.

'I had no intention of going north. I'd seen a couple of rugby league cup finals at Wembley in the late '60s and realised what a hard game it was. I wasn't that aggressive because union then wasn't what it's like now. I'd take a bump and give one, but no more than that.

'One question kept niggling away at the back of my mind: are you man enough to go and play that game? These offers kept coming in and deep down I was thinking: well, you've got to have a go.

'Why Barrow? Because they were at least £4,000 ahead of the field. For the money they paid me, you could have bought two of the more expensive Rolls-Royces. How much are they today? A week after signing I caught a train up there with a small suitcase and I envisaged seeing people in flat caps and mufflers, like out of a Lowry painting. I couldn't have been more wrong. The setting was beautiful, looking out across Morecambe Bay, with Lake Windermere 15 minutes away.

'Whichever rugby league club I went to, I knew I had to learn the game and where better to learn it than with a side of grafters? If I improved as I hoped I would, another club would come for me, which is what happened.'

By then, he was on borrowed time as a rugby player and there wasn't much of it left, not that Jarrett had any way of knowing. He moved from Barrow to Wigan shortly before the first of three strokes stopped him in his tracks at the age of 24, in March 1973.

'The first one came totally out of the blue,' he said. 'I had a disagreement with Barrow at the end of '72. They said they were building a side around me but, apart from a couple of minders in the first few months, they didn't put their hands in their pockets. I told them I wanted to go and eventually they did a deal with Wigan, in March '73.

'I was living in South Wales and it wasn't ideal to be travelling back and forth. To say I kept in full training would have been a lie, but I was keeping up to a certain level. All the travelling could have been one of the possible reasons why I was ill.

'We were playing against Salford on the Friday night. I'd had a bang on the head and I was given a couple of big aspirins to thin the blood. I drove home after the game for a rest because I'd been chosen to play against Bradford the following week in the Challenge Cup.

'I got up on the Monday morning, went downstairs to make a cup of coffee as normal, dropped the top of the coffee pot and bent down to pick it up. Then, bang! Beryl (Mrs Jarrett) was in the kitchen making toast. I was always larking about. She saw me and didn't take much notice, thinking it was another lark. When she saw I was in exactly the same position a couple of minutes later, she realised something was wrong. The doctor was there within ten–fifteen minutes at the very most, could have been less. I was in the Royal Gwent within half an hour. I couldn't speak properly. I'd go to say something and something else would come out. It was quite frightening.

'I had time to think, and then you begin to dwell on things, like: "How can I get back onto the rugby field? I'll tell them I've smoked a hell of a lot." I did smoke, but not as much as I told the doctors. I told them I'd smoked between 60 and 80 a day. I thought if I gave them up now, I can keep playing.

'That must have stuck because they thought that if I smoked that much, maybe it wasn't so surprising that this had happened. I didn't smoke anywhere near that many, rather between 20 or 30, which was still too many.

'Ever since the first stroke, I've always had certain problems. My right side, even now, is much weaker than the other side. My balance isn't brilliant. At the time I felt so fit, and that made it all the harder to accept the medical advice that I could not play rugby again. I was only 24.

'Within 12 months, I was playing cricket for Newport, as I did for several years after that. I wasn't quite as forceful a batsman as I had been earlier, but I could contribute. Then I had another stroke, in '79. I was in California with my wife and the two kids. We landed in LA and went down to San Diego. I didn't feel 100 per cent. I was walking into glass doors, going into the swimming pool with my watch on. I took the family to the zoo on this particular day and, coming back, something wasn't right. I made a beeline for the hotel and took a couple of aspirin for my headache. Ten days later I came up to San Francisco and we went across to Hawaii, but I was getting better all the time.

'The next year, 1980, was the big one. I was working in the scrap business, sitting in the office, and the headaches were terrible. I wanted to cover my head with something dark and curl up. It got so bad that I went to the doctor. Then I found out I'd had another serious stroke. I wasn't as fit then as I'd been before. I was almost a vegetable for most of 1981 and 1982, in that I wasn't capable of doing much at all.

'My speech took a long time to come back. If I did anything that made me tired, I'd start slurring my words and people thought I'd been drinking. A friend of mine said: "How do you fancy being a quantity surveyor?" That got me back to work and back to normality.

'People ask me whether I feel lucky to survive three strokes. Lots of people have strokes, the vast majority of them in excess of 60 years old. Being so young did help. The neurologist at the University of Wales Hospital in Cardiff, Robert Weekes, said: "All I can tell you is: bad luck."

'I didn't know I'd had the second one until I'd had the third one. The MRI scan showed up the one I'd had twelve months previously. The first and third were in exactly the same spot, at the junction of blood vessels in the brain. Mervyn Davies had a subarachnoid haemorrhage between the brain and the skull. Mine was in the brain. Between the brain and the skull you can operate, but of course you can't go into the brain unless it is a matter of life or death.

'I finally gave up cigarettes in '91. Like thousands of others, I'd tried to kick the habit so many times. I quietened down and made a conscious effort to try to stop rushing around. I'd go into the garden. If I did too much digging and started feeling light-headed, I paid attention to the alarm bells. I put my spade away and said: "That's enough for today."

Years of heavy smoking had taken a toll. 'Once or twice I'd get short of breath,' Jarrett said. 'I went to the doctor, saying I don't understand why I'm short of breath. He gave me a test that entailed blowing into a tube to measure lung capacity. Because of my smoking over the years, I'd lost about 20 to 25 per cent of my lung capacity. I wish I could speak to young people about cigarette smoking and warn them exactly what it means and what it can do to ruin your life. If I'd had my time over again, I'd never have smoked.'

Meteoric was hardly the word for Jarrett. His Newport and Wales careers came and went within three years, from his first match for the Black and Ambers at Ebbw Vale in December 1966 to his last, against Bath on 24 September 1969; from his Test debut in April 1967 to his last, against Australia at the Sydney Cricket Ground, on 21 June 1969.

He played his first game of rugby league at 21 in October 1969 and his last, for Wigan, in March 1973. Jarrett has no bitterness over the cruelty of a fate, which decreed he was all washed up as a rugby player at the ridiculously early age of 24. Instead, he counts his blessings – a Welsh championship title with his home-town club, a Lions tour, a Wales tour to New Zealand and surely the most sensational debut of all time.

No wonder they called him 'Batman'. It was so perfect in every sense that anything thereafter was always liable to suffer by comparison. 'I suspected that from the start and it wasn't long before I had to accept it,' he said. 'I was always striving to do something similar to that first England match and I think I achieved it once. Roger Young, an old friend who played for Ireland and the Lions, invited me to play in a match he organised to mark the centenary of Queen's University in Belfast.

'I played for an international team and it was uncanny. I scored exactly the same number of points I scored against England in exactly the same way, right down to the try. The match may not have been that important, but it still gave me a lot of pleasure.'

The early end to his rugby career served only to burnish the legend of Keith Jarrett. The best of the many stories spun around his prodigious first match for Wales is an apocryphal one. A Cardiff bus driver, taking his vehicle back to the terminus next door to where Ninian Park used to be, spots Jarrett walking along a street and offers him a lift.

As luck would have it, the driver also lives in Newport and offers to take his famous passenger home once he has clocked off. When the driver informs the duty inspector, he is told to take a double-decker instead.

'What would I need a double-decker for,' the driver says. 'There are only the two of us.'

'Because he can go upstairs,' the inspector says, 'and have a smoke . . .

13

DEATH ON THE TRACK

Tom Pryce

Born: Ruthin, 11 June 1949
Died: Kyalami, South Africa, 5 March 1977, aged 27

On a wintry Sunday afternoon in the middle of March 1975, a policeman's son from Ruthin stood on top of the podium at the Brands Hatch Grand Prix circuit. Tom Pryce, the victor's garland around his neck and a typically shy grin on his face, had become the first Welsh driver to win a Formula One race. It would, they all agreed, be the first of many.

Snow forced the delay of the annual Race of Champions before turning to heavy rain, another hazard for the drivers on a course already buffeted by high winds. A high calibre field featured the reigning world champion from Brazil, Emerson Fittipaldi, and a future world champion in the South African Jody Scheckter. Ronnie Peterson, the Swede who finished runner-up to Jackie Stewart in 1971, and the Belgian Jacky Ickx, runner-up to the Scot two years previously, headed the Continental challenge.

Before the end, none of them could see the winner, not because the spray from his slipstream obscured their view but because the newcomer with the Welsh flag embossed on his white helmet had left the field spreadeagled far behind. Pryce negotiated the 40 laps and 104.5 miles with such skill that fully 30 seconds elapsed before the nearest challenger, John Watson from Northern Ireland, took the chequered flag, with Peterson finishing third and Ickx, a full lap behind, fourth.

The Welshman's masterly defiance of the conditions confirmed what the experts had sensed all along, that he had the potential to beat the best anytime, anywhere. What Pryce did that day in Kent was a declaration of intent, not that the most self-effacing of sportsmen would have dared to say so. All he needed was a reasonable amount of time, enough to reinforce his natural ability with a little more experience.

He learnt about the fatal hazards of motor racing during his formative years in the '50s and '60s, when the sport claimed the lives of almost 30 Grand Prix drivers, among them young Tom's idol, Jim Clark, the former world champion from the Scottish Borders who was killed in a Formula Two race at Hockenheim in April 1968 at the age of 32. The family spoke of their son being 'very upset' at the death of the unassuming Scot and that of Jochen Rindt, killed at Monza two years later during the Italian Grand Prix.

Jack Pryce, who became a policeman in Ruthin after serving with the RAF in Bomber Command during the Second World War, knew that the tragedies would not deter his younger son, Thomas Maldwyn, from pursuing his passion for driving at high speed. His father had taken him to see the famous Isle of Man TT motorcycle races before young Maldwyn, as his parents called him, informed Mr and Mrs Pryce that he was going to be a racing driver, on four wheels, not two.

Pryce's mother, Gwyneth, a district nurse, convinced him to enrol at technical college as an apprentice tractor mechanic so he would have something to fall back on, even if it meant abandoning the idea of hurtling around in racing cars for fixing conked-out tractors instead. Maldwyn did study agricultural engineering, but motor racing was the only apprenticeship that really mattered to him.

He announced himself by winning the Crusaders Championship, a series of races for pupil drivers, which Pryce clinched at the age of 20, along with the prize, a Formula Ford Lola T200 worth £1,500. By then, he was known as Tom, if only because some of his English employers and sponsors decided that Maldwyn posed an enunciation issue.

He graduated to Formula One in 1974, making his debut at the Belgian Grand Prix for a racing team called Token, an amalgam of the first names of the joint owners, Tony Vlassopulos and Ken Grob.

Vlassopulos, Greek by birth, a shipping entrepreneur, barrister-at-law and occasional motor-racing commentator, had seen Pryce drive at Goodwood and made a mental note of his name. He and his partner Grob stepped in when the Berkshire-based Rondel Racing enterprise ran into financial problems exacerbated by the oil crisis of the time.

Rondel had been founded by a pair of mechanics, Ron Dennis and Neil Trundle, whose long association with motor racing began during the '60s, when they worked as mechanics for the Australian Jack Brabham, a triple world champion before launching his own racing team. Dennis, now executive chairman of McLaren Automotive, called in a designer, Ray Jessop, to create the Token built at premises in Walton-on-Thames by Trundle, who later became chief of McLaren Racing's special projects division.

'I was left with this hastily built F1 car,' Vlassopulos, the new part-owner, said. 'It was a lovely little car in the green and yellow colours of Lotus. I thought, it's a shame to waste it. I'd spotted Tom and decided he was exactly the sort of chap we needed.'

Car and driver had been entered to take their bow in a non-championship event at Silverstone on 7 April 1974, the International Trophy, as awarded annually by the British Racing Drivers' Club. The Token team had worked round the clock to be ready and finished in such a state of exhaustion that Pryce drove the truck containing the car from its Surrey base to Silverstone in Northamptonshire.

Gearbox problems forced Pryce to retire on the 16th lap from a race won by James Hunt, a dashing Englishman then revving up to be the next Briton to win the world title. The novice from Ruthin made a big enough impression on Vlassopulos at the Belgian Grand Prix for Token's joint-owner to decide they would enter him in the next race on the circuit, the Monaco Grand Prix.

'I went to the organisers and said: "We'll bring Tom and the car down to Monte Carlo tomorrow,"' Vlassopulos said. 'They refused his entry because they said he was too inexperienced. I should have taken the car down to Monaco anyway and put it on the grid. We did the next best thing, which was to enter the Formula Three race before the main event because I wanted everyone to see how good this fellow was and what they were missing.

'I said: "Tom, I'm going to send you to Monaco in our little Formula Three car on one condition. You *have* to win." You couldn't meet a nicer human being, but you couldn't get anything out of him. He was a man of very few words – but on this occasion he didn't utter one.

"'Tom, did you hear what I said? Win the race. And then, don't forget to give the sponsors a wave because that's important."

"'OK."'

Vlassopulos and an entourage of Indonesian sponsors watched the race unfold from their vantage point on the balcony of a hotel. 'After the first two laps, Tom was nowhere to be seen,' Vlassopulos said. 'We're going frantic with worry and then, all of a sudden, there he was leading the race. At the end, I asked him what happened on the first two laps.

'Tom was standing holding the horrible vase they'd given him for winning and said nothing. Trying to get an explanation out of him was like pulling teeth, but after a minute of silence, he finally said: "I missed a gear on the first lap!" Missed a gear and still won by a mile!'

Suddenly, Pryce was the talk of the sport. 'All the F1 teams were after him and no wonder,' Vlassopulos said. 'Some of the F1 drivers said: "My God, this boy is faster than us and he's in a Formula Three." He proved himself faster than many of them in practice.

'He did it, what's more, in a car that hadn't been tested, and he did it without a sponsor. All he got for winning was a ghastly vase from the sponsor and some prize money, how much I can't remember.

'Murray Walker, the commentator, reckoned Tom drove the finest race he had ever seen. Now, that's saying an awful lot; but you are talking about a young man who would have been world champion, without a doubt. He had all the qualities. Why did Tom go round a corner faster than anyone else? I don't know. It was something inbred.

'I'm 79 and have been watching motor racing all these years and I never saw anyone better than Jim Clark. Put him in a car and he knew instinctively what to do. He had it. Tom was exactly the same and he had the quiet, laid-back personality that reminded us so much of Clark. We already knew that here was a young man who knew how to drive a car very fast with great skill.'

Fast and skilful drivers had been losing their lives at an alarming frequency. The Italian world champion Alberto Ascari and the Englishman Peter Collins were among those killed during the '50s; the German Wolfgang von Trips and Clark, along with too many more throughout the '60s. It is a dreadful irony that one of the big F1 teams signed Pryce to replace a driver who had been killed at Kyalami; three years later, the Welshman would lose his life on the very same circuit.

The driver in question, Peter Revson, a native New Yorker and nephew of the Revlon cosmetics founder Charles Revlon, was also well known as the boyfriend of the reigning Miss World, Marjorie Wallace. He died at the age of 32 on the circuit near Johannesburg driving for the Shadow-Ford team in practice for the South African Grand Prix in March 1974.

In only his fourth race, at the Nurburgring in the German Grand Prix, Pryce ignored all manner of problems to win his first points in the World Drivers' Championship.

The following year, three weeks after his victory in the non-championship F1 Race of Champions, Pryce married Fenella (Nella) Warwick-Smith at St Bartholomew's Church in the Kent village of Otford, near Sevenoaks, after a two-year courtship.

'We met in a disco called Grasshopper,' she said. 'I was there with my sister and Thomas was there with a friend. We chatted a bit and he told me he was involved with cars on the sales side, which wasn't true. I didn't find out until much later that he was a motor-racing driver and when I asked him why he didn't tell me that at the start, he said: "I didn't like to mention it because it sounds rather big-headed."

'That was so typical of Thomas, always so modest, quiet and unassuming, but with a great sense of humour. I didn't particularly like motor racing. It wasn't my thing, but it gradually became my thing as Thomas made his way. He was very determined to do what he wanted to do, which was race. He had enormous talent and a great belief in his talent to make it to the very top. Naturally, he didn't say a word about that to anyone else.

'He knew he could do it, given the right car. His parents, especially his mother, who worked so hard running her own old people's home in Colwyn Bay, helped him greatly when he was starting up. He always used to say: "If I'm not very good, I'll give up rather than waste anyone's money."

'There were others in motor racing who didn't have the talent, but they had the money. They'd often be at the back of the starting grid, and Thomas would often be at or near the front, despite not having the best car. That's how good he was.

'I was just 18 when I went down to Monte Carlo to see him win the race there. I remember the sponsors saying to him: "Make sure you win. And then, when you've won, don't forget to give us a wave." He won and he waved and he received his trophy from Princess Grace. Pressure? What pressure?

'Wives and girlfriends always went to the races, but I was so shy I just wanted to keep out of the way. I was very young when I met Thomas and I came from a different background. I lived in the country, where I could indulge my passion for horses. Neither of us were used to being in the limelight, which was certainly the case for Thomas after his win in Monaco. All the big names wanted him to drive for them.

'Being young and naive, I didn't worry much about the dangers of the sport until I quickly worked out that the death of 28 drivers meant the stakes were dangerously high. Then it began to worry me. I remember another driver being killed in one of Thomas's early races, in Austria. We had all come to this race and someone would not be coming back. That was the awful reality. But when you're as young as we were then, you think you're going to live forever.'

There were two occasions during Pryce's formative racing years when the top drivers put their feet down. In 1969, they refused to compete on the fastest track of all, at Spa in Belgium, following an inspection by Jackie Stewart on behalf of the Grand Prix Drivers' Association. He demanded improvements in safety barriers and road surface.

A second boycott of Spa took place in 1971, forcing the Belgians to find an alternative venue. Spa was not reinstated until 1983, by which time its fourteen-kilometre circuit had been halved to seven. Asked in 1971 whether he would race at Spa, Pryce said: 'Yes, I would at the moment. I haven't been around long enough to argue against anybody about it. I have to learn about the driving and the people behind the teams and the organisation. Obviously, if things are ridiculous and all the other drivers are really against something I shall probably join them, but I'd race at Spa now.'

One of his contemporaries, Roger Williamson from Ashby de la Zouch, died in only his second Grand Prix, the Dutch at Zandvoort in July 1973. Like Pryce, he, too, had been destined for great things until his car overturned and he died from his injuries at the age of 25. Pryce, therefore, was acutely aware of the perils of his profession when another young English driver, Tony Brise, perished not in the cockpit of his racing car but in the passenger seat of an aircraft which crashed in thick fog near London. He was 23.

Despite her dislike of the sport, Nella was there wherever on the globe her husband happened to be racing, with one exception. 'I didn't go with him to Japan because I'd broken my hand riding my horse and decided to stay at home,' she said. 'As soon as he'd gone, I regretted it.

'I recognised the importance of the wives and girlfriends being there to support their men. People think of Grand Prix racing as terribly glamorous, but it isn't. You spend hours travelling and, after a while, the hotels all look the same. I used to do the lap timing, but there was always lots of time when you were just hanging around.

'Thomas always said that driving on the Grand Prix tracks was a lot safer than on the ordinary roads at home. He was such a safe driver that I could go to sleep in the back seat without the slightest fear, although he did lose his licence because of speeding offences. We were in a rush one day and the police stopped him. "Oh, you're Tom Pryce," the officer said. "My son's a great fan of yours. Can I trouble you for your autograph?"

'Thomas was happy to oblige. And then the policeman booked him!

'There was another occasion which also made us laugh. We were driving fast to catch the ferry at Dover for a Formula Two race and we came screeching to a halt when a policeman flagged us down. "Slow down," he said. "Who do you think you are? A motor-racing driver?" Thomas's modesty prevented him from saying: "Well, now that you mention it . . ."'

Pryce led the 1975 British Grand Prix at Silverstone going into the 21st lap before an accident put him out of the race, which was not the only indication of his rising status on and off the track. Soon he would be projected onto the silver screen, appearing in action as himself in the Sydney Pollack-directed film *Bobby Deerfield*, which starred Al Pacino in the title role as a racing driver obsessed by getting to the chequered flag before anyone else.

The film, based on the book *Heaven Has No Favourites*, written by the distinguished German novelist Erich Maria Remarque, the author of the anti-war classic *All Quiet on the Western Front*, dealt with the deathly nature of motor racing. It revolved around how the eponymous central figure's character changes after he witnessed a crash that kills a competitor.

Before the picture came out on general release, the third race of the 1977 F1 season took Mr and Mrs Pryce to Johannesburg for the South African Grand Prix. During the first practice session, in his favourite rain, the only Welsh-speaking driver on the circuit gave another impeccable demonstration of wet-weather driving, setting the fastest time, a full second quicker than the Austrian who would win the world title that year, Niki Lauda.

A Welsh teenager, Andrew Harris, who had emigrated to South Africa with his family three years previously, had followed Pryce from afar after seeing him race at Kyalami the previous year. 'The teams used to arrive at Kyalami about two weeks before the Grand Prix for an extended test session,' Harris wrote as part of a moving tribute, which he sent to BBC Wales. 'During this time, I took the odd day or so off school to visit the track.

'On arrival, I made a beeline for the Shadow pit, where I was very fortunate to meet Tom, talk, take photos and get his autograph. He seemed very relaxed and was looking forward to a good race. He tended to spend most of his time when out of the car just sitting on the garage wall, very quiet and relaxed.

'The night before the race I camped at the track, along with my father and a few of his Welsh friends, and it was very much a party atmosphere. The following morning, armed with my latest copy of *Autosport*, I slipped off into the pits just before the driver parade. I managed to get quite a few autographs – James Hunt, Niki Lauda, Emerson Fittipaldi, Mario Andretti, Jody Scheckter and a few others.

'Walking up to Tom, I noticed there wasn't a photo for him to sign, the only space being an unidentified car in the background. Tom and I agreed that this could be him, so he duly signed. He was very quiet but seemed relaxed and only smiled without saying anything when, in my best Welsh, I said: "*Diolch i chi*'. [Thank you.]" He was the last driver I met that morning. That autograph must have been one of the last he ever signed.

'As he was preparing to get into his car for the divers' parade, I ran back to our seats. We all yelled and waved when Tom came past. One in our group had a Welsh flag and Tom waved back.'

And so the time arrived on that fateful day, Sunday, 5 March 1977, for the main event. After a slow start, Pryce relied on sheer ability to drive his way from the rear of the 23-strong field towards halfway and was tracking Hans Joachim Stuck on the 21st lap when the Welshman's Shadow colleague, Renzo Zorzi, stopped opposite the pits with smoke billowing from the engine. The Italian's mishap triggered a chain of freakish events that resulted in a horrific double fatality.

When flames started to come out of the stricken Shadow's engine, two marshals decided to take their lives in their hands and run across the track as four cars, including Pryce's, hurtled towards them at a speed of almost 180 miles per hour. The first marshal, an unnamed 25 year old, made it across by the grace of God.

The second, Frederik Jansen van Vuuren, aged 19, made his mad dash across the 20 yards of track carrying a 40 lb fire extinguisher for what was later described as a 'minor fire'. Stuck, the German driver heading the four cars roaring towards the brow of a hill a split-second ahead of Pryce, saw van Vuuren, swerved and somehow missed him by a whisker. Pryce, in Stuck's slipstream a matter of feet behind, saw nothing but the rear of the Bavarian's Brabham.

Even had he seen the marshal, Pryce would have had no time to react. Nor was there any room for manoeuvre, with Stuck's car to his right and Zorzi's to his left. Both driver and marshal were killed instantly – van Vuuren by the car, Pryce by the fire extinguisher, which hit him in the face.

Stuck told of how he 'sensed' a marshal running across the track from his right carrying a fire extinguisher and how he missed him by an inch. 'Tom was running right in my slipstream and he had no chance,' Stuck said in David Tremayne's *The Lost Generation*. 'He would just suddenly have been confronted by this guy and hit him head-on. I saw Tom overtake me and I could see the state of the cockpit. I knew he was already dead. That was one of the saddest moments of my life.'

Nella had been in the pit area doing the job she always did when her husband raced. 'I was doing the lap chart,' she said. 'The first thing I noticed was that he didn't come round among the other drivers. I thought: "He'll be there any second."

'I realised within a few minutes that something serious had happened. Various people started coming into the pits. I saw one or two glance at me and I thought: "I don't like the look of this."

'Alan Rees, the Shadow team manager, came in and said: "There has been an accident. Tom has been killed."

'I said: "I don't believe you. I want to see Thomas. Take me to him." I can see that Alan was trying to protect me. I didn't know then that Thomas had been hit on the side of the head by a fire extinguisher and that Alan wanted to spare me any more trauma.

'After a while I went back to the hotel to get my things. Marcia Kerr, the wife of the team's chief mechanic, held my hand all the way back on the eleven-hour flight to London. I was in a profound state of shock. You are heartbroken and angry because that sort of accident should never have happened. It was all so unnecessary, which is what made me so angry.

'Our whole family were devastated. My father [Michael Warwick-Smith] pointed out one day that another family in South Africa were also grieving over the loss of a dear one, a boy of 19. Being kind and considerate, my father said: "Nella, we should write to them and send our sympathy."

'It was such a terrible accident, so brutal that it took many years for me to come to terms with the fact that Thomas had gone. I have had to console myself with the knowledge that he died doing what he loved. He used to say to me: "I'm so lucky. I'm doing what I love and I'm being well paid to do it."

'You get on with your life, but even now it's something which you never really completely get over. It was terrible for my parents-in-law. They were both lovely people who had lost their first son [David John] when he was three years old. They were like second parents and Jack had just retired when the accident happened.

'Like his father, Thomas had a lot of charm. Some in motor racing were affected by the adulation. It turned their heads. And I always said: "I hope it doesn't spoil Thomas." It wouldn't have done because he was never puffed up with his own importance.

'He was naturally a nice person, always one of the team. He wasn't a big drinker, but he'd buy them all a drink, even if he didn't have one himself, and then he'd slip off to bed.

'Welsh, of course, was his first language. He was always very proud of being Welsh and he had already built up a huge following there, which would have been colossal. They all said he would have been world champion.'

His death lent a cruel poignancy to the release shortly afterwards of *Bobby Deerfield*.

'I remember going to see it, thinking this is going to be terrible,' Nella said. 'The filming of Thomas racing had been done the previous year at Le Mans. I managed to sit through it, which included a couple of pieces of Thomas. You just saw his lovely big eyes looking out from underneath his helmet. When the credits rolled up at the end, there was a cross beside his name.'

More deaths followed. By the end of the '70s, the list included two of those whom Pryce had beaten during his victory in the Race of Champions. Ronnie Peterson, third at Brands Hatch and twice world champion runner-up, died, aged 34, following a crash during the 1978 Italian Grand Prix at Monza. Rolf Stommelen, the German who survived multiple injuries after a crash during the 1975 Spanish Grand Prix in Barcelona, was five years older than Peterson when he was killed in California in April 1983.

Pryce will never be forgotten, least of all in his home town. The local council in Ruthin commissioned artist Neil Dalrymple to create a permanent memorial at a place where locals and visitors alike could admire it – on the gable end at the junction of Clwyd Street and Upper Clwyd Street. The lovingly crafted memorial depicts a number of images, including one of a rain cloud, symbolic of Pryce being 'unbeatable in the rain', a point made at the opening ceremony by the driver's boyhood friend, Cledwyn Ashford.

The Formula One fraternity rallied round to meet the cost through a series of online auctions organised by David Richards, chairman of Aston Martin and the motor sport firm Prodrive. The cognoscenti in Ruthin that day were unanimous in their view that Pryce would have been world champion if only he had lived to make the talked-of graduation to the Frank Williams team. To reinforce their belief, they pointed to Alan Jones, the Australian who replaced Pryce and won the world title three years later in a Williams FW7 Cosworth.

As master of the ceremonies, Ashford called upon Nella, immaculate as always in a cream suit, to unveil the memorial on what would have been her husband's 60th birthday, 11 June 2009. Her widowed mother-in-law, Gwyneth, was there, even though she only had months to live.

'Gwyneth was a wonderful person,' Nella said. 'Despite her illness, she decided that nothing would stop her and she managed to stay for the whole day. It is very reassuring to know that Thomas will be remembered.'

Jack Pryce did not live to see his younger son honoured. The retired police sergeant died on 7 March 2007, two days after the 30th anniversary of Kyalami. Gwyneth passed away on 17 October 2009. Nella, who has not remarried, went into the antique business in London and now lives in the south of France, where she breeds Lusitano horses.

The boy who rose from the country lanes of Clwyd to become the finest racing driver produced in Wales – and arguably the world champion Britain never had – lies in the graveyard of the eleventh-century church in the Kent countryside where he and Nella tied the knot just short of two years before his last race.

14

THE MATCHSTICK MAN

Johnny Owen

Born: Merthyr Tydfil, 7 January 1956
Died: Los Angeles, 4 November 1980, aged 24

Johnny Owen's first professional fight outside Wales took him into what was then a war zone: Northern Ireland at the height of the Troubles. At a makeshift arena in a school on the outskirts of the ancient walled city of Derry or Londonderry, depending on political or religious persuasion, he boxed a draw over eight rounds with the former Irish Olympian Neil McLaughlin.

Getting there proved more alarming for the Welsh visitors than the fight itself. Twice, on their journey by car from Belfast airport, they were held up at roadblocks manned by the British Army, the first stops on an odyssey that would come to a tragic end in Los Angeles.

'They pointed their rifles through the window of the car and asked who we were,' Owen's trainer-manager, Dai Gardiner, remembered. 'I said: "We're just a couple of Welsh boys over to do some boxing." It was frightening because we'd never experienced anything like that before, but nothing seemed to ruffle Johnny.

'It was the same during the fight when the lights went out at the end of the third round because of a bomb scare. Everyone was a bit edgy because they didn't know what would happen next – everyone, that is, except Johnny. He was the calmest person in the place.'

The crowd that November night in 1976 had never seen a

bantamweight as tall as the spindly Welshman with the jug ears and the red dragon embossed on his shorts. Once the power supply to Templemore Secondary School had been restored, the contest went the distance without further disruption, apart from a short delay over that bomb scare.

'The Matchstick Man', who had been learning his craft from the age of eight through 126 amateur bouts, winning 108 of them, was on his way.

At 20, Owen had taken the first step on a journey that would lead him to the British, Commonwealth and European titles only to end in downtown Los Angeles with a fatal shot at the world crown held by the Mexican Lupe Pintor. Four years to the day after Owen's modest little entourage returned to his native Merthyr Tydfil from Northern Ireland's second city, they were burying him in a cemetery on a hillside overlooking his home town.

Nobody then could have imagined that the 5 ft 8 in. beanpole was embarking on a career that would take him from a local audience of a few hundred at an Irish school to a crowd of more than 15,000 crammed into the Grand Olympic Auditorium in the most populous city in the richest state in America. Jack Dempsey had been there for the grand opening of what was then the biggest indoor venue in America, built in 1925 for the summer Olympics seven years later.

That Owen fought McLaughlin twice more in a matter of weeks suggested a young man in a hurry to work his way through the ranks. At West Bromwich in January 1977, Owen out-pointed the Irishman over eight rounds and duly did so again barely a fortnight later at home in Merthyr.

'The first thing that struck me about Johnny was his height,' McLaughlin said. 'He was so gangling, and that made him very hard to hit. When I first fought him, nobody had really heard of him outside Wales, but I knew I wasn't being fed a sucker. I was more of a boxer than a fighter and I found him hard to get at.

'When the lights went out during that first fight, we had to hang around until they got them back on. Someone made a crack that I had a twin brother and he'd been slipped into the ring in the darkness because some people thought I was a different boxer when they got the electricity working again.

'I was nearing the end of my time as a boxer when he was just starting. He could string a few punches together, but he wasn't a big puncher. The second time I fought him over in England, he got very frustrated because he couldn't understand why he wasn't able to put me down. Whenever he caught me with a few shots, he'd keep saying: "You've got to go down."

'Normally, I would never speak a word in the ring because you need all your energy and concentration for the job in hand. But that night, for the only time, I did say something. I said: "You can't stop me." And he said: "I'll get you any minute."

'He was getting better with every fight and when I went in with him for the third time in his home town I knew I was up against it. Again, he couldn't stop me. I had a couple of chats with him and I remember he wore a red tie with a skeleton on it. He was a freak and he used his height to good advantage. I thought he was one to watch. He was a nice fella.'

Merthyr is a town steeped in boxing, whose champions include Howard Winstone, Eddie Thomas and the adopted Scot Ken Buchanan. The sport has long been a proud part of its heritage, a tradition that goes all the way back to the early nineteenth century, when the town found itself in the cradle of the Industrial Revolution. Jimmy Wilde, the greatest flyweight of all time, according to no less a judge than Nat Fleischer, founder of *Ring Magazine*, was born just outside the town at Quakers Yard before his family moved to Tylorstown in the Rhondda.

Wilde, whose fame earned him such wonderful nicknames as 'the Mighty Atom' and 'the Ghost with the Hammer in his Hand', was born more than 60 years before Owen and yet Johnny knew enough about him to draw inspiration from his success. He had read about him in a column featuring famous old fighters in the *Pink 'Un*, the *South Wales Echo*'s late, lamented Saturday night football edition. No wonder boxing became such a way of life in Merthyr that it used to be said some baby boys entered the world with their fists clenched.

It was probably the case, too, on 4 January 1956, when Edith Owens gave birth to the fourth of her eight children, John Richard. Boxing was an obsession from childhood and he pursued it with such unrelenting devotion that every waking hour away from his job as a machine operator was used to reach a phenomenal level of fitness. All those lung-searing runs up and down the Brecon Beacons gave him the stamina to unleash assaults of almost cyclonic force on opponents, ultimately wearing them all down, except for one.

The triple McLaughlin experience cleared the way for Owen to win the first of his titles before the end of March 1977, out-pointing George Sutton of Cardiff over ten rounds at Ebbw Vale to become Welsh bantamweight champion and leaving his Cardiff opponent well aware of the strength of the Owen chin. 'He had one of the best chins I ever hit,' Sutton said. 'He always came on strong towards the end.'

Eight months and four wins later, he took the British title from Paddy Maguire, stopping him in eleven rounds beneath the chandeliers at the National Sporting Club in the heart of London in Piccadilly. 'I'll have an orange juice,' an elated Owen said. 'There'll be plenty of time to celebrate when I retire.'

The old champion from West Belfast had been to the West End two years earlier, to Grosvenor House in Mayfair. He relieved Dave Needham of the crown via a technical knockout in the 14th round, thereby avenging his defeat the previous year in the Englishman's home town of Nottingham. And all that happened two years before Owen joined the paid ranks, by which time the Owens family had dropped the final 's' to avoid confusion with another boxer of the same name.

'You looked at Owen and there was nothing of him,' Maguire said at his home in Belfast, stretching his memory back over almost 35 years. 'You'd have thought that if you hit him hard, you'd maybe bust one of his ribs. He may not have looked strong, but I knew I was up against a tough cookie. The thing I remembered most about him was that he had very long arms, longer than I'd ever seen on any boxer.'

At 21, the Welsh challenger was eight years younger than the holder. 'I was finishing and he was on his way up, and in the end they stopped the fight because of a cut above the eye,' Maguire said. 'I don't mean to take anything away from Owen because I thought he was a great fighter. Afterwards, I went into his dressing-room and shook his hand and wished him all the best.'

A few months later, the new champion defended the title against

Wayne Evans, beating his compatriot from Gilfach Goch inside the distance at Ebbw Vale. By the following November, the classy Australian Paul Ferreri had been tempted to the steel town where Aneurin Bevan, the creator of the National Health Service, had been the sitting MP for more than 30 years. Owen saw Ferreri off over 15 rounds, which meant he had now conquered the Commonwealth. He kept busy, almost as if there was no time to lose, and in June 1979 made a successful first defence of both titles, stopping the Londoner Dave Smith in the 12th round at Heddwyn Taylor's promotion in Caerphilly.

At 23, Owen had made the Lonsdale Belt his own personal property. In February 1980, he added Europe to his empire, beating Juan Rodriguez on points and thereby avenging a controversial home-town defeat by the Spaniard in Almeria the previous March. After a third defence of his British title, against the No. 1 contender John Feeney in June of that year, Owen declared himself ready for the big one.

In four years as a professional, he had fought 27 times, winning 25, drawing one (to McLaughlin in Derry) and losing one (to Rodriguez on the Costa del Sol, where, despite a series of dirty tricks, one of which was designed to disrupt the challenger's sleep, Owen, according to British experts, used his superior ring-craft to give Rodriquez a lesson and win everything except the decision).

He had gone from nowhere to having a shot at the world title. Dai Gardiner, Owen's trainer-manager since the 17 year old dropped a points decision to Maurice Sullivan of Cardiff in the Welsh ABA final, found himself unsure about which way to turn next. Four months into his reign as champion of Europe, Owen put his titles on the line against Feeney from Hartlepool and duly out-pointed him over 12 rounds in London. The question then was whether to make a further defence or go for broke by fighting Pintor. The Mexican had won the belt in controversial circumstances the previous year, with a points verdict in Las Vegas over his fellow Mexican Carlos Zarate, the decision so angering the deposed champion that he retired on the spot in disgust.

That Zarate had achieved a unique feat in boxing – putting more than 20 successive opponents out for the full count and then subjecting another 20 to the same fate – gave a rough idea of Pintor's ability to look after himself. He was what they call in the trade 'a banger' – one tough hombre.

'We did have a chance to defend the Commonwealth title and, to be perfectly honest, that was the way I wanted to go,' Gardiner said in a candid interview. 'I would have taken it earlier in the year, but we'd already signed up for the Feeney fight with all titles up for grabs. Johnny won very comfortably and then Mickey Duff, the promoter, began to talk about a world title fight.

'My first reaction was no, because I'd more or less agreed through the agent Paddy Byrne to fight a Danish-African [Mike Irungu] and we'd have been getting pretty much the same amount of money. Duff then negotiated the world title fight.

'Johnny wanted it and he wanted it badly. He kept saying the same thing to me: "Take the world title shot, Dai." Then Johnny, his father and I went up to London to meet Duff. We signed that day and went to America about ten days before the fight.

'Johnny sparred with welterweights and middleweights, strong fighters who would try and push him back in the gym, but even they found that difficult. He was well prepared before we left and he was determined he wouldn't do any sparring in America. They wanted him to do some so the boxing reporters could see him, but he stuck to the pad-work.'

On the night of Friday, 19 September 1980, the Grand Olympic Auditorium was packed to the rafters, every one of the 15,300 seats occupied by Pintor supporters, save for the faithful few who had made the journey from the valleys. By the end, as the roar built to a crescendo, it must have sounded as if it was coming from the whole of Mexico City.

'When the day came, Johnny was like he always was before any fight – very calm,' Gardiner recalled. 'He was very confident and very cool. He always liked a little laugh before a fight because he was naturally very funny, with a great sense of humour. We'd seen some hostile crowds in our time, like the one in the Spanish bullring where he fought Rodriguez for the European, but never anything like the reaction we got from the crowd when we walked into the arena that night.

'I had to shout a bit to make myself heard – "You all right, John?"

'He said: "Aye, I'm fine. Mind, we'd better watch out with this lot."

'In his tracksuit, he didn't look like a fighter at all. He looked more like a greyhound. He was a freak because he was so strong. We'd stayed in the hotel right up until about an hour and a half before it was due to start. When the crowd saw Johnny, they gave him a lot of abuse because of his appearance; he was so different from any other fighter. They saw the way he was built and took the mickey. Everyone used to do that, probably out of ignorance. I don't think they realised how good he was. They soon found out.

'The fight was going pretty good. We got beyond the halfway stage and I thought we were in front. He got a split lip in the fourth or fifth round and he was spitting a fair bit of blood. Johnny had never been put down in his life, and when it happened in the ninth he was up at the count of four or five. He looked OK.

'Back in the corner, he wanted to know what all the fuss was about. I was telling him: "This man's a dangerous fighter, Johnny. He may not have looked one bit dangerous for the first eight rounds, but he's dangerous, so don't let him catch you again."

'He got annoyed with me. He thought I was panicking and he was arguing: "Why all the fuss? I'm all right. I know what I'm doing. Get my gumshield."

'He went out for the tenth and it went OK. Pintor was really trying to wind it up at that stage because he must have known he was behind on points. In the 11th, Johnny started to get on top again and then we came to the fateful 12th round.'

Ring Magazine, the pugilist's bible, reported the salient facts, as witnessed by their West Coast editor, the late Christopher Coats. His account gave due acknowledgement of the scrawny Welshman having posed a real threat to Pintor's status:

A typical Mexican banger, Pintor brought no new battle-plan into his fight against the light-hitting 5 ft 8 in. challenger. A good left hook and lots of courage have made Pintor what he is and he overcame his four-inch height deficit by pressing forward, looking to unload the harder punches.

But Owen, the Commonwealth champion, showed that, despite his ghostly pale and thin frame, he had serious ambitions for the world title. At times, he clearly out-boxed Pintor, not hitting him with anything hard but cutting the champion over his left eye in the third round and in the fourth round over the right eye. At the end of the sixth, the ringside doctor visited Pintor's corner to inspect the cuts.

Pintor turned the fight around with one roundhouse right in the ninth round, knocking Owen down on his backside. From then on, the challenger seemed to fade. The fight became a cat-and-mouse game, with Owen lacking the strength to keep Pintor at a respectful distance from him.

The tragic ending came quite suddenly. Owen held his own against the champion for much of the fight and though Pintor took charge from the ninth on, Owen was not taking a dreadful beating. A right hand to the head dropped Owen to the canvas a full two minutes into the 12th.

Referee Marty Denkin gave the mandatory eight count. Then, before allowing the fight to continue, he asked Owen if he wanted to go on. The Welshman did not appear seriously hurt at that point. But, seconds later, Pintor landed another right to the head and Owen crumbled to the canvas with an ugly shudder. He immediately lapsed into unconsciousness.

Gardiner has run that last round through his mind over and over again, wondering whether he had any reason, other than hindsight, to throw in the towel. The answer is always the same.

'There was no question there and then of pulling Johnny out of the fight at the end of the 11th,' Gardiner said. 'He was doing all right and he didn't give any signs that the punch that put him down had done any damage. I wish to God now that I had pulled him out but at the time there was no reason. If he'd come back to the corner in a groggy state at the end of the ninth, I would definitely have stopped it.

'The last words I said to him were: "Keep tight and try and push him back. Tight defence." We were about a minute into the round when he got hit on the jaw and he just crumpled. One punch on the jaw. His legs folded. I could see he was in trouble. I jumped into the ring. The fight was over. It was terrible. Everyone was working on him. I didn't think it was life or death at that stage. I thought he'd come round, but he didn't.'

By the time the stricken challenger lay on the canvas, somewhere between life and death, the Mexican crowd had worked themselves into a fury. 'It is part of the mystique of boxing to witness a crowd brought to the edge of hysteria, for that is a tribute to the courage of the fighters,' Coats reported. 'But there is always a dark side to a sporting crowd and when Owen went down for the second time in the 12th round, in a coma and near death, the partisan crowd became like a lynch mob. Owen's cornermen were shoved and drenched with beer.'

It was reported that at least one of the stretcher party bearing Owen out of the ring had his pockets picked. 'We had a lot of abuse from the crowd, throwing beer,' Gardiner said. 'All the gear from the corner was gone, all the first-aid stuff, towels, everything went. I went straight to the hospital. The way everyone was rushing about I knew that it was bad. But I didn't realise how bad until about five or six the next morning, when they said they'd operated and that he was on a life-support machine.'

The operation, for the removal of a blood clot from the brain, lasted three hours. 'The main man who did the operation said: "This is very serious." I asked him if there was any chance at all. He said: "The next 24 or 48 hours will be crucial."

'I didn't sleep. I couldn't. My emotions were all over the place. After two or three days, Johnny was still on the life-support machine. His mother and sister came over and the family moved about 40 miles away from the hospital to get a bit of peace.

'I went to the hospital every day to see Johnny. He was just lying there on the machine. I'd talk to him about his next fight, about getting back on the road and things like that. I hoped something might have triggered a flicker of recognition, but there was nothing. I had to go from my hotel, pick up Johnny's family, take them to the hospital and then take them back to their place.

'As time went on, there was talk of him recovering. I stayed out there for six weeks until I had to get back to attend to my family and my work. I hadn't been back two days when the phone rang and it was Dick to say he'd gone. In the end, I think it was pneumonia that got him.

'I was a fitter with the Gas Board and I was preparing to go to work when the call came through from America. I was shocked, then devastated. In previous phone calls, Dick kept saying Johnny was getting better and better. I didn't know he had pneumonia. I don't know how I got through that day or the days that followed.

'It came out at the inquest that Johnny had a particularly thin skull. All kinds of medical checks were made compulsory after that, like skull X-rays. Had Johnny been hoping to start out as a boxer today, he would never have been allowed.

'It made me wonder, and still makes me wonder, about all the bigger boys he used to spar with in the gym, top people like Wayne Bennett and Jeff Pritchard. He obviously took some shots, but I never ever saw Johnny hurt or bothered.'

When word of Owen's condition reached Maguire's home off the Falls Road in West Belfast, he went to his church, the Clonard Monastery. 'I lit a candle for Johnny and said prayers for him,' he said. 'The whole family joined in and we all prayed for him.

'I kept bumping into people, and sooner or later the conversation would come round to the same question: "What about Johnny Owen?" And I'd always say: "I hope to God he pulls through."

'He was in a coma for a long time and I don't mind admitting there were times when I almost didn't want to know because I didn't want to face the reality that he might not pull through. Talking to you about it now takes me right back to that time when he got killed.

'I loved it every time Owen won a fight. I loved it because he'd taken the title from me and every victory just proved how good he was. He defended the British title twice and won the [Lonsdale] belt. He went for the Commonwealth and won that. Then he went for the European and he won that, too. So the world title was the next step.

'It's easy now for me to say that maybe he was put in too quickly. I think he should have had a few more fights, but then I remember reading that he was five rounds clear at the time when he was knocked dead by Pintor. The damage might have been done before the knock-out blow.'

Maguire, still giving something back to the noble art of self-defence as a member of the Northern Ireland Area Council of the British Boxing Board of Control, does not blame the sport. 'It was just one of those horrible accidents,' he said. 'Johnny Owen was unlucky to be in the wrong place at the wrong time. He was only a young man and, ever since then, I always say: "I'm one of the lucky ones."'

Some 70 miles north of Belfast in the historic city of Derry, Neil McLaughlin was working as a duty officer at the school where he had fought Owen four years earlier when he heard the news.

'I remember feeling really sickened by it,' he said. 'It was terrible. I was fearful for him as soon as I heard that he'd been taken from the ring to the hospital in a coma. I didn't think he was ready for a world title fight.'

In the aftermath of a tragedy that shocked the nation, the British Medical Association called for boxing to be outlawed. Even the late Eddie Thomas, Merthyr's best-known son, who had been in the sport all his life, as a champion boxer in his own right before guiding a local boy, Howard Winstone, to the world featherweight title, began to have second thoughts.

'I had to ask myself whether boxing was worth the candle,' he said. 'But boxing is in me, as it was in Johnny. That isn't easy to express because there's more to it than money or fame or even the knowledge that people who follow boxing are living out a part of their lives through you. There is something mysterious deep inside that keeps leading you back to the ring.'

Gardiner never went back to the old gym in New Tredegar where he trained Owen. He gave the sport up for two years to cope with his grief and a complete breakdown in communication with Owen's father, Dick. Every attempt at reconciliation was met with a rebuff.

'I tried to speak to him quite a few times,' Gardiner said. 'It was a shame. Dick had to blame someone. I was very close to Johnny, and he blamed me a bit. Dick was all for the fight going ahead.

'Before Dick passed away in Merthyr Hospital, he asked to see me. Two days before he died, he shook my hand. He said: "I'm glad we're back as friends. Sorry for all that's happened. No hard feelings."'

On Friday, 1 November 2002, a tearful Lupe Pintor visited the Owen home, where he met the Matchstick Man's parents and his four surviving brothers and three sisters. When the Mexican broke down, one brother put an arm around him, with some consoling words: 'We all know that what happened was an accident, so please don't cry. You have come all this way to honour our brother and we thank you.'

Owen senior had nothing but praise for Pintor. 'He had nothing to do with John's death,' Dick said. 'There was a chink in John's armour and that is all there was to it.'

The next day, Pintor unveiled the Owen statue in the centre of Merthyr. 'I feel that Johnny's spirit has always been with me,' he said. 'We had a great fight, a gentleman's fight. I don't know what the decision would have been had the fight gone to the end, but I would have respected the decision if it had gone to Johnny because it was a gentleman's fight.'

Gardiner has learnt to live with the Owen tragedy, which does not make it any easier. 'We have to move on, but it's always there, every day. Johnny never saw much of life. He never drank, never went out with girls, never went nightclubbing, nothing. It was a damned shame. Twenty-four years of age. I think he would have gone on to win a world title because he was so determined. He loved the fight game. He never skipped training. Whatever road-running we put him on, he did, and he never complained.

'He'd always be wearing the big, heavy boots. You try and run on the sand in those or backwards up on the Beacons – but that's what he did week in, week out. He'd always have a laugh when he finished. In terms of fitness, there was nobody like Johnny Owen. His main motivation was to do something for his family and he'd started to do that with a grocery store that he'd bought for his parents to run. He'd planned bigger things.

'Johnny loved to eat a chocolate gateau and he liked a curry, but only when he wasn't training. People used to say he looked like he needed a good square meal, but, believe me, Johnny could eat for Wales, especially after a fight. In all the time I trained him, I never knew him to be out of the gym for more than seven days and that would be when he was supposed to be on holiday.

'He was so dedicated that he never touched alcohol. I'm not sure whether his father said that he would have a sherry on Christmas Day. If so, that would have been his one drink of the year. I never met anyone as dedicated as he was to boxing.

'He used to say to me: "I'll have my first drink and my first girlfriend when I retire." That's what makes his passing so sad. Everyone in the valleys loved him – and a lot of them were women, because they wanted to mother him.

'Should I have taken that world title fight? I've asked myself that question a few times. There again, if I'd gone for another Commonwealth defence instead, who knows, the problem over the thinness of his skull could have happened then. It could have happened any time.'

Owen died 46 days after being counted out, on 4 November 1980, aged 24. His funeral, six days later, brought Merthyr to a tearful standstill as the cortège made its way to High Street Baptist Church in the middle of the town, where Owen and his brothers had attended Sunday school. They laid the coffin, draped in the Welsh flag, in front of the pulpit, where the Reverend Herbert Price gave the eulogy.

He described Owen as a local boy whose charisma and honesty had made him a folk hero. 'He was committed, utterly and completely, to that which was his life,' the Revd Price said. 'Nothing else mattered. I don't think even the world championship mattered so much to Johnny as doing his absolute best.

'He was a man of courage who took whatever life dealt out to him and took it without flinching. Let the youth of Merthyr never forget that. There are lads here in Merthyr who are going to be better men because Johnny Owen lived.'

They sang 'Fight the Good Fight' and when the mourners made it up the hill to Pant Cemetery, they sang '*Cwm Rhondda*' as only the Welsh can. Even after all these years, Gardiner remembers the events of that day as though they happened a month ago.

'His sparring partners and his brothers carrying the coffin,' he said. 'It was terrible. I'd never felt before in my life the way I felt that day. My hair felt as if it was standing up all the time. My stomach was full of knots and that sickening feeling didn't go away for months.'

Nobody caught the essence of Owen more strikingly or poignantly than the sportswriter Hugh McIlvanney, the master craftsman, in the *Sunday Times*. Owen, he wrote, was 'possessed by a furious aggression that has driven his alarmingly thin and un-muscular body through the heaviest fire and into the swarming, crowding attacks.

'It was boxing that gave Johnny Owen his one positive means of self-expression. Outside the ring, he was an inaudible, almost invisible personality. Inside, he became astonishingly positive and self-assured. He seemed to be more at home there than anywhere else. It is his tragedy that he found himself articulate in such a dangerous language.'

On the morning of the fight, McIlvanney had jotted down a few notes, which pointed to some sort of premonition: 'I found myself writing: "Feel physical sickness at the thought of what might happen, the fear that this story might take us to a hospital room."'

Not for one moment, though, did the thought cross McIlvanney's mind that his anxiety would have a deadly ring to it, that he would end up writing about a matter of life and death. More than 30 years later, time has not dimmed his memory of the events that led to Owen being home flown in a coffin to a hero's funeral.

'I never imagined it would be as horrific as it turned out,' McIlvanney said. 'I had the feeling before the fight that Johnny was stepping into a different world and that it might be the end for him in terms of the world title, not the end of his life. The danger was that they would find out perhaps in a very cruel way that he should not have been exposed to boxing at that level.

'Johnny looked so frail, although you knew that could be deceptive, but he was going to fight a Mexican and they are the most terrifying warriors of all. I just had a sense that the energy which masked his physical frailty would not be sustained throughout his career. It was a horrible feeling and the fact that I was quite close to the Owen camp made it all the more so. Johnny fought with an exaggerated fury to prevent people getting to him and he did that very well. Pintor was getting closer as the fight progressed and you could see there was only going to be one winner.'

Owen's death and other subsequent ring fatalities led to questions being asked in the House of Commons. One of the leading proponents for the abolition of boxing, James Callaghan, the MP for Heywood and Middleton, not to be confused with the former member for Cardiff South-East, launched a debate in the House on 10 May 1994.

'Only when my attention was drawn to the present plight of Muhammad Ali was I totally converted with regard to the terrible hazards and tragedies connected with professional boxing,' Callaghan told the House. 'Muhammad Ali was known as "The Greatest". In my view, he is the greatest advertisement for the necessity to investigate the safety of boxing. One look at his condition is enough to register the insidious effect of a life spent absorbing blows to the head. His legs are leaden and his hands tremble. It is said that he has Parkinson's syndrome and that his condition is not due to boxing. However, I have video tapes of his later fights which would suggest otherwise and that he took one punch too many.

'There have been several deaths in boxing over the years. They include those of Steve Watt, Johnny Owen and the Nigerian Young Ali. The most recent death in boxing in Britain occurred when Bradley Stone, aged 23, died after being stopped in the tenth round. It was Bradley Stone's second stoppage in the space of only 53 days. The grim toll of death and injury in boxing make it unworthy of being called a sport.'

On behalf of the government, Iain Sproat, the parliamentary Undersecretary of State for National Heritage, told the House: 'Figures provided by coroners to the Office of Population Censuses and Surveys show that, from 1986 to 1992, there have been three deaths in England and Wales from boxing. In the same period, however, there have been 77 deaths in motor sports, 69 deaths in air sports, 54 deaths in mountaineering, 40 deaths in ball games and 28 deaths in horse riding.'

In the aftermath of Owen's burial, Gardiner had nothing to do with the sport, a decision influenced more by his period of mourning and his trying to come to terms with the crushing sense of loss than any Damascene conversion to the anti-boxing brigade. He returned to the challenge of training future champions but never again set foot in the gym where he had trained Owen for seven years.

'I did quit for a bit,' Gardiner said. 'And I never went back to the old gym. Too many memories, I suppose. I opened a new one about two years later and now the old one has been demolished. I had to prove to myself that I was capable of training another champion. That's why I went back. I think Johnny would have wanted me to carry on.'

Gardiner bred not one world champion but two. Steve Robinson, one of his brightest protégés, was working as a storeman in his native Cardiff in April 1993 when he was given two days' notice that he had a crack at the vacant WBO featherweight crown against Englishman John Davison. The holder, Ruben Palacios of Columbia, had been disqualified after failing a test for HIV. Robinson's reign lasted for almost 30 months before 'Prince' Naseem Hamed knocked him out in September 1995.

In that same year, another of Gardiner's stable, Robbie Regan from Caerphilly, won the IBF version of the world flyweight division. When he stepped up into the bantams the following year, Regan duly won the WBO title. By then, the first moves were being made to raise the money for a permanent memorial to the man who had made the supreme sacrifice.

The same Baptist chapel was packed to the rafters again 22 years later, on 2 November 2002, for a memorial service that preceded the unveiling of a statue of Merthyr's warrior bantamweight. Some £40,000 had been raised from public donation to pay for the life-sized bronze sculpture and who should be there to perform the opening ceremony but Lupe Pintor himself.

Dick Owen had made a pilgrimage to Mexico the previous summer to meet Pintor for the first time since the fight in Los Angeles. His mission was to ask the Mexican to come to Merthyr, a magnanimous gesture that made Pintor realise that nobody in the family, nor in the wider community, held him responsible for what had happened to their son, brother and inspiration.

Pintor, accompanied by his wife Virginia, met each of the four surviving sons and their mother Edith. 'I am sorry for what happened,' he said through an interpreter. 'I did not wish him any harm. I was just doing what I knew best, as Johnny was. He was a great warrior. This is a difficult moment for all of us, difficult because it is remembering what once happened in a very different situation. Johnny Owen's spirit will always be with me.'

Even the hardest of men shed tears and when the emotion of the occasion temporarily overtook Pintor, one of Owen's brothers kindly offered a few consoling words.

Pintor, born Jose Guadalupe Pintor Guzman in April 1955, had the same sort of working-class background as his Welsh opponent. The Mexican ruled the world bantamweight roost from June 1979, before vacating the title in 1982 after eight defences, presumably because he had eliminated every serious contender.

He stepped up into the super-bantamweight division for a crack at the holder, Wilfredo 'Bazooka' Gomez, in 1985. In what was to be acclaimed as one of the fights of the decade, Gomez knocked Pintor out in the 14th before proving himself one of the greats as a triple world champion, winning also the WBC featherweight and WBA junior lightweight crowns.

Owen's father Dick defended the sport to the hilt. 'Boxing helped make real men and good citizens out of the young and, very often, tearaway youths,' he told Rick Broadbent, author of an excellent biography of his son, *The Big If: The Life and Death of Johnny Owen*. 'Time and again, I saw how boxing in this tough town turned out better human beings. It rarely failed. To get to the top, a person has to be special. To become a champion, one has to have something extra. I only worked with one such champion in my times as a trainer, my son John. Mark my words, he was special.

'In this sport of boxing, you try to inflict harm on your opponent and generally endanger his very right to exist. But mostly, after the contest, you love one another like long-lost brothers.

'This is a fighter's respect. Lupe told me that he had carried Johnny's spirit around with him in his heart for years and hoped that, after our meeting, he could lay it to rest. For a father to lose a son is the most difficult of events to accept, but I believe there is a truth here that we can take some comfort from. Perhaps it is better to depart reaching for the stars, doing what your life dictates, following the instincts of your heart, than to live to a hundred years and be forever miserable, disappointed and embittered.'

Dick died in December 2005 after suffering a stroke and was buried alongside his son in the same grave at Pant Cemetery. Gardiner has been going there every year on 4 November now for more than 30 years to lay a single red rose on the grave. A little girl, the daughter of a local charity worker, had placed a red rose on Owen's coffin before it was lowered into the ground. It read: 'May God be with you, Johnny'.

'Johnny always liked red roses,' Gardiner said. 'He used to bring my wife a red rose on her birthday. There isn't a day goes by that I don't think of him.'

In Pant Cemetery, a bashful young man of extraordinary ability and endearing modesty, who died doing what he did best as only he knew how, rests in peace . . .

15

THE FIGHTING MASTER

Ian Woosnam

Born: Oswestry, 2 March 1958

When word got out among the members at Llanymynech golf club that Harold Woosnam's little lad was going to try his luck as a professional golfer, the majority were decidedly unimpressed. Far from rushing to congratulate him on the wisdom of his decision, there were those who questioned his sanity instead.

A number of his contemporaries at the club feared that the 16-year-old farmer's boy would be wasting time and money chasing what they considered an impossible dream, for the simple reason that, in their opinion, he was nowhere near good enough. A Welshman who could go from practising in a cow shed to taking a stellar role in a golden era for European golf? Please, pull the other one.

Far from changing their tune in retrospect, the consensus among the doubting Thomases, as well as the Joneses, of the early days has been threaded into the fabric of Llanymynech golf club. 'A group of former club mates and county player colleagues spent days pleading with him not to take such a drastic step,' the club states on its website. 'They reckoned he was no better than thousands of other single-figure amateurs, including themselves, and one day he would come to regret the foolish decision.'

Imagine, had Ian Woosnam peered some distance into the future and glimpsed the road that would take him out of Llanymynech and the Powys hills, their reaction to his prophecy: 'One day I shall win the US Masters and come home in a Green Jacket. And if that's not enough, on the very next day the news will go around the world that I am the No. 1 golfer on the planet.'

He could have gilded the lily by predicting eight consecutive Ryder Cup appearances, a stack of global tournament victories, including three World Match-Play Championships, more than £10 million in prize money and a winning Ryder Cup captaincy of Europe against America. Nobody would have believed him back then, in the early spring of 1973, least of all those well-meaning members who saw nothing particularly special in his ability to negotiate a golf ball around the courses of their border region.

Having questioned whether he would ever get close to scratching a living from the game, they would probably have exchanged knowing nods of the 'I-told-you-so' variety when Woosnam struggled in the early years. What they failed to appreciate, or certainly underestimated, was the one quality that drove the embryonic superstar through every setback.

From his mid-teens, Woosnam believed in his ability to earn a living as a touring professional. Fortunately for Welsh, British, European and world golf, he did not have anywhere near the same belief in his first sporting ambition, to be a boxer.

Andy Griffiths, a boyhood friend who has been club professional at Llanymynech for almost 40 years, did golf an almighty favour by disabusing his pal of any notion of being the first 'Mighty Atom' from Wales to climb into a boxing ring since Jimmy Wilde, the former world flyweight champion who climbed out for the last time in 1923.

'In the early days he always wanted to be a boxer,' Griffiths said. 'He kept going on about it until one day I said to him: "How are you going to box?"

'He's not very big now, but he was really tiny then, so I stretched out my left arm and put my hand on his head. He started flailing about and he was still flailing about when I slapped him a bit with my free hand. I did that to talk him out of boxing and into golf instead. I never heard another peep from him about being a boxer after that.'

The real fight began there and then. It was just as well that

Woosnam's inner strength came fortified with an endless supply of gravel and grit. He needed it by the bagful to cement the foundations of his game, shaken every time fate sent him crashing to the canvas. It was almost as if the golfing gods were trying to find out whether he had the stomach for an almost constant struggle to beat the odds.

The whispers around Llanymynech made him feel like a golfing prophet without honour in his own locker room. 'I can't remember them saying it to my face,' he said. 'I was a stubborn little bastard and that was the one thing which probably made all the difference in the end. Right from the start, I decided: "I'll show you lot."'

During the mid-'60s after yeoman service to St Martin's Football Club on the other side of the Welsh border in Shropshire, his father gave up kicking a moving ball to hit a smaller stationary one covered in dimples. Griffiths' father, who played in the same football team, persuaded Harold to watch an exhibition between the 1951 Open champion Max Faulkner and his successor nine years later, Kel Nagle from Australia.

Woosnam senior liked what he saw and made a mental note to buy himself a second-hand set of clubs. Fortuitous or not, it marked the creation of the greatest golfer ever made in Wales.

'My dad played soccer until he got to the stage of life where a lot of his friends started to play golf, so he thought: "I'll give it a try and see what happens." He went to the local club and took the rest of us with him – my mum, my sister Julie, my big brother Keith and myself, which was before the youngest of the family, Gareth, was born. I was seven when I hit my first shot.

'It's so long ago I can hardly even remember being a youngster, never mind my first shots. I had a little hickory-shafted driver, which was like a 2-wood. I used to drive, putt ... do everything with it. Then I got another hickory-shafted club, an 8-iron, and I used to do everything with that as well.

'I loved the game straight away. We used to go to the club on a Sunday after milking the cows, which took a bit longer than it should have done because I was so small. I couldn't reach above the cows to the pipeline that took the milk to a tank, so I had to wait for someone else to do it. It wasn't until I was 13 that I eventually became tall enough to do that myself.'

Llanymynech, where the boundary between the countries runs through part of the course, claims to offer the unique experience at its fourth hole of driving in Wales and putting in England. In hopping across the border for three of the outward nine holes, then back home for the rest, Woosnam developed a simple philosophy that underpinned the unshakeable nature of his self-belief from an early age.

'If I could hit one good shot, then I could hit another,' he said. 'If I could play one good round, then I could play another. That was where the self-belief came in. One thing I wasn't going to be was a farmer – too much like hard work, seven days a week. You've got to be born to play golf and I suppose I must have had something different. I worked fairly hard, but not day in, day out. I certainly didn't sacrifice every waking hour.

'Working on the farm was hard work. When you've been carrying bales of hay around all day, you're too tired for golf. I never really had much of a chance to practise. The only real practice I got was in the cow shed or hitting balls out of the long grass in a field.

'In the summer months, we'd maybe play golf on a Wednesday afternoon. As I got into my teens, I began playing junior competitions all over North Wales and Shropshire. I can remember winning a few of them. At 15, I decided I was going to be a professional golfer. I had the chance that year to play football for Shropshire or golf for Shropshire. I couldn't do both, so I had to make a choice. I chose golf because I thought I'd last longer at that than football.'

He left school at 16 and took his first step along the fairway to heaven on the English side of the border, at Hill Valley golf club, owned by the father of his close friend Tony Minshall, who would become a touring professional in his own right. When he wasn't playing or practising, the budding Masters champion doubled up as a part-time greenkeeper and occasional barman, on both sides of the counter. When he wasn't pulling pints, he'd be knocking them back.

'For the first time, I was able to practise regularly and start to understand the game,' he said. 'There were some wild days. I worked pretty hard at my game, but I was messing around too much. It wasn't until two years later that I really knuckled down and started to iron the faults out of my game.'

Life on the Shropshire circuit brought him into early contact with a contemporary who beat him in the Shropshire & Herefordshire Boys' Championship in 1970, when they were both 12 years old, and who would beat him to the Green Jacket at Augusta. Sandy Lyle may have been living just down the road but, compared with Woosnam's agricultural upbringing, he came from a different world.

'Sandy lived at a golf club,' Woosnam said. 'His dad was the professional and Sandy was on the course every day, practising before he went to school. We're the same age, but in terms of where we stood as fifteen year olds, I was five years behind Sandy, probably more, and eight years behind Seve.'

During the autumn of that same year, 1973, when Brian Huggett flew the flag for Wales, America duly recorded another victory over Great Britain and Ireland at Muirfield, extending their monopoly of the Ryder Cup, which left many on both sides of the Atlantic fearful that the biennial competition was dying on its feet. The USA, apparently invincible, with Arnold Palmer and Jack Nicklaus in their prime, had reason even then to be afraid, not that they had any way of knowing why.

In England, Spain, Germany and Wales, five extraordinary teenagers were serving apprenticeships that would make every one of them a golfing colossus. All five were born within 11 months of one another and the Americans would suffer at the hands of them all individually and, once the British and Irish team had been expanded to encompass Europe, collectively.

A boy from the tiny Basque fishing village of Pedrena was the first of the five – Severiano Ballesteros, born 9 April 1957. He was followed, in chronological order, on 18 July in Welwyn Garden City by Nick, later Sir Nicholas, Faldo; on 27 August in Anhausen, Germany, by Bernhard Langer; on 9 February 1958 in Shrewsbury, by Alexander Lyle; and, a shade over three weeks later, on 2 March in Oswestry, by Woosnam.

In the fullness of time, they would win an aggregate total of 16 major titles, more than 300 other tournaments and somewhere north of £100 million in prize money. Of the five, Woosnam had arguably more ground to make up than the other four put together – something that had nothing to do with his being the youngest.

Their respective earnings on the European Tour in 1978 told their own story. Ballesteros won £54,348; Faldo, £37,911; Langer, £7,006; Lyle, £5,233; and Woosnam, £409. He still barely had two pennies to rub together two years later, when Seve won his first US Masters, Faldo the PGA for the second time, Langer the Dunlop Masters at St Pierre, and Lyle topped the leaderboard for the individual competition at the World Cup.

'Woosie', fiercely proud of his Welsh identity, was just about up and running. 'We started with a caravan,' he said. 'My father drove me around the various tournaments until I got my licence. When I was 16, Dad decided to sell his herd of Friesian cows and downsize to an arable farm. He did that so he could reduce the workload and have more time to help me. Then we dropped the caravan and got a Volkswagen caravanette instead.'

While the big guns of the sport checked into five-star hotels and had chauffeur-driven cars put at their disposal, the Woosnams pulled into a lay-by within striking distance of the course where they were playing. As the stars enjoyed a bottle of wine with their meal, oblivious to the cost, Ian cut open a tin of baked beans.

'It was a case of whatever was easiest to cook and they didn't come any easier than baked beans,' he said. 'We'd always have a few eggs and some bacon, so whenever I got fed up with beans on toast, I'd make myself a bacon sandwich. That's how it was and I loved it. I was learning my trade and that was the cheapest way of doing it.

'I'd go to these tournaments and try as best as I could. When I ran out of money, I'd play in the Midlands region and try and earn something there. I'd win a couple of tournaments and that would support me to go and play a few more tournaments on the tour until the same thing happened again. My dad always said to me: "You've got to give yourself five years. This is an apprenticeship like any other."'

During those five years, Woosnam lost his tour card three times, which meant he had to go back to the end-of-season qualifying school and all the anxiety that entailed. Each time he held his nerve and retrieved the lost card, believing that next season would mark the breakthrough into the big time.

Only once did the fine margin between success and failure, a fortune and a pittance, drive him to the brink of despair. It happened during final qualifying for the 1981 Open championship, which had returned to Royal Sandwich for the first time since Bobby Locke won there in 1949. Prince's, on the same stretch of Kent coast, and an Open course in its own right, having hosted the event in 1932, promised much for Woosnam. He went there, along with 60 others, in the hope of a top-three finish and one of precious few places left in the championship itself. The other four – Ballesteros, Faldo, Langer and Lyle – were all safely through, their exemption from qualifying another example of Woosnam's continuing struggle to close the gap separating him from them.

The first round of the 36-hole competition could not have gone much better. Woosnam, his muscular forearms the result of all that manual farm work, led the field with a 67 and stood on the last tee the next day knowing he had no room for error. 'I hit it 20 yards out of bounds,' he said. 'And then I walked straight in. I thought: "This is the end. I'm going to give up." That night I drove all the way back from Kent to Oswestry. When I got home, I said to my dad: "I'm going to pack it in."'

His father, who had sold his cattle to help subsidise his second son's golfing education, might have drawn a national analogy of a dragon breathing too much fire. 'Being a Welshman is a disadvantage for a sportsman,' he said some years later. 'They are excitable people. Ian was that much better than the others before he made it big, but they used to qualify and he couldn't. I think that was because of his nervousness and his Welsh breeding.'

For all his bluster, Woosnam was never the quitting type. 'A couple of weeks after saying I was going to give up, I'd got some of the anger out of my system,' he said. 'There was a club job going for a pro at Oswestry and for a few days I thought I'd go for that. I considered a lot of things and, when I'd weighed up all the pros and cons, I thought: "I'll give it one more go."'

So he could always have lowered his sights and found a job somewhere as a club professional, but that would have been a tacit admission that those members at Llanymynech who had doubted him were right after all, that he didn't have what it took to be a touring professional. Woosie had vowed to 'show them' and now he was ready to do so in spectacular fashion.

It dawned on him, slowly, that he had the wrong attitude, that his anger levels had to be reduced if he was to keep his occasionally wayward game on the straight and narrow. He found the answer to both in Africa during the early months of 1982 on the Safari Tour and he would reap the reward millions of times over.

'I'd hit fantastic shots, but I couldn't keep them on the fairway,' he said. 'I knew my attitude was wrong, and I knew the very day when the penny dropped and I changed it. I'll never forget being on the practice ground before the third round of the Nigerian Open, standing beside Gordon Brand senior.

'Gordon's winning the tournament with a 66 followed by a 67. I've done 73–74. I'm standing on the range, hitting balls, and hitting them so well that my caddy hardly has to move to collect them. I thought: "What the hell am I practising for when I'm nailing them like this."

'Now I'm watching Gordon practise. His balls are missing his caddy by ten–fifteen yards on the right and the same margin on the left. He also hit a few over the fence and then I noticed that it didn't really bother him. I thought: "If he's playing like that and leading the tournament, what am I doing wrong?" That's when I realised I had to stop beating myself up every time I hit a bad shot. I was too angry all the time.'

Controlling his temper often proved more difficult than controlling the ball. 'Throwing my clubs in the early days was nothing unusual,' he said. 'You've got to have a fiery temperament because it gives you the drive to succeed, but it took me a while to learn that it's got to be kept in check. I suppose Sandy Lyle is the only top golfer who hasn't got a bad temper. If he'd had one, he would have been the best player in the world.

'Whenever something went wrong, I'd be hard on myself, asking tough questions like, "Why am I doing this?" I changed my attitude and became relaxed. I changed my way of thinking, so that I'd see everything in a different light. If I got four birdies, then four bogeys wouldn't be the end of the world because I'd still be level-par. I began to understand that I'd be better off if I looked at the flowers and smelt the roses.

'The great Ben Hogan never used to let himself get upset if he hit four or five bad shots a round because he'd be too busy concentrating on cancelling them out with good ones. If you shoot under-par, it doesn't matter how you do it. There are no pictures on your scorecard, just a number against each hole.'

In 1981, the year when one out-of-bounds tee shot cost him his place in the Open, Woosnam failed to make the top 100 on the European money list, slumping to 104th, with breadline earnings of £1,884. The following season, during which he first made a conscious effort to stop and smell the flowers, he came up roses, making 25 times as much by winning almost £50,000 in prize money and finishing in the top ten.

For the first time, he was quids-in; no longer forced to rely on loans from his father or the sort of deal from a local engineering firm in Oswestry that kept him going. 'They gave me five grand a year on the basis that I'd give them 50 per cent of my net earnings,' he said. 'It was a three-year deal and for the first two years they got no return on their money because 50 per cent of nothing is still nothing.

'Then, in 1982, when it began to happen for me, I paid them back a monster amount. The firm was really struggling then and down to a three-day week because of the recession at the time. So I ended up sponsoring them. At the same time I was also able to pay my dad back and all the interest. He charged me 10 per cent, but without his support I don't know how I'd have ever got going.'

Before his maiden tournament victory, in the Swiss Open at Crans-sur-Sierre, Woosnam knew he still had to catch up with those leading the Order of Merit – Ballesteros, Faldo, Langer and Lyle. 'I finished second five times and it took me quite a while to get over that hurdle,' he said. 'It was about coping with the pressure and I worked out my own kind of psychology to help me finish first.

'Part of it was to build myself up. I always seemed to be written off, so I'd talk to the press about me being like David against Goliath. I was always seen as this wild little Welsh guy who loved a pint, which I did – and still do. The reporters would take the mickey out of me and call me "Boozey Woosey" and all sorts of stuff like that.'

From the lows to the highs, Woosnam never lost his sense of fun while avoiding the rush to pump iron and pound the treadmill. 'Life's too short to spend all the time in the gym,' he said. 'I like to have a few beers and enjoy myself.'

The England cricketer Darren Gough can vouch for that. The Yorkshire fast bowler tells how he took the field in a Test match against South Africa in Pretoria with a severe hangover after a session with Woosnam in the hotel bar the previous night. 'I have never walked onto a cricket field in such a disgraceful, self-induced state of disrepair,' he wrote in his autobiography. 'I had already thrown up in the dressing-room and I felt so bad I wasn't sure whether I had a hangover or was still drunk.'

Woosnam chuckles at the story and rapidly points out that England still won. After the ice-breaking win in Switzerland, the next four years brought three more tournament victories, the first on Welsh soil at St Pierre, Chepstow, in June 1983, the year he married his wife, Glendryth. The lone Welshman went into the final round sharing the lead at nine-under with Scotland's Bernard Gallacher, one shot ahead of Faldo and Langer, two clear of the booming Australian Greg Norman. The new champion burned them all off to win by three, his seven-under finishing round of 65 contrasting with Langer's 76.

After conquering his homeland, it took him a little time to conquer the rest of Europe and a large chunk of southern Africa. No British golfer had ever delivered as spectacular a year as Woosnam did in 1987 and it all came about because of a chance discovery during a New Year's Eve party in Oswestry.

'I kept hooking the ball all the time,' he said. 'I tried everything, but I just couldn't get rid of it. I'd been to Japan and come home with a set of clubs with a different kind of metal which allowed the ball to come off the club face softer and that suited my game. A friend of mine suggested I take a swing on the lawn for a photo, along the lines of "driving into the New Year".

'I was standing there in my normal shoes for a swing at a soft silver ball. For some reason that I can't explain, I stayed on my right foot longer than usual and it gave me a really good feeling. I went out the next day to practise, staying longer on my right foot, and it cured my hook. One little swing change and everything clicked into place. It was like putting the last piece into the jigsaw. I thought then that '87 was going to be a big year.'

How big not even he can have imagined. He hit the jackpot early in the year and kept hitting it, winning the Hong Kong Open (£20,000), the Jersey Open (£16,160), the Madrid Open (£27,500), the Scottish Open (£33,330), the Lancome Trophy (£50,000) and, at Wentworth on 18 October, the World Match-Play Championship (£75,000). What's more, he did it by eliminating three of those he once considered way ahead of him.

He beat Faldo by one hole in the second round and Ballesteros by the same margin in the semi-final, each victory achieved by putts at the 18th of around six feet. In the final, he sank another of similar length for another one-hole victory, all the more satisfying because it came against the local rival who had beaten him 17 years earlier in the Shropshire & Herefordshire Boys' Championship, Sandy Lyle.

At long last, Woosnam proved as good as his word. 'One day, Sandy, I'm going to beat you,' he said in 1970. 'One day.' To which the ever-popular Lyle said, in his easy, relaxed way: 'You'll have to grow a bit first.'

According to the official PGA European Tour guide, Woosnam had grown by half an inch in four years – from 5 ft 4 in. in 1983 to 5 ft 4½ in. 1987.

Having won in Asia and all over Europe, he still found time after the Wentworth triumph to win in America and Africa and become the first golfer to win a million in one year.

On 21 November at Kapalua golf club in Hawaii, Wales won the World Cup for the first time, beating Scotland in a play-off at the second extra hole, where Sam Torrance three-putted. By winning the team event in tandem with David Llewellyn, Woosnam also took the individual title five shots clear of the other Scot, Lyle. That brought his winnings for the week to £85,000.

What he won a fortnight later, on 6 December in South Africa, made that look like a piece of small change. The Million Dollar Challenge, an annual event at the Gary Player country club in Sun City near Rustenburg, guaranteed a winner-takes-all outcome after 72 holes of stroke-play. Woosnam, having cleaned up just about everywhere else, duly won the lot, right down to the last dime of the 1,000,000th dollar. His 14-under-par for the four rounds made him the first Briton to win the biggest purse in golf, more than doubling the £439,074.76 he earned on the European Tour.

The world rankings had been calculated a week earlier, which might explain why Woosnam found himself behind Norman, Ballesteros, Langer, Lyle and the American Curtis Strange. A player who began his professional life barely the sixth best in Shropshire, now found himself the sixth best in the world. He had just served global notice that his arrival as the No. 1 on Earth was going to be only a matter of time.

When the day dawned and a Welsh dragon flew from the highest flag-mast in the golfing world, it coincided with Woosnam's greatest achievement, winning the US Masters at Augusta on Sunday, 2 April 1991. After 71 holes, he and Tom Watson, the Open champion five times over, stood on the 72nd tee, tied at 10-under for the championship. Jose Maria Olazabal had reached the sanctuary of the clubhouse on the same score.

Someone had to crack, and while the respective drives came to rest on the same continent, they were poles apart. Watson sliced his into the trees; Woosnam unleashed a monster that sailed beyond the bunker from which Sandy Lyle won the Masters three years earlier, some 40 yards further on up the hill towards the green. 'Tom was brilliant that day, in every way,' the new champion said of the genial American. 'What a nice man.'

In a classic case of 'cometh the hour, cometh the man', Woosnam had a seven-foot putt to win his elusive first major and avoid a play-off with Olazabal. Putting had been, and would continue to be, the Welshman's weak suit – and hadn't Doug Sanders missed one of not much more than two feet for the Open at St Andrews in 1970 before the American faded into obscurity?

'His putt was downhill, left to right,' Woosnam, who knows his history, said. 'Mine was uphill, slightly right to left, which was perfect for me as a right-hander. Having a putt like that to win a major was another of the things I used to dream about as a kid. I knew that if I missed it, I'd still be in a play-off, which took some of the anxiety away. But I knew I wasn't going to miss it. It was my time. The putt was perfect.'

When he dressed that morning, the new champion intended to be resplendent in his national colours, red and white, leaving the organisers to search in vain for a Green Jacket small enough to fit him. 'The check trousers had Welsh red,' he said. 'I was going to wear a white shirt until I put it on and noticed a stain on the front. So I wore a navy blue one instead – Seve navy blue, because that was his favourite colour.

'On the Monday, I became the world No. 1. I could stand on the first tee anywhere and think: "I'm the best player here." Another dream come true, and if some people thought it was the wildest one of all, then that made it all the better. I was born to play golf, but ability alone isn't enough. You've got to be born with something extra. You've got have an inner hunger driving you on. You've got to have what Seve had.'

They went back a long way, Ballesteros and Woosnam, especially in the Ryder Cup. As twin towers of European strength from the early '80s to the late '90s, they were two of those responsible for changing the course of history by inflicting five defeats on the Americans in seven matches from 1985.

The last in which both appeared, in 1997, proved to be another European triumph in spite of one of the untold rucks of the Ryder Cup, between a fiery Welshman and a dictatorial Spaniard. Ballesteros, a Spanish captain on Spanish soil at Valderrama, did not endear himself to every member of the team, including Woosie and Colin Montgomerie.

'There were a few arguments, all right, about his style of management,' Woosnam said. 'On the Monday of that week, I was having a couple of drinks in the hotel bar. Seve comes up to me and says: "You've got to stop drinking, all week. No drinking."

'I said: "What's the matter with you, Seve? I know how much I can drink and how much I can't. I know what I'm doing. I ain't the kind of guy who's going to let you down or the team down and I'm very disappointed that you seem to think I might. I can't drink? You must be joking."

'When he said he wasn't, I told him to get lost and change his attitude or I was going to go home. He came up to my room and he stayed there for two hours, persuading me not to go. Some guys, like your Langers and your Faldos, don't have a drink. Others, like Sam Torrance, Mark James, Howard Clark, Lee Westwood and myself, enjoy a drink as a form of relaxation.

'Often you've had a bloody hard day playing 36 holes and you have a couple of pints to wind down. Then you go to bed and get a good night's sleep. You have to stay normal. You might have two or three beers. You're not going to have nine or ten.

'But that's the way Seve was. He said to Westwood: "You have to eat salads all week. You're too fat."'

Woosnam found Ballesteros's captaincy too hands-on for his liking and said so publicly. A well-documented altercation with Montgomerie was a case in point, but what got Woosnam more than anything else was the lack of communication.

'Being an experienced player who had been No.1 in the world, I couldn't understand why he just wouldn't talk to me,' he said. 'He wouldn't discuss anything. He would be whispering to other players, so you didn't know what was going on. He treated Darren Clarke the same way. He didn't speak to Darren all week.

'That was how Seve wanted it, but I wasn't at all happy about it. I didn't even know the pairings for the first day until I got to the golf club that morning with Darren. He didn't have a clue either. When I caught up with Seve on the practice green, I said: "Am I playing this afternoon?" He said: "I don't know."

'I said: "Who will I be playing with?" He said: "I don't know."

'I still don't have a clue why he acted like that. If that was meant to fire me up, he certainly succeeded. The next day he paired me with Thomas Bjorn. It was a strange match-up because we'd lost in practice. We won, so Seve could say he'd got it right. I always got on well with Seve. We just had a disagreement at that Ryder Cup. He was under so much pressure not to lose.'

In his biography, Ballesteros defended his captaincy:

I believed I had to be close to these players because many were inexperienced and lacked tactical sense. They knew that and felt more at ease when they saw me around. Obviously the odd one, like Colin Montgomerie, felt that I was treating him like a child. Colin didn't like being given tips. I remember going over to him to discuss the tricky 17th. Before I could open my mouth he shouted angrily: 'Seve, I know what to do. I really do.'

'Colin,' I replied, also angrily. 'I know you do. I only want to remind you.'

The spectators around us laughed, but 'Monty' was in no laughing mood. As I have said, 'Monty' is a great player. He tends to react stormily.

Ian Woosnam criticised me as well, this time on more serious grounds. He told British journalists that 'Europe has a captain who goes around as if he were playing blind man's bluff'.

I imagine he said this because I drove around the course encouraging everyone, even on practice days. I set out the strategy that we would follow, which meant I had to take difficult decisions the players didn't always understand. For example I only played Ian Woosnam and Darren Clarke once, aside from the singles, because I opted for the players I thought were on best form. I put both of them out in the second fourballs on the Saturday – Woosie with Bjorn, Darren with Monty, and they won.

On Friday evening I told myself that if those two wanted to show me they are playing, that they should have been playing today, they now have their opportunity. As I imagined, they both played fantastically well. I was very pleased for both of them but my primary concern was always to do what I thought was right for the team.

Good communication between captain and team is essential to weld the team together and make it strong. And the captain must never take decisions unilaterally on a whim. They should arise from taking into account the views of the team, in particular those of the most experienced.

When he became Europe's Ryder Cup captain, at the K Club in September 2006, Woosnam drew up a battle plan based on a policy of non-interference. Before he could put it into action, he had some firefighting to do after being subjected to a bitter personal attack from Bjorn, provoked by the Dane's omission from the team to make way for Westwood. In his outburst, a 'shocked' Bjorn said he had 'lost respect' for Woosnam and that he needed 'to learn how to be a captain'.

The following day, after the European Tour fined him a 'substantial sum', Bjorn issued a public apology for the 'hurtful and personal nature' of his attack on Woosnam. It hurt the Welshman so much that he offered his resignation during a recce of the K Club with most of his team.

'I was feeling the pressure as it was when I made the decision to leave Thomas out,' Woosnam said. 'What he then said and did broke my heart. During dinner after a day's practice, I got up and said: "Look, you've all seen the comments of Thomas Bjorn. If you don't feel I'm up to the job, I will stand down."

'I meant it. If they were not happy with me, I'd have been out of it there and then. I had to know that they had complete faith in time. They told me: "Don't be so stupid. Thomas was way out of order." That was what I wanted to hear, but I had to be sure.

'I then set out to make sure nobody made the mistakes I made as a player in previous Ryder Cups. I didn't win a singles match because I put myself under too much pressure and tried too hard. I told the guys: "Don't do what I did. Do the opposite."

'I had my own views on the captaincy. I'd been vice-captain with Sam Torrance [in 2002] and my views were very similar to his. I wanted to get every player involved and let him have his way. I had people around me who I could really trust when it came to making decisions – people like Peter Baker, Des Smyth, D.J. Russell and Sandy Lyle. I relied on them to let me know whether I was doing the right thing or not.

'I didn't try to tell the players how to do their job because their achievements spoke for themselves. All I did was make sure I pointed them in the right direction.'

He did rather more than that while, in contrast to Ballesteros at Valderrama, keeping as low a profile as permitted in such a high-octane event. Woosnam chose his pairings with a skill and perception that laid the foundations for a European win not far off landslide proportions and his choice of Darren Clarke turned out to be as inspirational as everything else.

The Ulsterman had been mourning the death some weeks earlier in August 2006 of his wife, Heather, after a long illness. Woosnam knew his man and Clarke delivered in spades, winning his two fourballs and the singles, as Europe romped home by a record-equalling margin, 18½ to 9½.

'You only have to look at the scoreline to see what sort of job Ian Woosnam did as captain of the 2006 Ryder Cup,' Clarke, the 2011 Open champion, said. 'He was fantastic. Achieving the same result as we did in Detroit two years ago was incredible and that says everything about Woosie. He kept things plain and simple.

'He was always talking to us, telling us what to do but never interfering on the course. On the first tee and at other times in the round he would come and offer just the right words of encouragement. You would expect nothing less from someone who has been involved throughout Europe's reign of success in the Ryder Cup.

'As Sergio Garcia cheekily said: "He might be a small man, but he has a huge heart."

'That has been obvious since he left the family farm in Oswestry to make his way in golf. When I came on tour, his was the swing I wanted to watch on the driving range – so sweet, such rhythm – a thing of real beauty.'

Harold Woosnam died in August 2003 at the age of 74 and his wife, Joan, also a club captain at Llanymynech, passed away in April 2009. They had seen the middle of their three sons do famous things for Wales, Britain and Europe. Golf has given Woosnam a lifestyle beyond his wildest dreams – a grand home as a tax exile on Jersey, a winter refuge in Barbados, a private jet, a personal fortune according to the *Sunday Times Rich List* of £20 million and an enduring status as one of the all-time greats of the game.

But for one of the more outrageous slings of misfortune, he would have won the Open as well as the Masters. At Royal Lytham in July 2001, everyone's favourite 'Wee Welshman' started the final round one shot off the lead and duly drilled a 6-iron to within a foot of the opening hole and made birdie. At the second he discovered, to his horror, that his bag contained 15 clubs, one more than the maximum, an oversight on the part of his caddy, Miles Byrne, which meant a two-stroke penalty. He finished joint-third, three shots behind the winner, David Duval.

Nobody will ever know what would have happened had it not been for the 15th club. 'I tried another driver on the practice ground and put it in the bag,' Woosnam said. 'I told my caddy: "Make sure you put that other driver back in the locker."

'He was a bit nervous and forgot. What made it all the more annoying was that had the first hole been a par four, we'd have noticed it straight away and avoided any damage. But with it being a par three we didn't find out till it was too late. Ten years before, I probably would have knocked Miles's head off, but we all make mistakes. It took me a while to get going again because I kept thinking: "But for the two-stroke penalty, I'd be leading this damned thing."

'I had my chances to win more majors, but I wasn't a good enough putter. I was probably the worst putter to win the Green Jacket. If I had to pick someone to make a ten-foot putt to save my life, it would have to be Seve. If I'd had Seve's dedication, most probably I'd be playing better than I am now on the Seniors'Tour, but mainly I enjoy playing social golf with my friends.

'When I was a kid, my heroes were Muhammad Ali, Elvis Presley, Jack Nicklaus, Arnold Palmer, Gary Player and John Wayne. I'd have put Seve up there if I'd known him then. I first played with him in Yorkshire in 1983. I hit the first nine greens in regulation; he hit two. The only time I saw him was when he got to the green but, at the turn, he was two-under and I was one-under. I said to my caddy: "How the hell is this guy beating me?"

'It was a real privilege just to have been out there to see how he did it. The Americans gave the impression that we were second-class golfers on this side of the Atlantic. Seve came along, then Faldo, Langer and myself, and changed all that.'

Woosnam succeeded despite the diagnosis during the late '80s of an arthritic back condition, ankylosing spondylitis. The worst-case scenario, that it might confine him to a wheelchair, has been averted, thanks to the regular medication that has allowed the one-time aspiring flyweight to bestride the fairways of the world like a colossus.

Back home at Llanymynech, plans for a new clubhouse include a special room dedicated to the lad some said would never make it.

16

GRAND NATIONAL DOUBLE

Carl Llewellyn

Born: Hundleton, Pembrokeshire, 29 July 1965

As a boy of ten on the family farm in Pembrokeshire, Carl Llewellyn used to come home from school and saddle up his pony, Sparky. He would go for a gallop, wait until the horse had reached a top speed of 20–25 miles per hour and then jump off. Once he had dusted himself down, he got back on the pony and repeated the forced landing over and over again.

Even at such a tender age, he had made up his mind that he was going to be a jump jockey and that he would have to simulate accidents in readiness for joining one of the bravest breeds in sport. By the time Llewellyn was up and running as a professional jockey, all that falling off the pony at his home 'in the middle of nowhere' near the village of Hundleton stood him in good stead – especially when it came to the mightiest steeplechase on the planet.

In view of subsequent events, it can be said without fear of contradiction that the youngster knew what was heading his way: riding into steeplechase history as the only Welshman aboard the Grand National winner twice comes at an excruciating price.

By the time he rode his last winner, Llewellyn had broken or dislocated an assortment of bones at least 38 times. At his own conservative estimate, he has broken his nose eight times, seven of his ribs, his scaphoids six times, five fingers, four toes, his right ankle, left leg, left arm, jaw, cheekbone, collarbone and right wrist, and dislocated an elbow.

The list does not include the consequences of a nasty accident that left him suffering from crushed vertebrae, which required surgery, one of at least twelve operations on various parts of his anatomy. In his time, Llewellyn rode over the jumps at every National Hunt course in Britain with the solitary exception of Edinburgh and there were times when it felt as though he had broken a bone at every one.

If nothing else, all that diving off the pony ensured that when it came to parting company with the constant danger of half a ton of horse flesh landing on top of him, he had no fear. 'After school, I'd get the pony, gallop up the field and jump off,' he said. 'I thought stupidly, and naively, that I had to get used to it, to learn how to fall at anything up to 25 miles an hour.

'At the time I thought it was a requirement of the job. What an idiot! I look back now and think: "How crazy was that?" I had loads of falls as a kid, not counting the deliberate ones. None of them ever put me off. I realised from an early age that taking a tumble was part and parcel of what I wanted to do.'

His childhood on the family farm coincided with what was grandiosely referred to as the second Golden Era of Welsh rugby. 'My heroes were all rugby players, people like Gareth Edwards, JPR Williams, Barry John and Phil Bennett,' he said. 'I played rugby into secondary school, but I knew I'd never be good enough to go any further.

'By then, I was hooked on racing. A cousin gave me the pony and I started riding it when I was nine. I just loved the idea of riding and I never used to miss *The ITV Seven* racing programme every Saturday afternoon. John Francome was my hero. He was the best – the McCoy of his time.

'I was lucky to have grown up on a farm because we always had loads of space to put our own home-made obstacles. I wanted to get into racing, which meant I had to make do with point-to-point, gymkhanas and that sort of thing because I wasn't allowed to race professionally until I was 16. In the months before I became old enough, I wrote off to loads of trainers in the hope that someone would give me a job. Two of them replied.'

Stan Mellor, champion jockey three years in a row during the early '60s and the first to ride 1,000 winners over the jumps before becoming a trainer, took Llewellyn on as an amateur at his stables near Swindon. The then 20-year-old Welsh apprentice rode his first race over the flat at Doncaster, finishing fourth out of a field of 18. He began showing his gratitude to Mellor by reaching the winner's enclosure for the first time on Starjestic at Wolverhampton in March 1986.

Soon – all too soon – the occupational hazards of a precarious profession began to hit home. And kept on hitting, with one shattering accident after another testing his resolve to the hilt. The first, and the worst by more than a few lengths, happened during one of his early seasons at Market Rasen when he broke his left ankle so badly that surgeons performing an eight-hour operation said he would never ride again.

'My right foot was pointing one way and my right ankle the opposite way,' Llewellyn said. 'It was a very big operation and it took them eight hours to try and repair what was one hell of a mess. Before they'd finished, one of the surgeons said: "He'll never ride again."

'They never actually told me, but one of the nurses in the operating theatre that day was related to a good friend of mine. She told me what had been said. It didn't bother me that much because when you're young, you think you can overcome anything. It took me nine months before I could ride again.'

Further serious setbacks came thick and fast during the next two years, starting with a broken leg. 'I was walking into the stalls at Ascot when a horse kicked me,' he said. 'It took me another nine months to recover.'

After negotiating the first race of his comeback without mishap, Llewellyn suffered another painful blow in the second, at Newton Abbot, which again put him out of action for months on end. 'I dislocated my elbow in a fall,' he said. 'They manipulated it back into place, or they thought they did, but it came back out again. That meant it was dislocated for two days, which was not at all pleasant. In the end, they had to cut it open and operate, so I had two rides in twelve months.

'Worse still, I lost my job. I'd gone from riding 41 winners one season and being champion conditioner jockey to riding only 19. The toughest part after a long lay-off was trying to get going again. For a long time, I couldn't get enough rides, never mind good ones. I had a lot of falls during my early 20s and a bad time with injuries. People used to say to me: "You've got to stop. You can't go on like this."

'I can honestly say I never gave it a thought. Same as in any job: you have a setback, you regain your fitness and you get back to doing what you're paid to do, in my case riding winners.'

He had plenty of time to reflect on his misfortune and wonder whether it was entirely a case of bad luck or, just possibly, something to do with his horsemanship. 'Bad luck,' he said, matter-of-factly. 'Sometimes there might have been something wrong with your judgement, but you can't hold that against yourself.

'Every jockey makes mistakes in just about every race – small mistakes, most of the time. Some are more serious and you might lose the race, but you can't let it prey on your mind. You can't say: "Oh well, I can't ride." You have to have belief. Some are not good enough, but I never once thought that. I never doubted my ability as a jockey.'

Nor did he ever stop to think that perhaps a punishing business was exacting too severe a physical toll. 'I broke my nose eight times and had three operations to improve my breathing because it had been repeatedly smashed,' he said. 'I've broken both scaphoid bones at least six times, but then that's not unusual because, if you're lucky, you can use your hands to try and break a fall. It happened so often that I'd ride with a metal brace around both thumbs to minimise the risk of more fractures.

'I only broke my collarbone once, which was very unusual, mainly because the end of it would pop up and prevent it breaking. I was lucky in that respect and unlucky in others. I broke my jaw and cheekbone once in a fall at Taunton. I was unconscious on the ground, the horse was down as well, and he kicked me in the face. My jaw was smashed to bits. The owner of the horse has a video of the whole thing. I haven't seen it and I have no wish to.

'What I did learn was that the higher the broken bones in your body, the quicker they heal. The lower down, the slower the recovery. When I was 27, I went down head first at Cheltenham and crushed some vertebrae. I had to lie flat on my back in hospital for one whole month and during that time I was never once allowed to move my head from the pillow.'

The early years also brought the inevitable bouts of concussion. 'I got concussed a lot when I was young, about eight or ten times, and I suppose that was all part of the learning process,' he said. 'You could say the same for my ribs. I've broken loads of them, seven times, maybe more.'

Not surprisingly, they have left a mark that Llewellyn has to learn to cope with every night. 'I can't sleep on my left side because of the lingering effects of getting kicked in the ribs at Newton Abbot,' he said. 'If I try to lie to my left, it hurts. But then I knew the risks when I began. I knew jockeys were getting hurt all the time. I didn't need to be told.'

Llewellyn based an unshakeable belief that it would all be worth the pain on his boyhood dream of competing in the most punishing, most famous steeplechase of all – the Grand National. The visualisation process did not stretch the imagination far enough to jumping the last all alone and showing the rest the way home. Winning it was beyond his wildest dreams.

All the bad breaks left him overdue a good one and fate began to even up the score two months before the 1992 running of the Aintree classic, when Andy Adams broke a leg during a fall at Doncaster, which ensured, most regrettably, that his horse lived up to his name – Come Home Alone.

His misfortune left a vacancy on Adams' regular mount, a giant of a horse by the name of Party Politics. The larger the animal, the less he or she tends to be fancied, if only because the more he or she has to carry around, the greater the danger of clumsiness or a lack of balance unseating the jockey.

Party Politics stood marginally more than six feet tall at the withers – in equine parlance, the ridge between the horse's shoulder blades. If topicality was ever part of the criteria for a National winner, then whoever replaced Adams had a real chance because the race fell five days before the General Election, which, surprisingly, put the Conservatives back in power and John Major back at No. 10.

Llewellyn got the ride, one that would land him on the front and back pages of every national newspaper the next day. 'I had two ambitions when I started off riding Sparky on the farm as a kid,' he said. 'One was to be champion jockey. The other was to ride in the Grand National. As the years go by, you realise how much luck is involved in being champion jockey. Basically, you had to ride for Martin Pipe because he was so dominant. If you weren't riding enough horses trained by him, you didn't have a realistic chance.'

Some of the most celebrated jockeys in National Hunt history, such as Francome, Mellor, Terry Biddlecombe, Peter Scudamore, Josh Gifford and Richard Johnson, spent the best years of their lives trying to win the National and never managed it. Jonjo O'Neill tried 13 times and never completed the course. Llewellyn knew how he felt after his National baptism on Kumbi, a horse trained by Ginger McCain of Red Rum fame.

'Kumbi was a massive horse who'd been around the course in a shorter race, except that he never got right the way round. He had very little chance. Ginger asked a lot of people to ride him and they all refused because the horse's success rate was nil. Over the longer distance, his chances were even less, if you can have less than nil. But I was so keen to ride in the National I'd have ridden any bloody horse.

'I sprung my collarbone the week before and went home to Wales thinking I'd had it, as far as the big race was concerned. Luckily, a friend of a friend rang up to explain that I could have the damaged part of the collarbone strapped down and pinned. The problem then was that I could hardly lift my arm more than a few inches.

'My girlfriend at the time knew a doctor and he gave me some amazing painkillers. After that, I was able to swing my arm all over the place. All went well until I got to Becher's the second time round and he had a spectacular fall. The horse landed upside down and I just missed him, which was just as well because he weighed about 450 kilograms.

'When that happens, you pull your head in and curl up into a ball. The smaller you make yourself, the better the chance that any kick will be no more than a glancing blow.

'Despite that, I loved every minute of it. All that jumping off the pony as a boy held me in good stead, so maybe I wasn't as crazy as I felt at the time. Even so, the renewed damage to my collarbone meant

I couldn't ride for another ten days, but I didn't care. I'd achieved part of my great ambition by riding in the race.'

Another fall 12 months later, on Smart Tar, meant he still had to pass the National finishing post. After missing the next two Nationals, Llewellyn not only stayed the course at the third time of asking but came romping home to the alarming sound of Party Politics breathing so heavily that his mount could hear 'the racket' despite the thunderous cheers of 100,000 punters.

Those who jumped to the reasonable conclusion that the Welshman guided the horse over the most terrifying fences in the sport had got it wrong. According to Llewellyn, and he was there, after all, the opposite was the case. The horse took him home without his needing to use the whip or a single word of encouragement, not that Party Politics would have heard it above the noise of his own breathing. Towards the end, he rode with the fear of the wheezing animal sounding as though he might conk out at any second.

'I'd never ridden Party Politics before, so I took him home for a run before the big race. That's when I became aware of his breathing. It wasn't at all good and he didn't work particularly well. The signs weren't good. He didn't jump properly for me, but his breathing became such a problem that after the race they had to drill a hole in his throat and insert a tube.

'He was a horse who didn't want any help. Some have to be told what to do. Others need a lot of help and encouragement. This horse just wanted to be left alone. He wanted to do it his way and no other way. I learned to not touch him, not say anything, just leave it all to him. I just sat there.'

He was still sitting there when Party Politics hit the front four fences from home. 'Going into every remaining fence, you're praying and hoping and wishing you land all right on the other side. You're saying: "Please God, let me get over this one." And then you're saying it again until there are no more between you and the finishing post.

'Although it wasn't neck and neck, you're still thinking: "This can't be happening to me. This is too big a dream." You spend all the time worrying like hell and what's worrying the life out of you is the sound of his breathing. Horses do get their breathing out of sync every so often and then they clear it and get back to normal.

'That didn't happen with this horse. Instead his breathing got progressively noisier until he began to make a hell of a racket. With all that going on, I wasn't travelling well and he couldn't have gone any faster. As it turned out, he didn't need to, so we just kept hanging on till we got there.'

They made the run for home, at 474 yards the longest on the National Hunt circuit, with two and a half lengths to spare from Romany King. The 15–2 favourite, Docklands Express, with Richard Dunwoody on board, finished 27½ lengths behind, in fourth place.

'The dominant emotion when you get over the line is relief. You are so relieved that you can't believe it. You're thinking: "Have we just won the Grand National?" My realistic expectation for the race was to finish the course, no more than that. They have modified the course since then and made it easier to get round, but fewer and fewer were finishing 20 years ago.

'Getting round then was a major achievement. You did that and you were congratulated by everyone, even if you were tenth, eleventh or twelfth.'

He drove from Merseyside to his southern base, then at Faringdon in Oxfordshire, for the celebration. 'We went to a restaurant owned by a friend of mine, along with about 60 other people,' he said. 'I drank a lot, but the adrenalin was so great I didn't get drunk. I finished between two and three in the morning, woke really early and went straight down to the newsagent's to get all the papers. I just about had time to look at them all before going to the stables to welcome the horse home.'

The victory carried a first prize of £99,943, of which Llewellyn's cut was 7 per cent, and if that was rather less than a king's ransom, the words 'Grand National winner' on his CV did wonders for his professional status. 'The money doesn't change your life because there's not enough of it to go out and buy a big house,' he said. 'But it paves the way for you to get better rides in better races.

'An owner will say to his trainer: "Who's going to ride my horse?" The owner loves it when the trainer tells him: "Oh, I've got the Grand National-winning jockey." They loved that.'

Shortly after beginning his 19 years as stable jockey for his Welsh compatriot, Nigel Twiston-Davies, Llewellyn began to think his luck had begun to turn with a vengeance, but then fate played the dirtiest trick of all. Back on board the reigning champion of Aintree 12 months later, Llewellyn had a sneaking fancy that Party Politics would achieve the back-to-back winning double done by four other horses, including the greatest National winner of all, Red Rum.

The old warrior had been only the fourth horse to accomplish the feat since the first Grand National in 1839, emulating Reynoldstown (1935 and '36), The Colonel (1869 and '70) and Abd-el-Kader (1850 and '51). Llewellyn will go to his grave swearing that Party Politics would have been the fifth had he not been robbed in the unprecedented circumstances of the race that never was.

Thirty of the thirty-nine runners completed the first circuit blissfully unaware that all manner of flags and arms were being waved to inform them that there had been a false start. Party Politics, all the better for his tube-assisted breathing, reached the halfway stage amongst the leading group.

'Nobody would have touched him that day and nobody will ever convince me otherwise,' Llewellyn said. 'I rode him when he won his prep race at Haydock over three and a half miles in a snowstorm. The tube allowed him to breathe much more easily, with the result that he was a much better prospect than the year before.

'Going into the second half of the race, I was cruising. I'm thinking: "We're going to run away with this." The first circuit is when you expect to get most of the problems with other horses getting in your way. The second circuit, with fewer runners, is usually comparatively straightforward.

'If you could ever guarantee a horse was going to get round, it was Party Politics that day. His footwork was unbelievable. I was sure I would have won it. Just as I was thinking that, I saw a steward waving for the first time, then more stewards, all waving. We had to pull up. It was heartbreaking, absolutely heartbreaking.

'I didn't have a clue why I was being waved down. Then they told us there had been a false start and the race was going to be declared void. Suddenly, what I thought was going to be the best day of my life turned out to be the worst day of my life. It took an awful lot of believing and even after all these years I still can't believe my luck that day.

'It was a crying shame for the horse, the trainer, the owner and myself. I was in a hell of a mood for the rest of the day and a long time after that. It was impossible to look at it logically, but once I began to come to terms with what happened, it made me realise how tough a race it is and how much has to go right if you are to win it.'

Not all the horses could be stopped. Esha Ness, a 50–1 outsider, finished first past the post, ridden by John White. 'I could see there were only a few horses around,' he said. 'I thought the others had fallen or something.'

Unable to find a practical way of staging a re-run, bookmakers were left with no option but to refund bets totalling £75,000,000.

Exactly six years after winning the National for the first time, Llewellyn won it again. He became the first post-war Welsh jockey to do so, going one better than Neale Doughty on Hallo Dandy in 1984 and Hywel Davies on Last Suspect the year after. How Llewellyn and Earth Summit came to be an item for the 1998 race might have been engineered by the racing gods as belated compensation for the chaotic events of five years earlier.

The gelding's regular rider, Tom Jenks, broke a leg a few weeks before Aintree, like Andy Adams before him. 'I rode Earth Summit a lot as a young horse,' Llewellyn said. 'The only time he ever fell was at Worcester, in his first race. He was a very quiet horse, not particularly brave until he got the blinkers on and then he'd find the courage to jump the big fences. Tom was his regular jockey and he would have ridden him at Aintree if he hadn't been injured so, in that respect, I was a bit of a jammy git. The owners then offered me the ride. I took about a hundredth of a second to say yes.'

More luck followed with the weather, which went from wet to very wet to almost waterlogged. 'It rained all day on the Thursday and all day on the Friday,' Llewellyn said. 'The more it rained, the more it reduced the chances of the vast majority of the runners. Luckily, Earth Summit loved soft ground. He was never inconvenienced by rain one bit. So much of it came down that there was a doubt about whether the race would take place because there was a danger of parts of the course being flooded. Once the going had gone from soft to heavy, I knew there were not that many horses who would be able to handle it.'

The previous year, when the main event had been delayed until the Monday because of a bomb scare, Llewellyn had defied the odds by bringing the 100–1 no-hoper Camelot Knight home in third place, a triumph for the jockey on what he described as 'a clever horse with a strong sense of self-preservation'.

Twelve months later, thanks largely to the saturated turf, he found himself at the other end of the National spectrum. 'Earth Summit had been backed so heavily that he became the favourite,' Llewellyn said. 'Once we were off, it was a case of avoiding trouble and having the luck to get around.'

Had it not been so wet, the rest would probably not have seen him for dust. Llewellyn rode a patient race before romping home by 11 lengths from Suny Bay. It was a triumph for trainer Nigel Twiston-Davies and the horse.

The owners, a syndicate that included the footballer Ricky George, had been told that even if the animal survived injuries inflicted during a crushing fall at Haydock in February 1996, he would not race again. But after six months in a box, they nursed him back to health until, against all the odds, he was able to race again, all of twenty-one months later. In December 1997, a few weeks after his comeback, Earth Summit duly made it a winning return at the Welsh Grand National, four months before repeating the feat in the Real McCoy, not to be confused with the perennial champion jockey of recent times, AP. In the process, Earth Summit went one better than Red Rum, as the only horse to win the Grand National, as well as the Welsh and Scottish versions.

As soon as Llewellyn had taken care of business at Aintree, the double-winner jumped in his car and drove across country to keep a long-standing commitment to attend a black-tie dinner in honour of fellow jockey Mark Dwyer, who won the Cheltenham Gold Cup in 1985 on Forgive'N Forget. The next morning he had a longer drive, back to Twiston-Davies' yard at Grange Hill Farm in the Cotswolds.

'It was a hell of a night,' Llewellyn said. 'Hundreds of people were there and I knew them all. From memory, it went on until about five in the morning. I got an hour or two's sleep, then drove back to Nigel's place in Gloucestershire to welcome the horse home. We took him down to the pub and there were hundreds more there.'

Only one Welshman, Jack Anthony, the most celebrated member of a famous racing family who grew up on Cilveithy Farm near Carmarthen, has ridden three National winners – Glenside in 1911, Ally Sloper in 1915 and Troytown in 1920, a race witnessed by King George V, who responded by giving the victorious jockey a Royal seal of approval.

'The King shook hands with me and congratulated me,' said Anthony, the youngest of three racing sons, who died in 1954 at the age of 64. 'I am a Welshman and everyone who knows the emotional feeling in the blood of a Welshman realises what I felt as I shook hands with the King.'

Eight decades on from the 1920 race, Llewellyn had a fleeting sight of his own treble. With two-thirds of the fences behind him, he led the National on Beau, one of only a handful of runners to get that far. A slight twist on landing and difficulty with his reins conspired to unseat Llewellyn. He clung on grimly for a few yards, got back on his feet and ran after the horse in the despairing hope of remounting before the next fence.

Shouts for assistance came to nothing. Beau ran off to prove that four legs are faster than two. Llewellyn could only watch the race run away from him on a day when only four finished, twice as many as in 1928 and the miracle of the 100–1 winner, Tipperary Tim, ridden by Billy Dutton.

A day or two before the historic race, a friend said to Dutton: 'Billy boy, you'll only win if all the others fall down.' Everyone else duly fell down, including the only other horse to finish, Billy Barton, whose jockey remounted, if only to ensure Tipperary Tim was not entirely on his Jack Jones.

Of all the horses he saddled over a career that brought him 995 winners, Llewellyn puts one above them all. 'In my early days after the bad injuries, I wasn't getting any rides on the televised races,' he said. 'I was scraping by at the smaller meetings and then I came across a horse called Tipping Tim. He was the hardest, toughest horse I'd ever ridden. He was also the cleverest and the most streetwise.

'He ran on all sorts of ground. He'd see a tiny gap and he'd get through it. Every time I looked to be in a bit of trouble, he'd get me out of it. He would never fall. He was just a street fighter and I loved him. He was the one who got me out of being a run-of-the-mill jockey to a higher profile. That's why, after all these years, he's still my favourite horse.

'Some you feel like they are yours and you don't want anyone else to ride them. Others you don't feel a part of. I never felt part of Party Politics, mainly because I'd only sat on him twice before I rode him in a race. I took him for a gallop once and I schooled him once. That was it. I never felt attached to him, whereas I was attached to Earth Summit.

'Some are very intelligent, others less so – just like humans. I do talk to horses. They understand that if you shout at them, it's not as good as being patted and spoken to quietly. They respond better that way.'

Earth Summit enjoyed a five-year retirement before being put down in March 2005 at the age of 17, following the diagnosis of cancer in both his liver and spleen. He had been due to take one final bow at Aintree later that month in the Parade of Champions. Party Politics was in his 26th year when he died of old age in May 2010.

Llewellyn rode his last race the previous year at 43, ascribing his longevity to a 'brilliant diet'.

'I kept a constant weight, 9 st 10 lb. I was very fit, but then I had to be to keep up with guys who were better than me. I never thought I was a naturally gifted rider. I had to work at it and part of that was being strict on my diet, not eating any rubbish.

'I always made sure I had the right food and the right amount – a lot of fish, a lot of chicken, a lot of vegetables, pasta, baked potatoes and bananas. I didn't touch crisps, chocolate, cakes, chips, pizzas and takeaways.

'I did drink, but only on Saturday night. There was no Sunday racing then, so I'd have a good blow out – cider, gin, wine, champagne, although not all at once. I'd enjoy a nice glass of whisky as a nightcap, and if a few drinks made me two pounds heavier on the Monday morning, that would be it.'

He has no truck with the 'ban steeplechasing' brigade, in full voice again after a number of horses had been put down during the 2011 National. 'I did a radio interview a couple of days after the race and someone on the programme likened it to bullfighting,' he said. 'That was the most ridiculous statement I think I have ever heard in my life. Whoever said it had obviously never watched a bullfight.

'Racehorses have the best of everything – the best food, the best hay, the cleanest water, the cleanest bedding, the best rugs and duvets. They are kept in the equivalent of a five-star hotel every day of their racing lives because it's in everyone's interests to ensure they are as healthy as possible for as long as possible.

'If a small number get killed in action, then they will have had a fantastic life of great quality for anywhere from six years to ten. It's unfortunate, but it's something you have to accept. The horses love galloping and they love jumping. They do, on average, five, six or seven days' racing in a year when they are pushed to the limit. The rest of the time they are treated like kings. That's not a bad trade-off.'

Llewellyn, who rejoined forces with Twiston-Davies in June 2009 as his business partner at their Grange Hill Farm racing stables near Cheltenham, has stayed single. 'It's very difficult for me to find the right wife, anyway,' he said. 'To have found one to cope with my life as a jockey and now as a trainer would have been even more difficult.'

More than 20 years based in England has done nothing to dilute his Welsh identity. 'I love Wales and I'm very proud to be Welsh. I'd much prefer to be Welsh than English. I don't know why, I just do, and my family are massively important.

'My mother is one of ten, my father one of eleven, so I've got hundreds of relatives. They are really good, proper people. It doesn't matter what you've done or what you haven't done, they don't treat you any differently. I get back as often as I can and sometimes I see people I haven't seen for years. It's no big deal because they make you feel as though you've only been away for a week or so.'

The more senior members of the family remind him of the early days when he jumped off his pony in anticipation of all those broken bones. At least now they can appreciate the method to young Carl's madness.

17

UNITED'S MARATHON MAN

Ryan Giggs

Born: Cardiff, 29 November 1973

One evening during the spring of 1987, Eric Harrison took his seat at Old Trafford to watch a game strictly in the line of business as youth team manager of Manchester United. What he was about to witness would cause a significant shift in the club's fortunes from perennial underachievers to the most decorated in English football.

Salford Boys were playing their Warrington counterparts in the final of the English Schools' Shield for under-14s, the type of fixture that always raised the possibility, however distant, that those with an educated eye would somehow find an uncut diamond, perhaps another George Best, if that didn't sound too far-fetched.

Harrison knew the star-making business better than most, which was why the United manager, then plain Alex Ferguson, employed him to overhaul a youth system that, under the all-Celtic combination of Sir Matt Busby and Jimmy Murphy, had once been the envy of the British game.

Harrison, a no-nonsense Yorkshireman from Hebden Bridge, specialised in ensuring that gifted youngsters made the most of their gifts, while imbuing them with a strong sense of self-discipline. He had slogged his way around the nether regions of the Football League as a player without doing anything too fancy other than his very best for, in chronological order, Halifax Town, Hartlepool United, Barrow, Southport, back to Barrow and Scarborough United.

When he first saw the Salford Boys' left-winger at Old Trafford that night, he could hardly believe what he was seeing. They had heard of Ryan Wilson at United, thanks to a tip-off from a local newsagent, Harold Wood, who identified with the red part of Manchester and whose perseverance resulted in his making a personal plea to Ferguson. The only fly in the ointment, a potentially very large one, was that young Wilson had aligned himself with the blue part of the great northern metropolis, as a member of Manchester City's self-styled school of excellence.

'He was sensational, absolutely incredible', Harrison said. 'He took my breath away. He really did. We had him on our radar and when I saw him he was even better than the reports we'd been getting from various scouts. He was incredible. He picked the ball up that night and just went past opponents as if they weren't there. It was all so easy; it was almost unbelievable.

'I was very, very excited. He was so elegant when he ran with the ball. His balance, footwork, speed – all were absolutely brilliant. You could see straight away that he was going to make it and I had never said that about any kid on the strength of one look. Normally, you need several looks because, at that age, they can blow hot and cold. I knew with Ryan from that one look that he was going to be a star of the future.

'Nowadays clubs can sign players when they're still in nappies, but it was different then. Nobody was allowed to sign for any club under the age of 14. Ryan left a big, big impression on me and a lot of other people at United.'

That Ferguson made the Salford Boys' capture a top priority said everything about the depth of the impression. The Guv'nor from Govan had arrived at Old Trafford the previous year, in November 1986, assuming charge of a club second from bottom of the First Division. Ferguson knew that if he was going to succeed where Ron Atkinson, Dave Sexton and Tommy Docherty had all failed in the previous nine years, United would need to invest heavily in home-grown talent.

When he first clapped eyes on the Welsh schoolboy during a trial at United's training ground, the Cliff, Ferguson could barely contain his excitement. 'When I first saw Ryan in that game, he gave one of those rare and priceless moments that make all the sweat and frustration and misery of management worthwhile,' he said. 'I shall always remember my first sight of him, floating over the pitch so effortlessly that you would have sworn his feet weren't touching the ground.'

As soon as Giggs turned 14, on 29 November 1987, Ferguson, accompanied by chief scout Joe Brown, beat the well-worn path to the family home in Salford armed with a two-year contract. They left with the signature of Ryan Wilson, then using his father's surname. A fly-half of mercurial ability, who partnered Gareth Edwards for Cardiff during the latter half of the '70s, Danny Wilson had followed the yellow brick road north to pursue a professional career, starting with Swinton rugby league club.

Wilson, whose father came from Sierra Leone and mother from Wales, was just 17 when his girlfriend, Lynne Giggs, from the Fairwater district of Cardiff, gave birth to the elder of their sons. The couple never married and by the time Ferguson signed Giggs for United, his father had gone from the family home for good.

'We got a great piece of luck when we took Ryan Giggs from Manchester City,' Ferguson has said. 'If I hadn't have come to the club when I did, he would have ended up playing for them – no question. My first real challenge was to get Ryan Giggs signed on schoolboy forms and we worked very hard at that. We were up at Ryan's door every night until he signed.'

Ferguson deputed one of his senior players, Steve Bruce, to keep a protective eye on the new boy. 'I'll never forget the day he first turned up at United,' Bruce said. 'Fergie was trying to nick him from Manchester City and he said: "I've got this kid, so just look after him."

'He came in and trained with us and we were thinking: "Hang on a minute. Fourteen? Are you sure?" The first time he got the ball he dropped his shoulder and went effortlessly past Viv Anderson, who was England's right-back at the time. Then he did it again and again, and in the end Viv was trying to kick him because he was taking the mickey.

'When he ran, you could not hear him because he was so quiet and effortless. He could probably run with the ball quicker than anyone else could run without it. The ball was stuck to his foot. He is still spindly, but when you looked at him then he was probably half the size. When he is finished, he will be talked about in the same breath as Law, Best and Charlton.'

Back in the very early days, before he changed his name, the Cardiff boy had been singled out by one of the game's most respected managers, David Pleat, whose Leicester team had drawn United in the FA Youth Cup. 'They had a winger called Ryan Wilson and I knew as soon as I saw him he was going to be a star,' Pleat said. 'I told Alex [Ferguson] what I thought and he told me how special a player he was going to be. He changed his name, of course, to Giggs and went on to be as good as I had predicted.'

Giggs and United would never have been an item for so long had his father not upped sticks halfway through the 1980–81 season and joined Swinton rugby league club. Another huge slice of luck in the grand scheme of things, Wilson's move north took his eldest son, then a seven year old at primary school in the western Cardiff suburb of Ely, out of his home town and into the kingdom of Manchester United.

Ferguson had found someone with such ability that he would virtually bypass the reserve team and step straight out of the youth ranks into the first team, the kind of quantum leap George Best had made a generation earlier.

'It's always a big plus when the manager takes time out to see a 14-year-old boy,' Harrison said. 'Sir Alex convinced Ryan and his mother that Manchester United was the place for him. The result was that we got him within a few months of first seeing him. Fortunately, Ryan and all that famous class of '92 were level-headed guys who worked so hard to pursue their one ambition, of playing in the Manchester United first team. Ryan was, still is, a fabulous guy who would do anything for you, as he has shown with his work for charity.

'With Alex Ferguson in charge, discipline was a priority. People might have turned round behind my back, saying I was too hard on the young players, but we had to develop winners. They say it's not important at youth level to win games. At Manchester United, it is, but you've got to play the right way.

'They're right – it isn't only about winning. It's about winning and playing great football. We had some outstanding young players – Giggs, Scholes, Beckham, Gary Neville, Ben Thornley, who was destined for the first team but for a very bad injury. There were others, such as Robert Savage and Keith Gillespie, who had great careers elsewhere. It was a pleasure to wake up not just on a Saturday but on every weekday too because the standard of training was very high, the highest I've ever known.

'Ryan's attitude was always spot-on and Alex Ferguson knew that from the start. Training, remember, is very, very important. At times, because the players were so good, training matches would often be more competitive than the real thing on a Saturday. Ryan always came in every morning wide-eyed and as fit as a fiddle. He could have run forever. Whenever he played for the youth team, the Cliff would be packed because, more often than not, Ryan would put on an unbelievable show.

'Alex always found him very easy to deal with, although Ryan tells me that he still gets one or two rollickings from the manager, which he's used to. He's been brought up in a fair, but hard, school.'

On one particular morning when snow had obliterated the markings on the training pitches, Harrison strode out into the middle with a rugby ball. 'They must have thought I was crazy,' Harrison said. 'I'm a big rugby fan, more league than union, so the sight of a rugby ball being whizzed around was music to my ears. We had a lot of fun that day.

'A few rugby players think footballers are softies, but they are most definitely not. Show me a good header of the ball and I'll show you a brave player. When you go up for a ball with an opponent, or sometimes not realising an opponent is there because your eye is on the ball, you risk a clash of heads. Ryan never gets injured because they can't catch him.'

Giggs took the leap from age-group football to Premier League stardom and beyond, to the towering cathedrals of the European game, in his stride. Before the end of his 20th year as a first-team regular, he had played 136 matches in the Champions League, more than any other British footballer. By the summer of 2011, he stood third on the all-time list, within touching distance of the veteran

Italian Paolo Maldini, second behind the outright leader Raul.

'Ryan had all this business about being the new George Best, which was never easy to cope with,' Harrison said. 'I think his mother would have given him a slap on the backside if he'd ever got carried away and found himself in the newspapers for the wrong reasons.

'I'm still very friendly with his mother, an absolute darling of a lady. Ryan will tell you: "There's no way I can ever answer my mother back, even now." He's a very rounded lad who had a great upbringing, despite one or two things going wrong and his dad leaving. That must have been a body blow to Ryan, but he's got on with his life. He took after his mother and finished up a really good human being, for which Lynne deserves a lot of credit.

'Before we knew anything about Ryan, there were rumours of him becoming a rugby league player like his father. The word on the grapevine was that this boy had everything to be a top rugby player. He liked the game and he must have inherited his father's genes in terms of pace and balance, but there was never any chance of that happening once he came to United.'

Wilson junior, as he was known then, took to the oval ball so naturally that, in his early teens, he considered himself better at rugby than soccer – a mind-boggling thought, given his subsequent success. At high school in Salford, he played four games every weekend, dividing them up equally between the codes. On Saturday mornings, it would be Salford Boys' football team; Saturday afternoons, Salford Boys' rugby; Sunday mornings, Langworthy rugby league club; then Sunday afternoons, Dean's football club.

'For quite a while, nobody could tell which I'd be better at,' Giggs has said. 'I played rugby all the way through high school, from ten to fourteen, by which time I was playing for Lancashire Boys. They more or less told me I'd play for Great Britain if I stuck at it. I played stand-off like Dad, but for Lancashire, who had top young players from Wigan and St Helens. I was out on the wing and I was also the goal-kicker.'

All that changed the day Ferguson came a-knocking with the potential for a career that would change everything in the youngster's life, including his name. As captain of England Schoolboys, notably against Germany at Wembley, the soccer world at large was beginning to take note of the name Ryan Wilson. Shortly after that, during a United youth team trip to Switzerland, he adopted his mother's maiden name and returned home as Ryan Giggs.

It happened when the referee went into the United dressing-room carrying a stack of passports, which he opened one by one, calling out the name and checking it against the date of birth to make sure nobody was over-age. 'When they called out "Giggs", Ryan said: "Yeah, that's me." It came as a surprise because everyone knew him as Wilson,' Harrison said, 'but Giggs it was and Giggs it's been ever since.'

'I've been asked many times: "Were you the father figure to these kids?" I always said, no, I was the boss. There is a difference. There were things they had to do in training and things they had to do in games. They had to behave themselves off the field. There was no late drinking or nonsense like that. I think Sir Alex has spies all over Manchester which meant nobody could get away with it.

'Ryan had his little moments, but nothing serious. He would do things for a bit of a giggle. He and Nicky Butt were the pranksters in that youth team. If someone's underpants had gone missing after training, the lads knew who to go to. It was all good fun, which strengthened the camaraderie.

'People have asked me: "What did you do for Ryan Giggs?" My answer was always the same: very little, really. We had Brian Kidd and Nobby Stiles coaching at the same time, and basically all we did was teach him how to defend. The most time I spent with him was on defensive topics. He was so easy to work with.

'He's exaggerating when he talks about big bollockings. If there was something I didn't like on the field, I'd take him to task, same as I would with any other player. As manager, I had a duty to treat them all the same and that extended to those who didn't make it. I couldn't let the others know that Ryan Giggs was the best thing since sliced bread and the rest were only average. They were anything but average because you were talking about David Beckham, Paul Scholes, Nicky Butt and so forth. Ryan knew, as they all knew, that if he crossed that line, he would be dealt with. They all got the same treatment. When he played in the youth team he was absolutely sensational.'

Giggs made such a flying start that he began playing in the First

Division a full season before he and the rest of Ferguson's teenagers won the FA Youth Cup. His debut, at the age of 17, as a first-half substitute against Everton at Old Trafford on 2 March 1991, made him one of the youngest in the all-time list, headed, oddly enough, by a goalkeeper who finished his footballing days playing rugby union in the back row for Wrexham RFC.

Dave Gaskell had just turned 16 in October 1956 when he appeared for United in the FA Charity Shield match against Manchester City. In doing so, he eclipsed the club record set a few years earlier when Duncan Edwards, lauded by Sir Bobby Charlton as 'the only other player who ever made me feel inferior', introduced himself against Cardiff City at Old Trafford in April 1953.

Giggs had made his bow at almost exactly the same age as Best, against West Bromwich Albion in September 1963. Another of United's Northern Irish colony, Norman Whiteside, also started at 17, against Brighton in April 1982. David Beckham was another 17-year-old debutant, which made others appear positively late starters, notably Charlton, who had to wait until the ripe old age of 19, likewise Paul Scholes.

When Giggs set off on the marathon to beat all marathons the day after St David's Day in 1991, United were still a considerable distance away from winning their first League title since 1967. Everton having given the Welsh teenager a rapid introduction to the harsher realities of life in the top tier, their away win contributed to United finishing in the nowhere territory of sixth place, behind Arsenal, Liverpool, Crystal Palace, Leeds United and Manchester City.

They wound up 24 points behind Arsenal, a total that would have been higher still had the champions not been deducted two points to United's one for a brawl at Old Trafford in the early weeks of the season. Despite Norwich bundling his team out of the FA Cup in the fifth round, Ferguson finished the season with the first European trophy of his Old Trafford reign, a brace of goals from Mark Hughes clinching a 2–1 win over Barcelona in the final of the Cup-Winners' Cup.

Of the twelve other United players involved in Giggs's debut, the majority had left the club within four years – Les Sealey, Mal Donaghy, Clayton Blackmore, Danny Wallace, Russell Beardsmore,

Darren Ferguson and Paul Ince. Only one of the remainder, the Irish defender Denis Irwin, was still there when Giggs completed his first ten years.

Seven months after one baptism, still aged seventeen, he went to Nuremberg for another, with Wales in the European Championship, breaking John Charles's record as the youngest Welsh cap. By the time the new boy appeared for the last six minutes, West Germany had made his a lost cause, avenging their defeat in Cardiff the previous June with a 4–1 win that rendered any judgement of Giggs that night a futile exercise.

When he played his first full international, a World Cup qualifier against Belgium at Cardiff Arms Park in March 1993, Giggs, then still only 19, clinched a 2–0 home victory with one of his free-kick specials.

One Welshman appeared in both of Giggs's debuts for club and country. Kevin Ratcliffe was there at Old Trafford as captain of Everton and in Nuremberg as captain of Wales. The Belgium game turned out to be his international swansong, by which time he had dropped two divisions down the Football League for a crack at digging Cardiff City out of the Third after twelve years at Goodison Park and 459 first-team appearances.

During that time, he built an enviable reputation as a defender who could really shift, which made him impeccably qualified on the subject of Giggs and his pace.

Ratcliffe may have been the fastest Evertonian out of the blocks, but when Wales under Terry Yorath held a sprint competition to lighten up training, he was not about to put that on the line against the new boy and risk seeing nothing other than the cleanest pair of heels.

'Terry wanted everyone else in the squad to appreciate how quick this lad was,' Ratcliffe said. 'Everyone, myself included, was reluctant to get into a sprint with Ryan. I knew how quick he was and I had no wish to be shown up.

'The first time I'd seen him at Old Trafford I was struck by his speed. He pushed one ball too far past the full-back and then he almost got it before it went dead when he had no right to be anywhere near it. You could see he had something, even though he was very slight in build.

'He didn't have a chance to do anything in Nuremberg, but I noticed a big difference in him when he made his full debut for Wales the following season. He was at least half a stone heavier, a year older and much better. There was also something else different about him. He was the first of the kids who brought these Nintendo computer games and everyone else wanted to have a go because we'd never seen that sort of thing before.

'His first full game was my last, so at least I can tell the kids I played in the same team as Ryan Giggs. He had to cope with a high expectation level even then. To do that and win the game with a cracker of a free-kick says everything about him.'

In between his truncated first international in southern Germany and his headline act at the Arms Park, Giggs had passed another landmark, his driving test. That evening, for the first time in his young life, he drove himself to a home game, arriving at Old Trafford in his stepfather's Ford Sierra. He wanted a car of his own and, by a happy coincidence, he had just completed 25 first-team matches, which, according to an unwritten rule at the club, entitled him to a club car.

He put his case in the hands of the club captain, Bryan Robson.

'Listen,' said Giggs in his autobiography. 'I can't really afford a decent car yet. Do you think the gaffer would let me have a club car?'

'Bryan said: "Of course, he will, yeah. You deserve one, you're part of the team now."

'Steve Bruce walked in and Robbo called him over: "Giggsy wants a club car. What do you think?"

'Steve looks at me and says: "No problem at all. Just go and tell the gaffer."

Suitably encouraged, Giggs did exactly that, never imagining that he had allowed himself to be set up for exposure to the Ferguson hairdryer. According to Giggs, the manager 'went absolutely nuts'.

'Who the f*** do you think you are? You've played a handful of games and you're coming in here with your f****** demands. I wouldn't give you a club f****** bike!'

A few years later, he treated himself to a Ferrari. Today, if the fancy so took him, he could probably afford to buy his own starting grid of Ferraris, Lamborghinis, Bentleys and Rolls-Royces without batting an eyelid.

If a footballer's greatness is measured strictly on trophies won, Giggs is unquestionably the greatest British player of them all. If longevity is the single most important part of the criteria to define excellence, he is again in a class of his own. Nobody else comes close to matching Giggs's consistency over two decades and he is still not finished.

He has been an integral part of twelve Premier League titles, four winning FA Cup finals, two winning Champions League finals, eight winning FA Charity Shield matches, one UEFA Super Cup, one Intercontinental Cup and one FIFA World Club Cup.

Since the creation of the Premier League 19 seasons ago, Giggs and United have finished as follows: champions (1992–93), champions (1993–94), runners-up (1994–95), champions (1995–96), champions (1996–97), runners-up (1997–98), champions (1998–99), champions (1999–2000), champions (2000–01), third (2001–02), champions (2002–03), third (2003–04), third (2004–05), runners-up (2005–06), champions (2006–07), champions (2007–08), champions (2008-09), runners-up (2009–10), champions (2010–11).

His unprecedented success with a club that lays claim to being the most popular in the world is in sharp contrast to his record with Wales. Regrettably, but not at all surprisingly, he achieved nothing of international note with his country, just as George Best achieved nothing of international note with Northern Ireland.

There was the occasional notable win, like the one over Germany at Cardiff Arms Park made possible by a classic from Ian Rush. Berti Vogts, then more than halfway through his eight-year stretch of managing the Fatherland, left the Welsh capital scratching his head about one Welsh player above the rest.

'Giggs was a big problem for us,' he said. 'The biggest is that he doesn't have a German passport.' Vogts had good cause to be apprehensive. Some years later, in February 2004, when he returned to Cardiff during his unfortunate time in charge of Scotland, Giggs reappeared to haunt him again in the course of Wales compiling a 4–0 win.

By then he had experienced the eccentricities of travelling with the Welsh FA. On occasion the organisation left so much to be desired that there were times when the players must have thought they had been transferred to Fred Karno's circus. When in 1969 they boarded a bus in Berlin for a World Cup qualifying tie against East Germany in Dresden and crossed the Iron Curtain at 'Checkpoint Charlie', they had nine players and almost twice as many officials.

Not much had changed when Giggs and company checked in at Stansted Airport for their chartered flight to Belarus. When the team's baggage weighed in at more than a ton over their limit, they were given an ultimatum: either lose a lot of luggage or remove 11 passengers from the aircraft. Mark Hughes thus became the first national team manager to find himself doubling up as a travel agent.

Harrison remembers it as 'a horrible time'. 'Mark had to tell a number of fans who had booked their own seats that there wasn't any room for them and then explain the situation, which was not at all nice. He should never have had to be concerned with an issue like that.'

Further trouble then flared over a home friendly against Argentina. 'Because we didn't have a training ground of our own, we arranged for Argentina to train at the local university,' Harrison said. 'They said: "No, that's not good enough. We're Argentina. Get us on the next flight out of here." We asked Cardiff City if they could put their pitch at the disposal of the visitors. Fortunately, the club said yes. Otherwise the Argentinians would have been on their way home.

'I had a fantastic time with Wales. The only problem was that we didn't have our own training ground. Instead, we had to beg, steal and borrow and that grated. An international team deserved better than that. When you run out on a bowling green of a pitch, as they do at United, your confidence is higher than if you're having to put up with a bumpy pitch and the ball bobbling all over the place.'

Hughes and his coaches were not amused at John Toshack voicing some severe criticism in his role as a television analyst before taking over as manager. 'Toshack was harsh in his criticism,' Harrison said. 'I know people will say you should say what you're thinking, but on some occasions he was very, very harsh. There was no respect shown to Mark whatsoever.'

When Giggs retired from the international stage at the age of 33 after captaining Wales against the Czech Republic in Cardiff in May 2007, he did so after 64 matches and 12 goals. By then, he too, like a legion of lesser players, had travelled far and wide in the national cause without ever once arriving in the finals of a World Cup or a European Championship.

'I'm disappointed not to have done that,' he said at the time of his Wales retirement. 'But many players go through that and I've been fortunate to have had such a successful career, so I'm not going to grumble.'

Like John Charles and others before him, Giggs missed many more internationals because of his manager's aversion to releasing players for friendlies and thereby running the needless risk of Manchester United paying a price for injury or tiredness. Giggs's loyalty to Wales is to be admired. As an England schoolboy player of some renown, he had both feet in their camp and ample excuse to have carried on wearing the three lions instead of the Prince of Wales's feathers.

It can be revealed now that he had another compelling reason to stay with England, and his mentor, Eric Harrison, had raised the topic with him shortly after he had broken into the United first team. Harrison, too full of Yorkshire grit to be given to any flights of fancy, claims that England would have won either the World Cup or the European Championship, or both, had Giggs thrown in his lot with them.

Others would have been tempted to look at the professional sense of pinning their colours to an English mast, as well as the consequent commercial spin-offs, and gone for it. Giggs, his Cardiff accent long superseded by an unmistakably Mancunian one, was never interested in selling his birthright. It was, as the 'Sergeant Major' discovered, not an option.

'I must admit that I did discuss the possibility of his playing for England,' Harrison said. 'I felt a bit awkward doing so. I got a quick no. "I'm Welsh, my father's Welsh, my mother's Welsh and I was born in Wales. I'm playing for Wales. End of story." Those were his words and that was it.

'I never dreamt of asking him again. I didn't say: "You'd be a superstar playing for England" or anything like that. I just asked him the question round about the time he made his first-team debut and everyone was talking about him as the new George Best and all that business. The answer left no room for doubt. He said: "I'm passionate about playing for Wales and I hope the Welsh supporters understand that."

'At club level he has been seen as one of the best ever to play for Manchester United. I was fortunate enough to be assistant manager of Wales. Sometimes we'd travel down together, but I never asked him: "How many medals do you think you would have won with England?" That would have been arrogant.

'Had he played for England, he would have been unbelievable. When Ryan began establishing himself in the Premier League as an out-and-out left-winger, England had nobody like him who was going to play in that position for the next ten years. They tried John Barnes and many others.

'It is an absolute certainty that England with Ryan Giggs would have won at least one of the big tournaments. He would have been that last piece in the jigsaw. He would have made a bucketful of goals for people like Alan Shearer. He would have absolutely terrorised defenders. As a rule, foreign defenders are good going forward, but quite a lot are not really good when it comes to one-on-one, as Gareth Bale found out for Spurs in Milan.

'Ryan would have sorted them out, no question, and England would have had a field day as a result. I'm not bulling him up, because he's a mature lad who doesn't like any fuss. He would have been a wonderful asset for England, a player who would have made a massive difference. They would have won something with him, for sure.

'During my time with Wales as assistant manager to Mark Hughes, I travelled a lot with Ryan. On all those trips from Manchester to Cardiff, never once did he turn round and say: "What am I doing this for?" There never seemed to be any trace of frustration from him whenever he was on duty for Wales.'

When Giggs first emerged as a figure with the ability to win Premier Leagues during United's initial success in 1992–93, Best paid the youngster a handsome compliment with typical generosity: 'One day they might even say that I was another Ryan Giggs.'

The Welshman's capacity to score goals that bore the hallmark of Best's genius brought him one which, above all the rest, his Ulster predecessor would have been thrilled to call his own. For most of that FA Cup semi-final against Arsenal at Villa Park on 14 April 1999, it appeared as though Giggs would be fated to a mundane bit-part in a lost cause.

He spent the first hour watching from the touchline, and extra time would not have been necessary had Peter Schmeichel failed to save Dennis Bergkamp's eleventh-hour penalty for Arsenal. United had been reduced to ten men by Roy Keane's dismissal when Giggs seized the ball 60 yards out. What happened next explained what a colleague, Gary Pallister, meant when he spoke of Giggs 'giving defenders twisted blood'.

Having found the nerve to swerve past every challenger in solo defiance of the law of probability, he then found a finish so explosive that Arsenal's England goalkeeper David Seaman could do nothing to stop it.

'I expected him to lay it off,' Seaman said at the time. 'But he just kept on coming. It was a real shock when he beat the lot and was right in on goal.'

They kept showering him with honours over the next ten years, climaxing in the ultimate recognition of his popularity across the full breadth of the sporting spectrum, the BBC Sports Personality of the Year award for 2009. By then he had been presented to the Queen at Buckingham Palace after being appointed an OBE in Her Majesty's birthday honours list in 2007.

Three years later, in January 2010, Salford gave him the freedom of his adopted home city, an honour that they had conferred upon L.S. Lowry in 1965, when the artist was 78. Giggs had also emulated a Welsh compatriot, David Lloyd George, and Nelson Mandela.

The Mayor of Salford, Councillor Roger Lightup, said: 'Freedom of the city recognises people who have made an exceptional contribution to our community and Ryan has devoted a tremendous amount of his time to work with charities and children over a number of years.'

As the seasons went by, he was lauded as a paragon of virtue, a family man whose apparently wholesome image made him the perfect role model. It also made him the perfect choice for blue-chip companies careful to select the best vehicle in which to promote their products – a lucrative business, which has contributed handsomely to Giggs' overall fortune, put at £34 million by the *Sunday Times Rich List* in May 2011.

For years, he went about his business on and off the field without the merest whiff of a scandal. While others made the front page, and several pages inside, of the *News of the World* over various indiscretions, Giggs took care to avoid making the same mistake.

'I was a lad growing up in public and it was a culture shock,' he said in an interview in 2008. 'I was cocky, confident. I'd just left school and I wanted to go out with my mates. Then you get recognised and followed or photographed. Girls sell their stories to newspapers. I rapidly realised it was something I didn't really like, so I made a conscious effort to settle down and keep a lower profile.'

A more recent interview, two years later, reinforced the point. 'I didn't become a footballer to be famous,' he told *The Guardian*. 'I became a footballer to be successful. I didn't want to be famous. Now people want to be famous. Why? Why would you want people following you about all day? I couldn't think of anything worse.'

How ironic that in trying to keep a lid on his extramarital activities, Giggs should unwittingly put himself in the eye of blizzards of damaging publicity. The lengths to which he went in an expensive attempt to stop the kiss-and-tell stories from seeing the light of day succeeded only in gaining him the notoriety associated with a cause célèbre.

Giggs, who married Stacey Cooke, the mother of his two children, in a private ceremony in September 2007, obtained a High Court super-injunction on 14 April to cover up an alleged affair. Within a matter of hours, he had been identified on the social-networking site Twitter.

Some five weeks later, Giggs's lawyers took legal action against Twitter, the first of its kind against the American company, and its users. On 22 May 2011, the Scottish *Sunday Herald* published a front-page photograph of Giggs, with the word 'Censored' over his eyes. The following day, the Liberal Democrat MP John Hemming used parliamentary privilege to break the court order and name Giggs in the House of Commons. He said it would not be practical to imprison the 75,000 Twitter users who had named the player.

Once the dam had burst, another damaging allegation came out in the flood, that the footballer had conducted an eight-year affair with his sister-in-law. Not for nothing did public-relations guru Max Clifford refer to it as 'the biggest own goal' he could remember.

The public soiling of his reputation as a man who stood for family values may have taken a severe battering, but nothing can besmirch his achievements on the football field. On 31 January 2011, a worldwide poll conducted by the club's magazine and website revealed that Giggs had been voted the greatest Manchester United player of all time.

Polls tend to lose historical perspective and while putting him ahead of the incomparable Bobby Charlton was going a step too far, there can be no doubt that when historians get round to judging the best players over the first 20 years of the Premier League, a Welshman from Cardiff whose father played rugby will be uppermost in their minds. One former colleague from the Old Trafford dressing-room, the ex-England striker Andrew Cole, puts Giggs above everyone else.

'I wouldn't be surprised if he was the best Premier League player of them all.' Cole said. 'I can't think of anyone you'd put above him. He's stood the test of time and now that he's getting towards the end of his career, he's receiving the plaudits for what he's achieved. I've had the pleasure of playing alongside him and being his friend for a long time and he's a bundle of laughs.'

Kevin Ratcliffe, whose captaincy of Everton against Watford in the 1984 final at the age of 23 made him the youngest FA Cup-winning skipper since Bobby Moore, goes a step further than those who bracket Giggs alongside Best, Charlton and Law as United's greatest. 'For me, he is the best player who has ever played for Manchester United. You only need to count the medals he has won to appreciate that he's in a class of his own.'

Harrison, old enough to remember all the outstanding players of the immediate post-war era, grew up idolising another Welsh footballer who, for all his qualities, never won the League Championship, the FA Cup or the European Cup. 'There is no question in my mind that Ryan Giggs is in the top ten of the all-time British greats, as a left-winger.

'I have to put John Charles in there because he was my hero,' said Harrison. 'Living in Yorkshire, I used to go to Leeds as a lad and watch him. But imagine a team with Best on one wing and Giggs on the other. Dear me, they'd be unstoppable . . .'

There is a story from one of Giggs's earliest matches, against Liverpool at Anfield, when he was given a cruel reminder of the credibility gap between the clubs at the time. When, after a home win, a few Liverpool fans asked three United players for their autographs, the trio, including Giggs, duly signed. No sooner had they done so than the fans took great delight in ripping up the paper containing their signatures and taunting the United trio with the jibe: "You're a bunch of f***** losers. Why would we want your autographs?"

When word of the exchange reached Ferguson, he told the three to store the experience in their memory bank and use it as a source of motivation for future visits. At that time, Liverpool had won the League Championship a record eighteen times compared with United's seven. Giggs learnt the lesson so well that his 12th Premier League title in May 2011 meant United had wiped their Merseyside rivals from the record book, overtaking them with a 19th League title.

Of all the statistics generated by a phenomenal one-club career, not least his superseding Sir Bobby Charlton's 758-match record and raising it towards 900, coming from so far behind to eclipse Liverpool on the domestic title front is surely the greatest one of all.

BIBLIOGRAPHY

Ballesteros, Severiano *Seve: The Official Autobiography* (Yellow Jersey Press, 2007)

Bennett, Phil *Everywhere for Wales* (Stanley Paul, 1981)

Bradman, Don *Farewell to Cricket* (Hodder & Stoughton, 1950)

Broadbent, Rick *The Big If: The Life and Death of Johnny Owen* (Pan Books, 2007)

Charlton, Sir Bobby with James Lawton *The Autobiography: My Manchester United Years* (Headline, 2007)

Clarke, Darren *My Ryder Cup Story* (Hodder & Stoughton, 2006)

Connor, Jeff *The Lost Babes: Manchester United and the Forgotten Victims of Munich* (HarperSport, 2006)

Davies, Mervyn and David Roach *In Strength and Shadow: The Mervyn Davies Story* (Mainstream Publishing, 2004)

Evans, Richard *Open Tennis: The First Twenty Years* (Bloomsbury Publishing plc, 1988)

Gate, Robert *Billy Boston* (London League Publications Ltd, 2009)

Giggs, Ryan with Joe Lovejoy *Giggs: The Autobiography* (Penguin Books, 2005)

Gough, Darren with David Norrie *Dazzler: The Autobiography* (Michael Joseph Ltd, 2001)

Hughes, Brian *Starmaker: The Untold Story of Jimmy Murphy* (Empire Publications Ltd, 2004)

Jackson, Peter *Lions of Wales: A Celebration of Welsh Rugby Legends* (Mainstream Publishing, 1998)

Large, David Clay *Nazi Games: The Olympics of 1936* (W.W. Norton & Company, 2007)

McLean, T.P. *The All Blacks* (Sidgwick & Jackson, 1991)

Miller, Douglas *Born to Bowl: The Life and Times of Don Shepherd*

(Fairfield Books, 2004)

Moorhouse, Geoffrey *The Official History of Rugby League* (Hodder & Stoughton, 1995)

Morgan, Cliff *The Autobiography* (Hodder & Stoughton, 1996)

Risoli, Mario *John Charles: Gentle Giant* (Mainstream Publishing, 2003)

Roberts, John *The Team that Wouldn't Die: The Story of the Busby Babes* (Arthur Barker Ltd, 1975)

Samuel, Bill *Rugby: Body and Soul* (Gomer Press, 1998)

Tait, Alistair *Seve: A Biography of Severiano Ballesteros* (Virgin Books, 2005)

Thomas, Clem and Greg Thomas *The History of the British and Irish Lions* (Mainstream Publishing, 2005)

Tremayne, David *The Lost Generation* (Haynes Publishing, 2009)

Williams, Charles *Bradman: An Australian Hero* (Abacus, 1996)

Williams, Peter *Winner Stakes All* (Pelham Books, 1970)

INDEX

298

INDEX

Tanner, Haydn 51
Tattersall, Roy 55
Taylor, Ernie 26
Taylor, Heddwyn 227
Taylor, Joe 92, 94
Taylor, Ken 61
Taylor, Roger 114, 119
Taylor, Tommy 23–4, 123–6, 129
Ter-Ovanesyan, Igor 136–9, 141–2,
  144–6, 148
Thomas, Clem 176
Thomas, Dylan 106, 118
Thomas, Eddie 225, 233
Thomas, Gareth 177
Thompson, Daley 150
Thornley, Ben 277
Tingle, Dick 14, 159
Titmus, Fred 54–5
Torino FC 74–5
Torrance, Sam 181, 251, 256
Toshack, John 284
Tottenham Hotspur FC 11, 29, 132,
  159, 183, 286
Trautmann, Bert 132
Treharne, Gwilym 206
Tremayne, David 15, 220
Treorchy Juniors FC 18
Trott, Frank 88
Trueman, Fred 42, 54, 56, 61, 64
Tulloh, Bruce 146
Trundle, Neil 213
Twiston-Davies, Nigel 266, 269, 272
Tyson, Frank 11, 56, 58, 62

Udinese FC 73
Underwood, Derek 54–5
University of Wales Hospital 173, 209
Uttley, Roger 177
Uzzell, John 'Dick' 200

Valentine, Alf 58
van Basten, Marco 85

van Vollenhoven, Tom 92
van Vuuren, Frederick Jansen 219
Vero, Glenda 84, 86
Verona FC 73
Violett, Denis 125, 127–8
Vlassopulos, Tony 14, 212–14
Vogts, Berti 283
von Schirach, Baldur 145
von Trips, Wolfgang 215

Wade, Virginia 17
Wakefield Trinity 94, 99, 140–1, 160
Walcott, Clyde 58–9, 65
Wales at FIFA World Cup, 26, 28, 75,
  124, 129
Walker, Billy 101–2
Walker, Murray 214
Walker, Oliver 44
Walker, Peter 14, 43, 46, 55, 61, 64
Wallace, Danny 280
Wallace, Marjorie 215
Wardle, Johnny 55
Warrington RL 96
Warwick-Smith, Michael 220
Warwick-Smith, Nella 215
Warwickshire CCC 57, 99, 195
Watford FC 289
Watkins, Allan 13–14, 35–49, 63
Watkins, David 14, 189, 196–8, 200–1,
  206
Watkins, Molly 41
Watkins, Stuart 195, 198
Watson, John 211
Watson, Tom 252
Watson, Willie 42, 48
Watt, Steve 237
Wayne, John 258
Webb Ellis, William 187
Webster, Colin 23, 27
Weekes, Everton 65
Weekes, Robert 173, 209
Welsh LTA 109

303